Frantz Fanon

Global Critical Caribbean Thought

Series Editors: Lewis R. Gordon, Professor of Philosophy, UCONN-Storrs, and Honorary Professor, Rhodes University, South Africa; Jane Anna Gordon, Professor of Political Science, UCONN-Storrs; Nelson Maldonado-Torres, Professor in the Department of Latino and Caribbean Studies and the Comparative Literature Program, Rutgers University, New Brunswick

This series, published in partnership with the Caribbean Philosophical Association, turns the lens on the unfolding nature and potential future shape of the globe by taking concepts and ideas that while originating out of very specific contexts share features that lend them transnational utility. Works in the series engage with figures including Frantz Fanon, C.L.R James, Paulo Freire, Aimé Césaire, Edouard Glissant, and Walter Rodney, and concepts such as coloniality, creolization, decoloniality, double consciousness, and la facultad.

Titles in the Series

Race, Rights and Rebels: Alternatives to Human Rights and Development from the Global South, Julia Suárez Krabbe

Decolonizing Democracy: Power in a Solid State, Ricardo Sanin-Restrepo

Geopolitics and Decolonization: Perspectives from the Global South, Edited by Lewis R. Gordon and Fernanda Bragato

The Existence of the Mixed Race Damnés: Decolonialism, Class, Gender, Race, Daphne V. Taylor-Garcia

The Desiring Modes of Being Black: Literature and Critical Theory, Jean-Paul Rocchi

Decrypting Power, Edited by Ricardo Sanín-Restrepo

Looking Through Philosophy in Black: Memoirs, Mabogo Percy More

Black Existentialism: Essays on the Transformative Thought of Lewis R. Gordon, Edited by danielle davis

A Decolonial Philosophy of Indigenous Colombia: Time, Beauty, and Spirit in Kamëntšá Culture, Juan Alejandro Chindoy Chindoy

Blackening Britain: Caribbean Radicalism from Windrush to Decolonization, James G. Cantres

Systemic Violence of the Law: Colonialism and International Investment, Enrique Prieto-Rios

Frantz Fanon: The Politics and Poetics of the Postcolonial Subject, Alejandro J. De Oto

Frantz Fanon

The Politics and Poetics of the Postcolonial Subject

Alejandro J. De Oto
Translated by Karina Alma

ROWMAN & LITTLEFIELD
Lanham • Boulder • New York • London

Published by Rowman & Littlefield
An imprint of The Rowman & Littlefield Publishing Group, Inc.
4501 Forbes Boulevard, Suite 200, Lanham, Maryland 20706
www.rowman.com

86-90 Paul Street, London EC2A 4NE

This translation copyright © 2022 by Karina Alma
Originally published in Spanish as *Frantz Fanon: política y poética del sujeto poscolonial* by El Centro de Estudios de Asia y Africa © Alejandro J. De Oto 2003

All rights reserved. No part of this book may be reproduced in any form or by any electronic or mechanical means, including information storage and retrieval systems, without written permission from the publisher, except by a reviewer who may quote passages in a review.

British Library Cataloguing in Publication Information Available

Library of Congress Cataloging-in-Publication Data

Names: Oto, Alejandro J. de, author. | Alma, Karina, translator.
Title: Frantz Fanon : the politics and poetics of the postcolonial subject / Alejandro J. De Oto ; translated by Karina Alma.
Other titles: Frantz Fanon. English | Politics and poetics of the postcolonial subject
Description: Lanham : Rowman & Littlefield, [2022] | Series: Global critical Caribbean thought | Includes bibliographical references and index.
Identifiers: LCCN 2021043946 (print) | LCCN 2021043947 (ebook) | ISBN 9781786613486 (cloth) | ISBN 9781538199152 (paperback) | ISBN 9781786613509 (epub)
Subjects: LCSH: Fanon, Frantz, 1925-1961—Political and social views. | Fanon, Frantz, 1925-1961—Influence. | Postcolonialism—Africa.
Classification: LCC CT2628.F35 O7613 2022 (print) | LCC CT2628.F35 (ebook) | DDC 320.9/045—dc23
LC record available at https://lccn.loc.gov/2021043946
LC ebook record available at https://lccn.loc.gov/2021043947

Contents

Translator's Note	vii
Note to the English Edition	xi
Acknowledgments	xv
Foreword	xix

Introduction
    On the "Uses" of Fanon   1
    Between Fanon and Us   3
    Reading Fanon: Some Derivations   5
    On Diversities and Divergences   10

I Fanon and Some Environments of Historicity:
    The First Displacements   11
    Spaces of Historicity   12

II Writing and Urgencies: On Ethics and Works: Readings   19

III Histories of Ambivalence   55
    Sartrean Routes, Fanonian Strategies   68

IV Historicity and Contingency   75

V Contingency, Identity, and Alienation: The Challenge
    of the Specters   95
    Impulses, Agency, and Subjects: An Unfinished Plot   102

VI Memory, Oblivion, and the Subject	119
By Way of Conclusion	129
Frantz Fanon: A Biography	135
Works of Frantz Fanon	139
Notes	141
Bibliography	163
Index	175
About the Author	183
About the Translator	185

Translator's Note

This book is a Spanish-to-English translation of Latin American historian and philosopher Alejandro J. De Oto's *Frantz Fanon: Política y poética del sujeto poscolonial,* published in 2003. The primary concern from the original text was its use of idioms and its density of language. The use of idioms in Spanish gave the original a sense of intimacy between the reader and author, a sense of familiarity as a reader from the same language community, and a conversational tone that balanced out the density or, rather, intricacy of De Oto's thought. I derived pleasure in reading De Oto's original text and his twist of phrase that welcomed the reader to follow his logic. Thus, my concern in translating his writing (and speaking since his text contains much of his speaking voice) was to retain the imprint of his voice while removing idioms and turns in sentence and paragraph structure that blocked comprehension when translated into English. Clarity became the prime goal and, therefore, I removed most idioms throughout the text and attempted to make sure that the sentence structure used English syntax.

    Density of language is an odd concept when applied to the works of philosophers who work through the intricacy of thought to make their point. Density of language usually refers to verbosity or the use of unnecessary jargons that block readability and comprehension. De Oto's work is no denser than works by other literary, philosophical, or cultural theorists. Additionally, he brings into conversation terms that are familiar to readers of Frantz Fanon and Jean-Paul Sartre, among others.

However, intricacy of thought can be complicated in Spanish by what in English is considered a run-on sentence. Possibly, there is no sentence that is too long in Spanish. This makes for a syntactical density that packs modifiers and begins to obscure the subject of the sentence. Therefore, whenever necessary, I divided sentences so that the subject and object as well as the subject-verb agreement remained clear. For clarity, I removed, and when not needed, transitional adverbs, dashes, numerical points, and other punctuation marks.

At the same time, I believe in the complexity of Alejandro De Oto's thoughts as he has phrased them. Breaking down a sentence or unpacking meaning is what scholars, readers, and professors do, for our students for example. So, in some instances, I think there is something valuable to keeping some of that dense phrasing. Additionally, there is a balance in De Oto's language between passages that are dense and a breeze.

The translation retains all of De Oto's notes as written in the original. Any and all notes that I have added are in brackets. However, these are minimal. I avoided adding notes unless it was to translate a title. For quotations, wherever and whenever possible, I cited the English version texts when the original was written in English to avoid two layers of translation with the first layer being De Oto's translation of English and the second, my translation of his translation back to English. This means that I read both the original source and De Oto's translation of it. When I was not able to locate the book or article, I kept De Oto's translation of the original. To avoid several layers of translation of Fanon's words, and the possibility of warping the original quotation, I cited directly from an English version of *Black Skin, White Masks* (1967) and *The Wretched of the Earth* (1963), which I added to the bibliography. However, I retained De Oto's citation from his source and included the page citation from my English version source, for example: *The Wretched*, originally cited, 127; 138. "Originally cited" refers to De Oto's citation. The second page number following the semicolon refers to the source I used. I did this so that readers may readily access an English version of Fanon's book.

Lastly, the bibliography remains the same as the original. However, I added the translation of titles in brackets and, whenever possible, the English version source also listed in brackets. For example:

De Beauvoir, Simone. 1986. *La fuerza de las cosas*, Ezequiel de Olaso (trad). Ciudad de México: Editorial Hermes.
[_____. 1965. *The Force of Circumstance*. Trans. by R. Howard. New York: Harper Collins.]

Readers can locate her book by using its English title *The Force of Circumstance*.

In closing, I would like to thank Jane Anna Gordon and Lewis R. Gordon, for inviting me to be part of this project, and Alejandro De Oto, and Jane and Lewis, for trusting me with his words. I am especially grateful as a reader of Fanon whose work and thought continue to inform my own in several meaningful ways.

Karina Alma

Note to the English Edition

Much has transpired since *Frantz Fanon: The Poetics and Politics of the Postcolonial Subject* appeared in Spanish in 2003.

First what could be described as an avalanche of works about the writing of Fanon was inspired by the decolonial turn. It was a movement produced by the proposal to find the marks critical to a Eurocentric vision of modernity and the production of knowledge. Understanding the role played by the colonial and imperial difference was key to re-inscribing Fanon's writing as a genealogical marker of the relationship between modernity and coloniality.

Second, there was the addition of Fanon's writings that had remained out of the public eye, or were difficult to access, which made it possible to reconstruct the debates and itineraries of Fanon's complex intellectual life. At the same time, this made it possible to trace with greater precision the critical processes that are at the foundation of his core works, especially *Black Skin, White Masks*. Central to this is the contribution made by *Frantz Fanon: Alienation and Freedom* (2018), which includes texts by Fanon collected and introduced by Jean Khalfa and Robert J.C. Young.

A third space for interaction around Fanonian writing continued to unfold under the wide umbrella of phenomenological readings undertaken in a postcolonial key. It is not necessary to investigate very far to find the powerful saga that Lewis R. Gordon inaugurated in the mid-1990s. It is one of which, in large part, this book is a part. I do not intend to adjudicate regarding correct readings of Fanon, but I do show that his writing continues to be projected as an arena of cultural, ideological, and political disagreement, which has major consequences in contemporary intellectual debate. For an update on substantial interventions in the field, I highly recommend reading the introduction to *What Fanon Said* (2015, 1–7) by Gordon.

In Latin America, which was the first intellectual home for this book, at the end of the twentieth century and the beginning of the twenty-first, in the midst of neoliberal deployments, Fanon's presence in intellectual traditions had a double character. On the one hand, it was seen as a kind of hindrance, situated in the confines of emancipatory political practices, which, if they had any place to take effect, was no longer in revolutionary rhetoric. In that sense, reading Fanon was, above all else, a nostalgic exercise. On the other hand, memory of his major contributions to understanding themes of decolonization and racialization survived in the intellectual records linked to African diasporic organizations, with the cases of Colombia and Brazil as perhaps the most significant. Fanon's impact on the intellectual agendas of South American countries was very limited in those years, and the presence of his writing was also muted. Even today, outside the circles where his writings are actively circulated, things have not changed much.

Taking that context and that of the present into account, one of the central tasks to be undertaken continues to be that of stabilizing a decolonizing philosophical, political, and cultural library. Of that there is no doubt. What is more debatable is the way that such a library should be constructed. It is in this situation that the value of this book appears. I have tried, through all the means in my power, not to read Fanon as an exception (although for many genuinely merited reasons he is exceptional), or as someone marginal to the intellectual matrices that make up the global humanities and social sciences. On the contrary, I have read him by thinking about the ways in which his writing can be summoned to analyze concrete problems in any academic research, in the same way that one might summon Clifford Geertz if one is doing ethnographic work, or Jacques Derrida if one is doing deconstruction, or Enrique Dussel if one is grappling with the problem of transmodernity. In other words, as a key tool in that kit of which Michel Foucault wrote. In this sense, continued engagement with Fanon's works is inevitable if one intends to discuss processes that affect the forms of producing subjectivity in the contemporary world. In my case, a key problem related to the said production of subjectivities, and for which much work remains to be done, is regarding historicity or, in more historiographical terms, temporality. Fanon makes crucial contributions to such considerations.

I do not rule out the value of works that focus on discussing Fanon's thought as a source for understanding the debates that arose in the context of the decolonization processes of the mid-twentieth century. I just think that context is a powerful dimension when one doesn't confine the writing to a limited number of movements. On the contrary, the context may be one of the most significant dimensions in disputes with discourses that present themselves as universal and certainly are not. It is always an open dimension in Fanon's writing, because in it, historicity and temporality are also open. Therein lies their extraordinary power.

In sum, this book is an open invitation to think seriously about the crossroads of time, space, ambivalence, and subjectivity through the two major works of Frantz Fanon, *Black Skin, White Masks* and *The Wretched of the Earth*.

For financial support for the translation of this work, I would like to thank the Williams College W. Ford Schumann '50 Program in Democratic Studies.

Alejandro J. De Oto

Acknowledgments

Writing an appreciation list that includes the many people who assisted in some way in the preparation of a work like this means that someone may be left out. This case is no exception.

Having explained this possibility, the following does not imply a hierarchy, but, instead, a chronology. I thank Hilda Varela of the Center for Studies in Asia and Africa (Centro de Estudios de Asia y África, CEAA), who, for three years, was my counsel as she listened attentively to my more challenging arguments, helping me to return to those topics in my discussion. She is now a good friend. With the friendship of Romer Cornejo, also of CEAA, I learned that academia (of which we are both members) can be manifested in a way that does not resemble accustomed discourses. Through laughter, he made the best and most complex comments on my work, which made for more productive workdays.

I share mutual respect for Benjamin Preciado and admiration of his work. Benjamin's writings on India were highly inspiring in keeping me focused on this manuscript.

It is not easy to convey the adventure I experienced studying in a liminal place such as the Center of Asian and African Studies at the College of Mexico (Centro de Estudios de Asia y África de El Colegio de México). Perhaps one of the characteristics of the impossibility of translation to which I allude in some passages of my text can be exemplified by this experience. Investigating and studying there was one of the most powerful intellectual journeys that I have ever experienced.

Celma Agüero, Flora Botton, Jorge Silva, Susana Devalle, among others, remain part of my journey and personal transformation.

Guillermo Zermeño, historian of the Center for Historical Studies at the College of Mexico (Centro de Estudios Históricos de El Colegio de México), was and is one of my central intellectual references. His work inspired many ideas in this text.

I received the support of different people in other geographies but with the same impulse. I want to thank them all. John Noyes, who took the risk of having me present the topics of this study in the African Series Seminar at the University of Cape Town. George Landow, who agreed to be my academic contact, enabled me to spend almost a year at Brown University preparing the manuscript and exposing it to different audiences.

I want to make special mention of Professor Lemuel Johnson of Ann Arbor. With him I had the opportunity, years before this work, to conduct a seminar on African literature. He later became the external reader of my dissertation. Though our face-to-face meetings were rare, in those moments, I realized his enormous human and intellectual capacity. His books had already revealed this to me. Beyond the transcontinental distances that separated us, his death was an unexpected loss. However, his memory inhabits the best moments of this study. I remember a meeting with him in 1998 in Ann Arbor to work on the manuscript. His comments were so enlightening that I fear that I may never live up to them. The space left with his departure is now inhabited by our memory and by meaningful remembrance.

Marcelo Eckhardt of the University of Patagonia in Argentina is another person I want to thank. His friendship and permanent contact with his literature opened my eyes to the possible aesthetic and political experiences that have more than one point in common with the works of Fanon, Césaire, and Depestre, among others. When we talk about colonial experiences and resistance, it is remarkable how close the encounter truly is with what otherwise might seem so distant.

Horacio González, a sociologist at the University of Buenos Aires, persisted, with chivalry, through almost five days of conversation and readings at my home in Mexico. We discussed arguments on national culture, postcolonial critique, and the need to reread Sartre. His incredible erudition and his kind criticism allowed me to change some of my points. I am sure that when he reads the final version, we will maintain a friendly disagreement. It is not easy to find a friendship and a critique of this nature. He and Liliana Herrero, his companion, hold my strongest affection.

Esteban Vernik is a partner in intellectual and life adventures. I thank you for the years of friendship and the time spent discussing the itineraries of this book.

The intellectual challenges of my students in Trelew and Comodoro Rivadavia in the history program (2002 class) of the University of Patagonia during the final stages of revision of the manuscript were the reason for some changes in some passages. They are the clearest signal that there is still much to write about.

I also want to thank Gabriela Lara of the College of Mexico (El Colegio de México) who, with her friendly and efficient work, removed my doubts and lack of knowledge of publishing. Thanks to the support of the Antorchas Foundation (Fundación Antorchas), which allowed me to complete the research and writing of this manuscript.

The staff of the Library Cosío Villegas of the College of Mexico deserve a separate paragraph. Thanks to them, I was able to find the material for my research that would otherwise have been impossible to locate.

In these final paragraphs, I thank my parents, José Alberto and Providencia Esther, and my brother José Alberto, who have always been a source of inspiration and love that far exceeds these pages.

Lastly, I dedicate this work to Ivan and Milton, the children of two of my dearest friends, Marcelo Eckhardt and Esteban Vernik. They recently entered an uncertain world where dilemmas are often addressed with intolerance, violence, and cynicism. The war in Iraq since 2003 is a horrible example of a world that places us at the crossroads of vital political and moral urgencies that seem astonishingly like those Frantz Fanon analyzed. Though the world has changed from Fanon's time to today and thus claims to offer a better present and future, we still debate similar issues faced then with the same intensity and, in turn, encounter the same sense of survival. Ivan and Milton still do not know this, but their presence signals that our search for dialogue, home, understanding, tolerance, and affection continues.

Foreword

Amid the avalanche of printed paper that invades culture, Italo Calvino recommends a return to the "classics." However, how are we to return to them when all works are impregnated by the historicity of the very act of reading? "A classic is a book that never exhausts all it can say," Calvino tells us. The importance of encountering a classic is that it allows us to relate to it as we also distance ourselves from it.[1] Classics of modern sociological and anthropological literature are the works of Frantz Fanon. Undoubtedly, his corpus remains a wellspring to understanding the nature of colonialism in the era of scientific and technological modernity.

To become familiar with the classics, however, it is recommended that one mark the distance separating the reader of today from the works of the past. Every reading is an act that produces meaning. Not to assume this would contradict Fanon's critical appeal inspired by the phenomenological movement that also stimulated Sartre, which is the opening to the radical historicity of the subject and of the work itself. Fanon's is distinguished from other works, because he avoids falling into an extreme defense of the colonial subject that would otherwise exceed a protocol of good intentions. The radicalism of his thought consists in pre-positioning the principle of historicity that surrounds the colonizer as well as the colonized. As such, temporality imprints his work. His thought constitutes the history that traces modern colonialism and its disorders on the skin and bodies of the colonized, but also on the society of the colonizers.

Since the publication of Fanon's final work in 1961, crucial events have transformed the face of the earth and affected critical intellectual work. South African apartheid ended. Algeria has changed. Sartre is no longer with us. Many of the wars of liberation withered while others triumphed. Most significantly, the Soviet Union ceased to exist. These displacements drew an abyss separating us from the historical experience formed during the period of the so-called Cold War.

However, this does not mean that bridges cannot be drawn between the two shores that separate us. The "originals" remain for us fortunately to resume the dialogue of the present with its past. In this sense, Fanon's work constitutes the archive that allows Alejandro J. De Oto to form his own inscription on postcolonial memory. His inquiry delineates from the intention to betray the "originals" as little as possible but without falling into the disingenuous thought that these are transparently offered up to his immediate gaze. For that reason, he dedicates a good part of his exploration to analyzing the use of Fanon's work. Like Calvino, De Oto proposes that every work arrives "bringing the imprint of the readings that have preceded ours, and after, leaving an imprint in the culture or cultures it traversed, (or more simply, in its language or customs)."[2]

In consequence, the trail left by Fanon's writings is transformed in this book into the archive of a memory oriented to the rescue of critical thinking during the postcolonial period.

It is also true that these approaches cannot ignore recent shifts in world geopolitics. However, without having to enter into discussion of all the recent developments, we know that the discursive plot of modern colonialism survives on its margins. It is exactly in that tissue into which Fanon made an incision to try to cure the sick body represented in that time not only by Africa and Europe but also by Latin America.

Fanon's work was followed by an overabundance of response from writers and thinkers, critics, and commentators. We are made aware of them in detail so that we may proceed, from our present, in dialogue with Fanon's work from his zones of indetermination. Considering this distance, Alejandro J. De Oto asks himself what is left to rescue from the author of the *Wretched of the Earth* in facing the ethical and political urgencies of our present. Fundamentally, De Oto's work signals, perhaps because of its obviousness, what many of its critics neglected: the relationship between the subject who writes and the subject of the written work. At present, writing plays a major part of contemporary cultural critique. Historian and anthropologist Michel de Certeau emphasized not long ago that his subject of study was in fact "orality," a point which does not cease to surprise since this is in consideration of the "writer." The paradox arises in that the "orality" or the gestures of the tortured faces, starving or made neurotic, cannot be understood without considering the "three or four centuries of Western work" woven into literature.[3]

Frantz Fanon: The Politics and Poetics of the Postcolonial Subject seeks primarily to do justice to its title; it is beautifully written and demanding. Through its journey, the readings convey a feeling of floating in a flowing river. Perhaps for that reason, De Oto's reading of Fanon's work emphasizes not its "essentialist" enunciations, characteristic of the time, but rather the ethical features contained in its narrative strategy. De Oto sees it, following Adorno, as a possible way of "responding to the monstrosity of certain historical, cultural and social projects" inscribed in modern colonialism. De Oto prefers the areas of uncertainty rather than to be situated in the prescriptive angles of discourse. Thus, De Oto's Fanon reveals himself in embarking on his own journey of writing on the alienated subject—and its revolutionary potential framed by the national liberation wars of the decades of the 1950s and 1960s. The challenge of this new reading of Fanon consists therefore in explaining why the transformation of the political and cultural situation of "the wretched of the earth" does not necessarily coincide with modifications in the epistemological devices that produce knowledge. Alejandro J. De Oto's reflections are situated at this crossroads of writing in general and its ethical and political functions framed by a postcolonial critique.

Guillermo Zermeño

Introduction

ON THE "USES" OF FANON

In recent years, several texts have appeared that invoke Fanon in their titles. The invocation does not necessarily imply that these studies strictly represent a quasi-internal analysis of Fanon's writing.[1] What could this "use" of Fanon mean? The answer usually relies on a series of considerations linked to intellectual geographies and eras. However, a particularly interesting result of Fanon's "uses" is that including his name in a title implies a starting point from which one can discuss issues such as identities, discourses on the nation, perspectives on gender, and theoretical crossroads. In that sense, the presence of Fanon invites different regions of knowledge without necessarily being faithful to a supposed primary Fanon, as the producer of authorial authority.

Fanon's "uses" in these works reveal greater efforts toward discord than accordance and are directed, in many cases, to exterior spaces of Fanonian writing. The ambivalent character of Fanon's own writing, a problem that we will explore here exhaustively, makes this possible. We could say my "use" in this study is of the same nature. The use links to problems such as thought on the form of the subject in the historical space that may possibly redeem the subject, alienation as a process that does not allow, due to its plot, for thinking of subjects outside of historicity, the very historicity of that subject, and the scenarios of the cultural imagination against the problem of confinement and openness.

These are problems and questions that exceed the more defined contexts of Fanon's writing, though to exceed does not mean to surpass them.

However, notwithstanding this "excess," Fanon's works overall (especially his two most important books, *Black Skin, White Masks* and *The Wretched of the Earth*) remain central to a strong plea against colonialism, as the site of a resolute and powerful voice embedded in political and moral urgency and in the cultural and political project. This is a constitutive moment of his texts. There is no doubt about that.

The crossroads that form that moment and the historical and political differences that unfold in the plot of his texts make his writing a peculiar place.

In analytical terms, historical Fanon is perfectly distinguishable from Fanon the author. Although I do not intend to discuss the function of the author, the peculiarity of Fanon's writing resides in the intersection between the discourse that impugns the colonial regime and the biographical trace in which it is imparted, especially in *Black Skin, White Masks*. It is at that crossroads, as I said above, that we question the subject, the historicity, the identities, the poetics, and the politics of his writing.

To read Fanon means subjecting oneself to a dislocation that produces a thought that is, as Homi Bhabha states, "authentically radical," in that it projects an "uncertain dark" ("Interrogating Identity: Frantz Fanon," 40).[2] Experiencing such displacement is to experience the extensive significance of a historicity that, in Fanon, resists remaining as annotations with capital letters, as with words like "History," "Identity," "Race," and "Revolution," among others.

However, the question—which I have yet to ask—persists: Why Fanon and not others? This question can be answered with complete bibliographies that assume different directions. We will resort to these bibliographies. However, the most important reason is not subtractive, nor additive; it is not to argue for or against. It is not about broaching issues that others have not considered, though there is some of that in my analysis.

The reason for choosing Fanon and his writing to enact a textual, political, and cultural heterological study and to re-encounter key theories capable of displacing our firmest positivity is because of the immeasurable fact, in terms of its value and radical thinking, that it places us at the limits of its revelation (revolution) with a dimension more acute, cataclysmic, unexpected, and full of uncertainties (of the national culture) that are impossible to leave unless at the cost of renouncing Fanon.

BETWEEN FANON AND US

Writing about Fanon always means to write about something else. This simple phrase, which brushes against the limits of the absurd, defies any attempt to agree, no matter what is being argued, on some of the most enigmatic writings of the twentieth century. Enigmatic more for what they do to their readers than for any secrets or riddles they may contain and offer as a challenge.[3] This is because the specters of Fanon's writing are more extensive, diverse, and resistant than we suspect.

It is, in turn, the memory of our intellectual, historical, and cultural needs at an end/beginning of the century that appear to throw us into terrains that any modern classic would not envy. In this case, as in many others, the specters are not strange figures that only haunt our texts. No. They are also signs. References that recall the inevitable and the impossible.

As Leonard Harris and Carolyn Johnson state, in thinking analogously of Derrida and the specters of Marx in their foreword to *Fanon: A Critical Reader*: "A haunting in memory, empowered to shape our identity but empty as a theoretical source describing who or what we are, the why of our predicament, or the what of our particular theater" (xv).

In the Derridean imagination, specters are, after all, those figures that besiege (haunt/*hanter*) without inhabiting the besieged (haunted/*hanté*) place.[4] They inhabit the siege (haunting).

The specters of Fanon's writing, which are Fanonian possibilities, besiege our writing and our political and moral urgencies with uncertainty. The latter, which seems like an oxymoron, is less so if our efforts to translate become historical by making Fanon's writing more a place of "use" and less a place of dictates.

In that sense, to speak of Fanon is inevitable, and it is impossible to speak of him and his texts while feigning fidelity to them. The inevitability responds, in my case, to the problem of "displacement," a word that readers of this study will see with excessive frequency. I refer here to our displacements and later to Fanon's. Our own writings are included in a sort of failed translation of history. Not only translation in brass terms, to say, the one that composes the texts and the attempts of representation that surround them but also the cultural translation, the most difficult and elusive of which puts the discussion in the field of the ineffable. My translations in this study are attempts made from fragile coordinates that run through my own tenuous (and spectral) cultural and theoretical belonging. This is a difficult, perhaps impossible, point to make when we face writings that apparently and primarily offer a sort of catalog of certainties. If I continue the dialogue, it is to do so within the Fanonian zones that vigorously rest in certitudes. This is not exactly a conciliatory gesture made with certain metaphors about the end of modernity but, instead, a statement of how things are. However, if in traversing the text one can perceive an attitude of its nature, then the attempt goes far beyond any parochial vision. Nonetheless, as we know, intentions are one and what derives from those intentions is another.

The fragility of the theory to which I allude links more to the difficulty of reconstructing the cultural traversals in Fanon's texts than to a fact of an absence of theory. It will become apparent that theory invades and shapes the body of this text. To problematize, I do not mean to renounce the possible homogeneity of my own reading, but, instead, to move toward an orientation that allows me ambiguity, theoretical license, and cultural, historical, and geographical uncertainty. In short, I try to learn from Fanon. Each of these aspects allow, in my opinion, a more profitable dialogue with its specters. You will not find any fidelity here for that reason. Nor is there an explicit attempt to be unfaithful; instead, things only happen. In this fictional happening, a paradoxical Fanon exists that is always possible. Or, to put it bluntly, that is always available. It is the Fanon who resists the logics of confinement by some of his readers and by the logics of confinement within the disciplines. Yet, this is a logic without method, because his texts, despite the incendiary and programmatic tone of many passages, are not arranged from coordinates situated from the emblematic questions of "What to do?" or of "how to do it." These two questions are included in the catalog of confinement. For example, these allow, in several cases, for the exclusion of the figure of Jean-Paul Sartre from the "pantheon" of colonial discourse. Ultimately, confinement serves to remove possibilities. But the idea of a pedagogy persists even in the face of a lack of methods. This issue is explored here in various ways with the aim of being strategic.

In this way, this study textually approaches a type of value that traverses Fanon's writing—a translated value, by the way—which considers his works (and writings) as a space of exclusion rather than opening, as a space of differentiation. The problem of translation shifts to another sphere. It is no longer that of representation in a strict sense but that of evocation because that allows for greater learning from Fanon. From there, his texts sometimes become unthinkable spaces where seemingly incompatible traditions meet if the problem of fidelity continues to be engaged.

READING FANON: SOME DERIVATIONS

To study Fanon's two most important texts, *Black Skin, White Masks* and *The Wretched of the Earth*, is to contend with several problems.[5] The first of these deals with the types of texts, sometimes open and sometimes not, in which a dialogue can be established. This is not a minor problem because it implies considering the main direction of my work. While Fanon's texts are central to the arguments and substance of the pages that follow, the lines of thought that they produce often dissolve or do so to the initial questions that seemed directly to challenge these. I refer here to the fact that talking about Fanon's texts or, more precisely, his writing is also to speak about those that speak on Fanon or that, at least, propose to do so. To put it simply, a relatively extensive set of texts has been produced on Fanon between different eras and traditions. This has meant having to prioritize certain readings which, of course, depend exclusively on the preferences that the reader-author assigns to them compared to others.

The field of Fanon studies too often encounters extensive disputes over the correct interpretation of his writings, expressed in articles and books that seek to revise prior readings in relation to specific passages. This process, otherwise familiar in any field of study, contains an additional, associated difficulty of having to work with texts—to say, doing so with meanings, signifiers, discourses, which, as we know, can be interpolated from the most diverse and divergent directions. Thus, for example, almost two decades after his death (1961), we find a series of studies that treat Fanon and his writing from the perspective of political projects tied directly to revolutionary theory. The biographical genre and studies share to a considerable degree the theoretical and ideological expectations of these works.[6] I dedicate a considerable space to discussing some of these works, as they allow us to perceive more clearly than others, how approaches vary not only in terms of theoretical and general political positions but also, and fundamentally, in relation to the ways these approaches constitute the object/subject of Fanonian writing. Additionally, they are a good mirror in that they reflect—and in many cases refract—strategies that we could call textualist in their approach to Fanon. Although in a nuanced way, that approach includes mine.

A greater emphasis on the "how" rather than on the "what" of Fanon's writing allows us to see the political and theoretical displacements of his texts and to reinvent dialogue among different temporal regions. In dealing with these readings, I am not suggesting that they constitute a sort of erroneous perspective or that they are necessarily part of a dialectical process, such as suggested in the prologue of *Fanon: A Critical Reader* (7), a dialectical process which, in this case, ultimately seems to confirm the best and most accurate of these readings. On the contrary, when I say that it is a matter of emphasis, I mean that matters look very different (and I apologize for the extensive use of visual metaphors) when the inquiry shifts from the contents that should be known to the way that these contents work. In this sense, without renouncing discussion on the diverse interpretations of Fanon's texts, when opportunity affords it, I focus here on the possible ways these are articulated in relationship to other texts including, of course, mine.

In another sense, the works encompassing this perspective are those that come closer to the idea of textual fidelity, producing additional reinforcement of Fanon's authorial authority. Moreover, they allow, in the general context of my study, a possible discussion about what we call political and moral urgencies.

However, the proposal is not to categorize the readings by common characteristics of their theoretical and political contexts. That is neither my claim nor objective since it would imply a restriction on the freedom to connect cultural scenarios, texts, and readings from diverse areas. A certain historiographic attitude toward Fanon's thinking and writing generates, from my perspective, a reduction in the possible spheres through which his work could be explored. I am referring concretely to the problematic idea of gradation or that each reading and period constitutes an advance on the path to a more complete understanding of his work. Although this is not the general rule crossing contemporary historiographic thought, the descent from the rules of a methodology that proclaims a kind of state-of-the-art toward an affirmation of the last works as the most finished and faithful is latent.

To a large extent, readings on Fanon propose that these be differentiated from the project of postcolonial criticism.[7] But, even within this criticism, Gordon, Sharpley-Whiting, and White, for example, distinguish in their description of possible stages of thought on Fanon between those that correspond to postmodern cultural studies and postcolonial studies. The figures that mark this stage are Homi Bhabha, Henry Louis Gates Jr., Abdul JanMohamed, Benita Parry, Edward Said, Gayatri Spivak, and, from a Marxist perspective, Cedric Robinson. According to Gordon, Sharpley-Whiting, and White, these authors, exempting JanMohamed, Parry, and Said, have made Fanon the object of numerous attacks based on fashionable political claims, such as misogyny or homophobia. Characteristic of these studies, except those of the last-named authors, is that Fanon is read through the lens of literature. Generally, the attacks correspond to a postmodern devaluation of theorists of liberation, following certain teachings of Lyotard, under the argument that they must, among other damning limitations, be totalizing and structurally modern. One of the readings that one can obtain from the perspective of considering Fanon's texts as an example of totalizing discourses is that they threaten marginalized groups, especially women (6). In considering this argument, it is possible to find concrete examples of the same critique in works by, among others, Rey Chow, bell hooks, Kobena Mercer, and Lola Young.[8]

Gordon, Sharpley-Whiting, and White's argument involves the question of fidelity. If scholarly authors can make claims that result in anachronisms, when speaking of Fanon, thus imposing demands that did not appear in his cultural horizon, then their arguments become debatable. At the end of the day, however, every reading is a sort of anachronism. Let us not forget that, if the intention is to polemicize Fanon, this starts from Fanon, a point often avoided. In other words, in defending him from "fashionable political designations," we cannot say that these issues were not present in Fanon. On the contrary, the aim is to think about Fanon in tension with his own arguments.

The group of readings assembled around this fifth (and presumably last) stage of academic thinking on Fanon is characterized, perhaps better than others, by a Fanon who has something to teach in different areas of thought.[9] In this stage, there is a Fanon available to the study of oppression, an endeavor that is certainly very sound, and of racism within intellectual genealogies involving Black Americans. Du Bois is a figure permanently associated with Fanonian thought.[10] Parallel to this, there is a Fanon read through the key lens of phenomenological existentialism, particularly by Lewis R. Gordon. In my study, I almost take his *Frantz Fanon and the Crisis of European Man* as my starting point. Gordon is a new and important voice in studies of Fanon, because he has rescued its Sartrean proximity for academic and political discussion, a particularly absent point in some of the postcolonial critiques represented clearly by Homi Bhabha. Additionally, Gordon's texts reclaim Fanon from the spirit of dialogue and the challenges these offer in philosophy, in his specific case, and for discussions involving the social sciences in general. It is a "use" of Fanon neither detained nor enclosed by the thematic of bibliography. Françoise Vergès, for example, in her contribution to *Fanon: A Critical Reader*, works from a similar position in thinking of Fanon through a history of psychiatry, but her questions, broaching the space of a disciplinary field, point to extra-disciplinary concerns that inevitably emerge from literature on Fanon's texts, especially *Black Skin, White Masks*. Questions within the boundary of a disciplinary discussion are raised but engaged from a different site: What kind of psychiatry do we face in the environment and production of a postcolonial culture; what are the legacies of postcolonial psychiatry in the general framework of psychiatry; what are its primary links with psychoanalysis (85, 91–3)?

In the same manner, in the same anthology, Renée T. White considers Fanon's *Sociologie d'un révolution* (sociology of a revolution) as staging theoretical and methodological learning that sociology can generally draw from his work (101). Gordon, Sharpley-Whiting, and White identify the positions in this moment as new readings on and from Fanon which are extremely varied. Perhaps most interesting is that the thematic diversity encourages a double possibility. First, it contributes directly to releasing Fanon of his postmortem theoretical and political duties particularly strong in the readings of the two decades after his death.[11] Second, it opens the possibility of discussing what happens within the disciplines and our experiences when they are crossed with writings that, in many ways, resist simple thematic and methodological reductions. This is a seemingly promising aspect when facing an increasing awareness of the problem of defining the strategies of authorizing authority in the order of textual discipline.

What seems to be closer to methodological and theoretical rigor does not always help one to consider the limits and challenges of a knowledge. This insight can be observed more clearly in the extensive compilation of Gordon, Sharpley-Whiting, and White.[12]

In this brief introduction of translations of Fanon, I must also highlight two sets of texts, grouped according to different logics. The first of these is the compilation edited by Nigel C. Gibson, *Rethinking Fanon: The Continuing Dialogue* and the second is the volume edited by Anthony Alessandrini titled *Frantz Fanon*.

Gibson's text tries to traverse with breadth the intellectual circuits linked to Fanon from the late 1970s through 1990s. The thematic organization of the text aims to not privilege some perspectives over others. However, linkages to so-called colonial discourse (postcolonial critique) are at the fore, and the reading by Homi Bhabha is regarded as a central point of discussion (14). Perhaps Gordon, Sharpley-Whiting, and White imagine thought on Fanon as a process that has not been interrupted, so that talking about a resurgence may seem incongruent. Nevertheless, most of the names that compose the complete circuit of authors who work with and from Fanon reappear in each compilation in attempts to summarize the main tendencies of analysis of his work. This persistent circulation, rather than to indicate a continuity of debate, summarizes the group of intellectuals who are presently responsible for a broadened discussion of Frantz Fanon. It may not be a resurgence, but it is an insistent reappearance. In the case of the compilation by Gibson, the names of Homi Bhabha, Diana Fuss, Henry Louis Gates Jr., Anne McClintock, and Edward Said appear, including those who relate to the most recent thought on Fanon. Among others, Emmanuel Hansen is linked to the genre of the readings that privilege the problem of revolutionary discourse and Nigel Gibson in his discussion about the problem of new humanism and the spaces of representation for a dialectic of history.

Something similar happens with the second compilation by Alessandrini.[13] His project advances on the ground of what I referred to earlier as the uses of Fanon. It is not simply, suggests Alessandrini, about working on the presupposition that each reading is somehow an incorrect appropriation, or a betrayal of Fanon, thus supporting a kind of easy pluralism, but to consider the implications of the uses of Fanon, their successes and limitations in reflecting on his texts on the stage of contemporary cultural politics (1). As he points out, not everyone in his book shares that project; for example, Gibson in "Fanon and the Pitfalls of Cultural Studies" claims a use of Fanon that polemicizes with invented Fanons. However, it is worth mentioning, among other points, that Alessandrini's volume represents an attempt to debate among theoretical positions without a rigid distinction among contemporary uses of Fanon.

ON DIVERSITIES AND DIVERGENCES

Possibly the most fruitful point for my study links to the problem of Fanon's uses and the possibility of imagining diverse and divergent scenarios that centralize the politics in my text. Regarding the theoretical problem, again, I have not been faithful to two types of issues—one, to the traditions in the texts of Fanon, and the other, to a specific reading or theory elaborated from Fanon's texts. With fidelity, I prefer to be faithful to what I already invoked as specters. Again, specters do not serve only as a reminder, as a mere presence that is simply there. Rather, they organize the concerns of everyone who, in one way or another, works with Fanon.

Thus, the central points of this study, namely, the problem of ambivalence between a transnational sphere and nativism, the question of agency for the colonized subject, the belief of a subject (say, of the theoretical and political necessity of relying on a subject) despite the devastating critique of colonial modernism and classical humanism, the imaginary of a contingent historicity and the permanent opening of cultural and historical strategies that this implies, were treated at different registers.

This theoretical license is inevitable if we want to take advantage of discussions that emerge from different spheres and if we want to inaugurate some form of dialogue. The political question associated with this type of work is evident. If at the end/start of the century we reread Fanon, it is to reflect from a different historicity on problems that, in many ways, seem to have absolute validity.

I

Fanon and Some Environments of Historicity

The First Displacements

> *I think: I wanted to live outside history. I wanted to live outside the history that Empire imposes on its subjects, even its lost subjects. I never wished it for the barbarians that they should have the history of Empire laid upon them. How can I believe that that is cause for shame?*
>
> —J. M. COETZEE, *Waiting for the Barbarians*

One of the questions that runs throughout this study is about the possible ways in which Sartre's existentialism is articulated in Fanon's writing. Although I have not limited the problem to a specific chapter, the presence of questions and positions that come from the extensive dialogue that Fanon maintains with Sartre is inescapable. The absence of Sartre in many of the contemporary works on Fanon corresponds more to a distance with respect to Sartre than in connection with Fanon's writing. The readings of Homi Bhabha and others close to certain poststructuralist contexts serve as examples, but this is also true of those readings to which I dedicate a considerable part of my analysis, those that can be encompassed in what I call a "postmortem ethics." Most of them link in their reflective mode to Marxism. The reason for this absence is also in the difficulty of connecting the individual dimensions of existential experience with the collective dimensions of that experience, at least, in an assessment of Sartre's writing that is not worth rearguing, as it was based more on a series of partial readings than on a complete review of his work. A certain ahistorical critique of existentialist arguments ties to this point. Poststructuralist readings regard the reason for the absence of existentialism as a problem in Fanon's texts to a critique of Sartre's extreme confidence in the subject. Both perspectives, which have been argued regarding most of Fanon's writing, suffer on this specific point due to the same problem. The following question may seem naïve. Even when considering the existentialist dimensions that inevitably inhabit Fanon's texts, can a dialogue be established with readings that omit the Sartrean presence or criticize it as a so-called deviation from Fanon's writing? All our readings, after all, compose new Fanonian texts. I would like to consider the possibility of dialogue among positions and readings that apparently exclude each other even at the risk of this study being considered uselessly contrary or as a theory of excessive uncertainty.

SPACES OF HISTORICITY

Additionally, I am interested in discussing Fanon as a thinker of the temporal, as one who knows the plots of historicity and whose subjects unfold in them. This temporal link emerges from its proximity to Sartrean existentialism or with existentialist phenomenology.[1]

Lewis Gordon indicates that Fanon privileges an existentialist perspective while rejecting the ontological dimensions of human beings (10). In his book *Fanon and the Crisis of European Man*, Gordon addresses the problem of whether Fanon's critical project can be read from an existentialist matrix, which would highlight Fanon's proximity with Sartre and Maurice Merleau-Ponty. Gordon's central argument posits that Fanon, by rejecting an ontological matrix of Being, questions and opens, in turn, the possibilities of imagining the universe of representations in what Gordon defines as a new humanism. The rejection of an ontological matrix implies a separation with respect to the study of Being in the texts of Husserl and Heidegger, articulated in Fanon with an existentialism that recognizes the historical dimension in which subjects act, but with a phenomenological dimension in which "he does not reject . . . what he 'sees'" (10).

Gordon invokes Sartre to propose that in Sartrean philosophy human being is never what ontological tradition says it is. It is not Being in ontological terms, but to be human in the moment of crisis that implies its existence through its negation (17). At this point, the ontological tradition is basically a theodicy that seeks the primacy of Being, of presence, and considers all Others as problems, in their foreclosure of having been shown as non-existent in the first place (17). Let's read Fanon:

> I came to the world, imbued with the will to find a meaning of things, my spirit filled with the desire to attain to the source of the world, and then I found that I was an object in the midst of other objects.
> Sealed into that crushing objecthood, I turned beseechingly to others. Their attention was a liberation, running over my body suddenly abraded into nonbeing, endowing me once more with an agility that I had thought lost, and by taking me into the world, restoring me to it. But just as I reached the other side, I stumbled, and the movements, the attitudes, the glances of the other fixed me there, in the sense in which a chemical solution is fixed by a dye. (*Black Skin*, originally cited 101; 109)

Here, I am particularly interested in Gordon's argument that defends the implication of the concrete in Fanon. What Fanon "sees" as a form of existential resistance against the hierarchical dimensions of an ontology are the effects of colonial society. These effects constitute the material with which *Black Skin* and *The Wretched* are constructed. First, through analysis of alienation in colonial society and second, in the analysis of colonial society as a "Manichean world." Let's look at this in more detail. The alienation that Fanon reviews in *Black Skin* regards the lived experience of blacks.[2] This experience, in the characters of Mayotte Capécia and Jean Veneuse, designates a separation.[3] The particularity of this separation is that it does not occur with respect to an original nucleus from which all experience deviates, as can be read in some recurring arguments of Négritude or in the foundation of an urgent national culture. The separation regards the impossibility of establishing a representation in which the subjects do not have to renounce, as Marc Bloch would say, the "sensitive features of the landscape." These features are in these texts much more than the object of an elusive geography. These are the traits of a historical landscape and experience defined by the fact of subordination, historical estrangement, and displacement.

> I could no longer laugh, because I already knew that there were legends, stories, history, and above all historicity, which I had learned about from Jaspers. Then assailed from various points, the corporeal schema crumbled, its place taken by a racial epidermal scheme. In the train it was

no longer a question of being aware of my body in third person but in the triple person. (*Black Skin*, originally cited 103; 112)

In the context of such a landscape, the body separates from its perceptible traits also because there is no possibility of restoring lost or imagined orderings, nor representations that could dissolve the opacity of the colonized subject (almost objectified) through the visible. Not to what Fanon "sees" as Gordon would say but, because of its implied visibility: "I subjected myself to an objective examination, I discovered my blackness, my ethnic characteristics; and I was battered down by tom-toms, cannibalism, intellectual deficiency . . . and above all else, above all: 'Sho' good eatin'" ("*Y a bon Banania*,"[4] originally cited 104; 112). An exterior linked to Fanon's reading of Sartre's *Réflexions sur la question juive* where "they [the Jews] have allowed themselves to be poisoned by the stereotype that others have of them, and they live in fear that their acts will correspond to this stereotype. . . . We may say that their conduct is perpetually overdetermined from the inside" (quoted by Fanon, *Black Skin*, originally cited 106; 115).[5]

Despite the differences that Fanon encounters between this situation and the "lived experience of the Negro," the possibility of an ontology remains outside his strategy in not even beginning to recognize the idea of an omnipresent being beyond all historicity (a complex problem in *The Wretched* that allows an existential critique by Fanon with the Hegelian dialectic of the Master and the Slave). That could also be the reason for Fanon's estrangement from the historicity of Jaspers's use of *Geschichtlichkeit*, a historicity that refers to the union of the self with the *Dasein* (literally, "being-there"), with existing or presence, a *Dasein* represented as appearance.[6] In Jaspers's terms, historicity arises from that union.

In this sense, there is no possibility of imagining a place for the colonized subject in Fanon since not experiencing the displacement of all historicity, but particularly of a Jaspersian historicity, attacks the corporal schema. We could say that *Black Skin, White Masks* begins to enunciate a double critical movement by means of a metaphor of disappointment, as it appears in the idea of an external representation that locates corporality and any feature of identity in triple person. It is an historical realization (*Geschichtsbewusstein*) that warns that what exists within history for the figure of a black subject thrown into the world is, precisely, an absence of history (*Geschichtslosigkeit*). However, this absence is with respect to the model of a history and a historicity lodged by various traditions of modernity that include Hegel and, as part of the existentialist inheritance, Jaspers.

For Jaspers, repetitions or regular causalities, as he called them, are not material of history. On the contrary, singularity becomes historical in the happening. Historical consciousness reconsiders what is "irreplaceable, peculiar, individual" and, in doing so, gives it a value that does not perish with time. The peculiar must be appropriated. In the process, what it reveals is its permanence. Thus, in a sense, the historical implies an abolition of time because, by means of its appropriation, it shows its enduring character beyond all events and repetition. Jaspers will say that the historical is that which becomes frustrated, which is not easily revealed. Abolishing temporality exposes its eternal character. The idea is that finite man, as "unfinished and unending," must realize the timelessness of the eternal (*Origin and Goal of*, 300). Hence, there is a coincidence between the unfinished character of man and his historicity (*Geschichtlichkeit*). Since there are no perfect final endings, history is inconclusive. It is change and transformation; it constantly pushes us to seek the eternal that is in fact impossible to grasp (301). But this transformation, despite Jaspers, is not eventful but conditioned by the existence of the eternal or of the historical on its terms. One could say that there is a kind of relationship between the peculiarity of existence, even of individual existence, and the awareness of that existence that always refers to the eternal by the pursuit of its search and by its very inconclusion. The eternal in Jaspers may be the Self, but that Self resembles greatly the humanist tradition of man, and the idea of the presence of metaphysics. The problem always returns to a place that is the transcendence of the context of the conditions in which our lives are resolved. Jaspers' entreaty to the dominion of history is the basis of a philosophy of existence that while seemingly enunciating respect for that which is near, dilutes it in the transcendent act of a historical depth that offers, supposedly, better and broader reasons for our existence: "we cannot let slip away what we can be during our time, submitting to it before we try to penetrate, by illuminating the time, to that place where we can live from a profound depth" (*Philosophy of Existence*, 90). Thus, when Fanon moves away from Jaspers's historicity, Fanon signals the impossibility of the colonized establishing the link between the peculiarity of existence, the consciousness of that existence, and the possible scenario of transcending the nearest contextual boundaries.

The historicity Jaspers taught Fanon becomes a burden in the moment of imagining his position in the world as black and colonized. The separation of the body from its immediate references, the gaps left in physical terms as representational for the body of the colonized, in the triple person, are the factors that do not allow for the Jaspersian idea of a historicity that is almost equivalent for all subjects, a historicity that can transcend the immediate contexts because of the search for the eternally historical, beyond the regular causalities.

In this first moment of *Black Skin* there is no room for transcendence because what Fanon proposes to show is the nature of alienation. It is the paradoxical return to a memory because a lack, or absence, in a sense, a non-place within historicity designates the memory. As such, it can affect the strategy of representation that the idea of presence (*Dasein*) entails. As we will see later, Fanon insinuates here a double impossibility, that of recovering lost orders and that of restoring pasts in the present.

The emptiness generated by the racial epidermal schema is much more than the realization of a racist worldview. Fanon advances a critique of the historicity of classical humanism from this place. The abandonment of the historicity of Jaspers by Fanon is a sort of scission and rupture with the representational orders of modern society. Any displacement to that non-place becomes a critique and evidence of political and moral urgencies. It is the raising of consciousness of a history, not necessarily of history in general, but of one that writes modernity as a project that casts difference to the exterior, to an indeterminate space. The political and moral urgencies are inscribed in the awareness of an absence of participation in the construction of history, if the model of historicity that is imposed is that which claims a link between the peculiarity of existence and the awareness of that existence. Fanon's consciousness, then, is negative at this point, not necessarily dialectic, since it inhabits not the borders of the representation, nor the borders of the colonial system, but rather an imperceptible place shown by the fact of questioning what discourses and modern historicity repress.

It is not, of course, to think that the abandonment, the distance, or the impossibility that the Jaspersian historicity imposes on Fanon's reading should be interpreted as an antimodernist reaction by Fanon. It is a negation that is articulated by figures of difference that inevitably arise when the model of historicity is summarized (in a complex way, of course) in a determined movement, despite everything, in a kind of perpetual actuality.

This type of historicity removes the positive historical ground from the political and cultural imagination of the subject (our ways of imagining the subject) in which his figure unfolds. At this point, it is not about seeing what Jaspersian historicity represses to understand the place of Fanon's political imagination, in a question like that of Michel Foucault in relation to madness, which suggests, for example, that to understand what our societies call sanity, it is necessary to explore madness ("The Subject and Power," 779–80).

Although it must be recognized that this type of analysis is attractive, because it offers with relative transparency the constituent relations between what is remitted to oblivion and what appears as the reason for it, this historicity becomes impossible when the question of the subject refers to a triple person. The impossibility of thinking of any possible figure of the subject when the type of representation it relies on does not make him into one is a Fanonian claim. The space that is left free in the "triple person" is a sign of that impossibility.

There is at that moment in the Fanonian narrative almost none of the two aspects that Foucault assigns to the word "subject": "subject to someone else by control and dependence; and tied to his own identity by a conscience or self-knowledge" (*ibid*, 781). With this, I do not mean that Fanon does not note on the first condition of the subject and of being represented within it, when extending its categories to the stage of his individualization. However, as an extreme of his critique, and as an expression of his political and moral urgencies, what appears in front of what he "sees" is precisely a lack or absence of subjectivization, whichever direction it assumes. Nor, as we shall see, will there be room for any transcendence in the Jaspersian sense.[7] There is no transcendence functioning in a situation of experience that does not recognize any possible state for the subject.

If historicity is found in a determined course or in the confrontation with this course, then there is no place to experience it. In the passage of *Black Skin, White Masks*, the subject of interrogation no longer faces the displacement of his own beliefs on the location he occupies, but its representational emptiness. The vacuum precisely foreshadows the content as traversed by, and as the product of, political and moral urgencies.

II

Writing and Urgencies
On Ethics and Works: Readings

> *Kafka's writings are by their nature parables. But it is their misery and their beauty that they had to become more than parables. They do not modestly lie at the feet of the doctrine, as the Haggadah lies at the feet of the Halacha. Though apparently reduced to submission, they unexpectedly raise a mighty paw against it.*
>
> —Walter Benjamin, "Some Reflections on Kafka" in *Illuminations*

The political and moral urgencies in Fanon's texts have been the subject of various readings. However, in the approximately two decades following his death, these urgencies were read as an emancipatory project inserted in the logic of a rising historicity (which we will discuss with the question of Sartre) by most voices contemporary with Fanon and those who followed.

Fanon was portrayed as the romantic hero of a situation explained in the articulations of the modes of production and in the theory of revolution. He was, however, a romantic hero also in his devastating critique not only of a state of things that confronted the historical text of colonialism and the developments of an idea of emancipation beyond national independence (especially for *The Wretched* and for the African revolution), but also of his own existence, his own life.

The romantic hero echoes, for example, certain Latin American perspectives like those mapped by Ricardo Córdoba in the prologue to the book directed to Frantz Fanon militants and the Anti-Colonial Revolution in which the poet Juan Gelman translates the essay by Peter Geismar, author of a semi-biographical work that Irene Gendzier recognizes as one of the most extensive studies on Fanon (*Frantz Fanon*, 16). However, I situate Córdoba's argument in disaccord with readings that romanticize Fanon because of its definite distancing from the real conditions of existence (8) in a construction of Fanon that is ideal but not applicable.

The literature of the two decades after Fanon's death has, from my perspective, a problem with its language. I hold a negative suspicion, in more than one sense, on the nature of the ambivalent language in them because what is to be explained, and the word is not casual, are not textual forms (and their contents) but what seems transparent: the resource of action and the fraternal dimension in struggles for liberation (8–9).

In a way, what Fanon "must" do in these years is build a postmortem ethic and a delimitation of its political and moral urgencies. Córdoba's critique covers these.

Beyond this dimension, the prologue's writer is caught in the same grammar that he tries to reject. The idea of parallel lives fed by the same "fire" between Fanon and Che Guevara results in a romantic image rather than a leveled representation of individuals and collective forces (7). And this romantic image comes at a time when romanticism is rejected by much of the traditional European left because of its supposed antimodern content. This left includes those committed to the socialist project (16).

However, the article by Peter Geismar, "Frantz Fanon: Evolution of a Revolutionary: A Biographical Sketch," inevitably approaches a Fanon who must, in one way or another, honor a certain romantic tradition. He is seen as the key intellectual of the Algerian revolutionary process (that of *El Moudhajid*) and his absence, in some way, hastens "the collapse of progressive forces" (29). But Geismar quickly restores the exigency of the literature of those years on Fanon, which obliges us to present his thought first and fundamentally from its political stance, more than from any other (30).[1] Fanon's subsequent absence emerges in the double condition of a process of a central subject and as a builder of a postmortem ethic that cannot be evaded.

In the same collection, Enrica Coletti Pischel points out that romanticism in Fanon, or of the figure of Fanon, is a characteristic shared by other revolutionary leaders of the Third World, due to the historical and material conditions in the colonial world that liberation movements must face. For example, they must have a discourse that highlights the predominance of the new versus the old and the exaltation of human freedom (64). She qualifies this attitude in Fanon as "moralistic romanticism" (65).

Nevertheless, valorizing Fanon's romanticism accomplishes, according to Coletti Pischel, the exigencies of his times. Appealing to romanticism and to statements linked to it, such as "New Man," "morally integrative," and "for the people," is done, as in some colonial societies, if they comply with an "objective revolutionary function" (65). Coletti Pischel reinstates the double condition to which Fanon's figure is subjected. Fanon may be seen as romantic, but "independent of this human and existential problematic" (65), his contribution is placed within Marxism (66).

Coletti Pichel sees in Fanon's texts an instrument to validate the base that produced the appropriation of Marxism in the colonies (66). Additionally, from this perspective, Fanon's texts would also be a critical control for those versions of Marxism that Eric Hobsbawm called, in a famous article, "vulgar Marxism."[2]

Though its existentialist dimensions and, we could say, its cultural Antillean background are rarely agreed upon, despite mentioning the specificity of his discourse, there is no possibility to think of his texts and figure on unstable terrain. For example, Césaire could have seen Fanon beyond the implicit suspicion that poetic language contains, as found in Geismar's quote (see note 7).

In *The Predicament of Culture*, James Clifford suggests further thought on the Antillean political text, of which Fanon is part, with Césaire's notion of marronage, which is presented as a permanent transgression against the colonial order and hierarchy. The word marronage and the associated verb maroon were coined by Aimé Césaire, one of the creators of Négritude. As Clifford points out, Césaire evokes with marronage (which can be read in the sense of the Cimarrón, derived from the escape of black slaves in the Antilles and in the swamps of Guyana) not only an escape from the order and impositions of slavery but an experience of transgression and the reconstruction of culture (220).

The point here, then, is not an ex post facto critique of attempts to understand Fanon's political perspective and theoretical contribution, but, instead, to think about the challenges his writing has permanently deployed for some of the most relevant readings.

What I mention as the imposition of a postmortem ethic has several meanings. First, it implies reading Fanon through the obligations of political and moral urgencies (that are no longer his, but all of ours) that have him enter a tradition, either theoretical or political, to which he must respond. Second, this investment maintains the tone of the characteristics of the period.

Fanon, who has given little sign in his texts about this, is almost compulsorily read from the specificity of the anticolonial struggle. But, in this reading, a hierarchy is imposed on his texts ordered in successive "intakes of consciousness." From *Black Skin* until the final manifesto of *The Wretched*, what is highlighted is the growing immersion in revolutionary processes that express a strong categorization of his work, the text that his life writes, as well as the text of his life.

A brief paragraph of Peter Geismar's biographical essay reads:

> Fanon's life seems to have four stages: a conventional bourgeois youth; an introspective period during which he realized the extent of his neurosis as he prepared to be a psychiatrist; a revolutionary, cathartic break with the past; a more definitive African revolutionary ending. (21–2)

Each moment implies an organization of Fanon's textuality and, of course, a hierarchy. This organization, inevitably ascending, will contain romanticism in some place in the text, although the tone of the time of these writings immediately restores the transparency of the Fanonian project.

Fanon's biographies always contain a precarious balance between the political theoretical dimensions of his work and his personal history implicated in the phenomena and processes to which his writing refers. The *Frantz Fanon* of Irene Gendzier is perhaps the best example of this. This point is relevant to what I discuss here because of the depths of a life that seeks to be explained in the world, in some way, with the pace and organization of a biography that authorizes it and in the concrete case of a theoretical, political, and cultural project. This authorization responds, from my perspective, to the forms and fundamentals expressed in Fanon's postmortem ethics. If his texts have any use of this ethic, it is in the confirmation and originality of a set of texts supported by a life.

However, the act of explaining the directions Fanon's texts take is to inevitably link them with his personal history and, by extension and content, with certain ideological and political projects, such as Marxist theory, existentialism, and blackness.

Gendzier explains Fanon from this lens, producing an organization and a reading like Geismar's. Chapter I of her book, titled "In the Beginning: The Search for Roots, 1925–1952," makes an important point: if we must search for the ways in which dramatic tension enters the founding of a new humanism, and if colonial violence establishes a way of life and an exercise of reflection, then these must necessarily be found in the life experiences of the author. If this is the foundation, his work inevitably always refers to the scenarios his life faces. From there, the biographical exercise advances on the direction of a growing consciousness as a result of self-reflection and of a way of writing associated with it:

> Very early in his life and in his writing, Fanon arrived at the conclusion that he needed to understand himself as he was, as he believed himself to be, and as the world saw him. For this, he chose to write. Not as a way of describing the world or himself, but as a way of understanding it, its absurdities, and the possibilities of its rationalizations. To write was a form of action; it was in its origins self-centered and reflexive. But by its very nature it was also a method of communicating, a reaching out to tell and to teach others. (Gendzier, originally cited, 24; 4)

Perhaps this process was as described by Gendzier, which is not in question, but what matters is that he (himself) is associated with the critical space of a life read from rationalizations. In this sense, the tension and ambivalence that inundate Fanon's texts seem to move in a peculiar way to the texts of his commentators, as an attempt to restore the "anomaly" that such tension and ambivalence represent. I say an anomaly in quotation marks because, as we will soon see, this only exists if we accept certain restrictions from the start, such as the suppression of ambivalence in Fanonian discourse.

It is also true that Gendzier's biography highlights the intellectual circuits that Fanon travels and inhabits. For example, the connections with *Les Temps Modernes, Présence Africaine*, the Hegel of the French reading of Merleau-Ponty and Sartre, Marx, and Freud. However, the relationship between Fanon's existential situation and his political and philosophical discourses is what contains the weight of his figure for Gendzier. In a way, the representation of Fanon that emerges from

Gendzier's work suggests that his texts are always the result of that crossroads. Gendzier carries the weight of Fanon's growing consciousness until the last pages. The consequence of this is that, despite the multiple circuits of Fanon's texts and life, everything converges in an ascending project and in a series of proposals for the future:

> He understood that his own conception of neutrality should somehow be more than a guarantee of permanent poverty. . . . Militant and uncompromising as he was in his beliefs, Fanon was not beyond recognizing that the new dawn was filled with threats that were as capable of breaking and killing men as those of an earlier day. That he did not live to see the aftermath of Algerian independence did not deprive him from understanding as much. (Originally cited, 361; 269–70)

That is, beyond the obstacles that a quasi-romantic disposition of Fanon produces, the rise of a consciousness makes it possible to better and more precisely see their deployment of the future. In other words, it is not exactly the space opened by the multiple texts that intersect in his life (and I use here a metaphor of a wide text) and the confusion that they hold which allow us to see the consequences of the policies carried out in post-independence Algeria, but rather the exorcism of all these texts in view of a consciousness reminiscent of the Hegelian "spirit" after having traversed the ordeal of history.

Fanon's return from the "anomaly" becomes complete. It is a return because the prescriptive tone of postmortem ethics must organize its knowledge out of the "failures" that an extremely mixed and diverse life contains. Or better, the life must be organized into a coherent and directed set of knowledge. Benita Parry, as we will see later, uses a term to describe the particularity of Fanon. For her, the tension existing in his texts between the transnational and specific acquires the name of an "impulse." The impulse in the literature relevant to Fanon in the two decades following his death remains. In some places, it cannot be domesticated. Ultimately, this literature faces problems related to romantic visions not so much in the dimension that these have in a liberation or revolutionary project but in the almost radical instability that they provoke in the discourse of modern reason and in the colonial text.

For example, Córdoba's prologue, quoted earlier, fears Fanon's romantic heroic mutation, because it would dismantle the most profoundly transformative contents of his discourse. He therefore does not warn of the romantic instability that the subject represents and even, of the individual subject at the limits of his moral, vital, and historical strength that results and is the cause of a textuality and writings that insistently depart from the canon.

The exorcism of the anomalous represents a displacement of Fanon's writing in terms of order. In other words, his writing decenters claims that pretend to be true to them. If the romantic facet of his personality encompasses, as Coletti Pichel says, a necessary and objective moment of the revolutionary process, then this idea definitely leaves out the possibility of writing immersed in ambivalence and irony. But, even before that, it leaves out the representation of Fanon's writing in terms of their simultaneous tragedy and irony. Of tragedy, because the supposed escalation of his consciousness from *Black Skin* to *The Wretched* could be represented as the impossibility of separating the problem of alienation from the subject. Of irony, because it is in the folds of that alienation that the most cutting critique emerges of a subject willed in the world. The exclusion of these two dimensions in the reading of his texts obliges a traversal of circuits that must confirm, at each step, the certainties of a consciousness that separates slowly but inexorably from the charges which bring it back to situations of subordination and alienation. The "colonized" is the figure that would help to trace this journey. However, the romantic dimension has an extra consequence.

The romantic hero of the late eighteenth and nineteenth centuries does not always win battles and, when he does, it is only to warn that the forces he faces have an even wider dimension than he had suspected. The figure of Goethe's Faust or Carlyle's hero inexorably faces at the end of their heroic acts the tragedy and the irony of them. There is no restitution of an ideal world at the conclusion of the adventures they undertake. There is no return to any desired past nor to a possible future since they, as unstable texts before the forces of history, can only deal with them. They do not aspire to a definitive victory; there, however, lies their originality. Faust will discover, in his hands, the result of history beyond the illusions that derive from the power of the pact. Carlyle, for example, will construct a figure of the hero like one who emerges from epoch to epoch, of temporality in temporality, of divine adscriptions:[3]

> In the history of the world there will not again be any man, never so great, whose fellowmen will take for a god. Nay we might rationally ask, Did

any set of human beings ever really think the man they *saw* there standing beside them a god, the maker of this world? . . . a rude gross error that of counting the great man a god. (35)

This image of someone in a growing process of secularization represents Carlyle's conception of history in which the individual subject faces history. But, as Hayden White points out, the subject of Carlyle's history is not exactly history in general but rather the one capable of leading it. Carlyle had, says White, a critical principle that would individualize "the man who accomplishes something against history" (148).

In that sense, Fanon, or rather, colonized Fanon, that personage who travels through all of his writing, is always at the crossroads of facing history, even at the risk of suspecting the limits that history imposes. A crossroads reminiscent of Jaspersian historicity, despite Fanon's displacement of it, present beyond the project of liberation and the founding of a new humanism; however, a crossroads that is also present within these two central elements of his writing and his political and cultural imagination. From this point of view, then, the organization of knowledge on Fanon and his texts require that what I have called postmortem ethics be based on excluding that which represents risk and instability for the political project that it embodies.

The emerging order resembles that of an inflexible and hidden chronology that marks the key moments of the rising movement. Fanon's texts are from there the register of events of the consciousness of the colonized in their struggle to delink from the bonds that constitute the colonized as such. If they are to become, this word, becoming, links with historicism. This evocation of historicism is not, as is often the case, a sort of strategy to rule out a possible look at historicity, but to revise the problem underlying Fanon's readings in relation to the imagination of historical time. If the temporally smooth and plain sequence does not seem to organize the postmortem ethics that his writing must fulfill, then what remains unspoken is a temporal imaginary. This representation is more complex in not only confirming a course for history but also for consciousness and, in doing so, designs a hierarchy that inevitably fulfills stages that, in a self-created gesture, consolidates them. For that reason, no reading could privilege or focus on *Black Skin, White Masks*, for example, without experiencing the sense of disorder and scarcity in the thematic organization that, as we know, is often seen as a metaphor for other shortcomings. Rupturing the temporal order of Fanon's readings would reveal such shortcomings and betray the text of Fanon's consciousness and his intentionality as an author. At that moment, the result is silence. It is a silence from which I will speak later, which is very much like colonial silence.

Thus, faced with the challenges against the temporal imaginary of historicism or against any seduction of rhetoric, a response is to rectify this anomaly by means of enunciating the "true" elements at stake, what I had referred to as the exorcism of the anomaly. This is not the elimination of the textual but of the meaning of Fanon's enunciations and histories that seem to take divergent paths. Thinking through Jacques Derrida, what works as supplemental must be eliminated so that the "true nature" of Fanon's project may emerge.

Examples of this abound. Gendzier points out that Fanon's preoccupation with the Antilles does not seem to have disappeared despite his displacements (30–31). That is, beyond the legitimate description of this process by Gendzier, the problem lies in the territorialization of Fanon and his writing. Displaced Fanon is one that does not coincide with an ethics and a politics that is situational. Neither does his writing, unless it functions under a claim that permanently obligates a reference to its limits. Renate Zahar imposes such a point:

> Any research into colonial phenomena runs the risk of getting bogged down in colonial, racialist or paternalistic categories if the psychological processes of oppression discussed by Fanon are neglected or passed over in silence. His theories are, however, limited in scope by the fact of their being based on the historico-economic and political conditions he encountered in *his own revolutionary activity*. His description of the processes of alienation can in the first instance only claim validity for *those areas that he knew from firsthand experience*. (xxi; my italics)

Different from what Gordon establishes regarding what Fanon "sees," this experience, located both within "his revolutionary activity" and in "firsthand experience," creates locations in his writing. These function as signs in the readings and as an undisguised presence of a temporal imaginary that organizes his texts as a project. If the revolution fails, Fanon remains available for the social sciences.

In other words, if one location fails, the location of disciplines remains. As we know from Michel Foucault's *The Birth of The Clinic*, disciplines have more than one way of regulating knowledge and its provisions. The function of territorialization explains successive contexts in which the consciousness of the colonized subject emerges. Each step confirms that a different moment has been reached. But more than explaining the succession of contexts, territorialization is above all a way of giving identity to what seems elusive and unstable.

The romantic figure evokes an elusive ethos in which community and the subject merge but never in a final and defined way. For this reason, the traits that refer to romanticism as a form of displacement are abolished or, more precisely, displaced according to a project that must account for its rationality at every moment. This perspective proposes that rationality is situational and culturally and discursively localizable. In that sense, it should also be noted that modern aesthetic and political experiences could be considered as journeys and as almost permanent drifts, that is, from the aesthetic experiences of Johann Wolfgang von Goethe's literature, particularly of *Faust*, to the dissolution of the limits of anarchists' political and cultural representations where there is a huge field of completely modern drifts. This is also evident in the representations of the voyage to imperial territories of the nineteenth century that abound with what Mary Louise Pratt called "The Imperial Eyes" and the spaces of dissolution and disintegration of claims more resistant to difference, as is the case of the travel writing by Richard Francis Burton.[4] Alternately, drifts in the persistent presence, deferred in postcolonial African, specifically Nigerian, literature, of the ambiguity in Conrad's *The Heart of Darkness* as the means of a metaphor that builds the others but also destabilizes its own. This paradox dwells in the Fanonian postmortem ethics. All forms of displacement can be made regardless of the other side of modern traditions, which, paradoxically, they seem to defend. The cases I mentioned above are only a few markers in an immense cultural territory in which the figures, practices, and displaced discourses are constitutive of the very critical traditions of modernity. After all, extending the image of travel and displacement to its cultural limits, one could say that the intellectual and cultural adventures of modernity were marked by both ideas: traveling and displacing of, among others, Marx, Burton, Bakunin, Baudelaire's *flâneur*, Rimbaud, Miranda, and Sarmiento. The quests on each trip differ and have divergent results. For example, as Marx inaugurates his physical and intellectual journey from the Neue Rheinische

Zeitung, which takes him to France and later to England, Richard Francis Burton begins his journeys (after a long defeat by continental Europe) from England toward the limits of the British Empire. Both will visit the British Museum Library[5] during the same period as they prepare their moves. One travels toward the center of the most extensive "civilizing" project of the nineteenth century and the other toward its margins. Bakunin will deploy its failed revolutionary energies in various European regions; Baudelaire's *flâneur* (magnificently studied by Walter Benjamin) will be displaced inside a nineteenth-century Paris that illuminates the model of the new modern city. Their journeys will wander through the alleys until the markers of modernity imposed by the "passages" confine them in their interiors and then in the bazaars, the central space of merchandise. Benjamin thought like no one else about merchandise as a form of territorialization, when imagining it as an extension of the spirit of the *flâneur* or his equal, a last refuge that paradoxically disperses desire in its labyrinthic provisions (*Poetry and Capitalism*, 71).

The street, as a place of cultural experimentation characteristic of modernity, represented in the poetry of Baudelaire by the figure of the *flâneur* that Benjamin studied, is a very important trope in one of the readings by Bhabha on Fanon. Not because they look like those Fanon theorized from what he "sees" or the Baudelairean *flâneur* (perhaps no more distant), but because both find in the figure of the street the dimensions of historicity in a sort of day-to-day, which contingent as it may appear is simultaneously a symptom of more profound situations and a place for critique of homogeneous and univocal projects. Bhabha states regarding Fanon:

> For a writer and a political activist, some of whose most salutary scenes of political engagement/encounter have typically happened while walking down the street ("'Look, a Negro!'" being the seminal moment of racist recognition in *Black Skin, White Masks*), Fanon's emergent insurgent day-to-day resembles Michel de Certeau's concept of "local authority" as he elaborates it in his essay on the politics of the everyday, "Walking in The City": a discourse of local authority compromises the "univocality" of historicism, universalism or, in this case, nationalism. It functions as a "crack in the system" that disturbs functionalistic and totalitarian systems of signification and spaces of enunciation by inserting local authorities "above and below" and "in excess." ("Day by day . . . ," 189)

The street as a place that defies the constitution of homogeneous forms of signification has journeyed in many modern scenes. Dostoevsky in *Notes from Underground* will construct Nevsky Prospect Avenue of St. Petersburg as the political and cultural space for the encounter and conflict between social classes where the problem of recognition between different forms of historicity and temporalities are staked.[6] The street will also be the place of tragedy for a consciousness that tries to surpass the narrow limits homogeneous meanings impose on identity. Fanon will recognize in it that his figure is represented not in double- but in triple-person. In responding to Perry Anderson's criticisms of the modernity project of development, Marshall Berman delineates in *All that Is Solid Melts into Air* an almost Fanonian style to extend the representational space of the street to our daily experiences (the two sites, we could say, where Fanon will develop both his idea of historicity and his theoretical perception) and our critical reflections that must contend with the "substance and the flow of daily life" (130). Berman notes with sharpness that before learning to read contemporary critical texts, like Marx's *Capital*, for example, it is necessary to learn to identify the signs of the street, because these may provide the diverse and divergent forms of cultural and political significance acquired by the subjects (130).[7]

But the voyages and displacement continue. Rimbaud finds in the displacement of the self a place to enunciate the futility of fixations. In the voyage that confirms his suspicion of "barbarity" is Sarmiento, someone who writes and thinks from a decentered place, who must obligatorily find the fundamentals of the center, reinventing it even beyond his original text. The idea of civilization and barbarity in *Facundo* cross this path, an extensive icon in the close of nineteenth-century Latin America. There are plenty of cultural and temporal examples, but their abundance informs us of something that belongs to Fanonian thought: the marks of the modernity which inhabit these texts should not be thought, read, or imagined only as places that concentrate and stabilize meanings.

The place of ambivalence, of which I will speak later, is a kind of "non-place" that disputes its centrality and intents because his biography, constituted by both his life and texts, stabilizes its political and cultural imagination. Ambivalence implies considering what Bhabha, in his critique of Edward Said's *Orientalism*, mentions, which is how, in the process of subjectification, the colonial discourse destined for the dominated subjects contains the "dominant being" within it (24–5). Thus, by extension, it can be understood that critical discourses are inhabited by the reasons that make them such. However, Bhabha's critical point should not be understood as the failing fixation of a component of subordination in any practice of resistance but as an unavoidable analytical reference. It is a key argument to displace, in turn, any reading that evokes Fanon from a perspective that defends Manichaeism.

The Tunisian writer Albert Memmi, a contemporary of Fanon, in *The Colonizer and the Colonized* (*Portrait du Colonisé précédé de Portrait du Colonisateur*), describes the enormous variety of situations that indicate the concrete possibility of existence to which Bhabha refers. Although Memmi has a closer concern for the sociological/psychological types that inhabit the colonial world, the situation of ambivalence is present in all of the categories chosen: the colonizer, the colonist, the colonized. Although Memmi situates the colonial relation in a bipolar situation, the plot of this bipolarity is so complex that it is impossible to think about without the dimensions of ambivalence that inhabit the subjects of the colonial situation and without the role that alienation plays in them. Memmi chooses, almost in the same way that Fanon would, to dream of the "complete cure of the colonized" when all forms of alienation cease (Memmi, 141). The variety of elements and factors at stake in the colonial relation and in the forms that identities assume, among which are found ambivalence, can be unfolded by means of scrutiny of the dream. However, this is no longer to denote a problem to be solved but to understand the cultural processes that are at issue when it comes to thinking, even, in categories of an all-encompassing character, such as colonizer and colonized, and in the interstices in which alienation is historically produced.

While alienation produces itself, it also informs and is articulated with the strategies of resistance to discourses that territorialize subjects in identity attributes (whatever they are) and in defined temporal trajectories. At that point, the idea of alienation implies that we must pay more attention to the complex form in which difference is articulated and expressed.

Rather than design a homogeneous figure of the colonized, or of any of the other colonial categories, Memmi and Fanon construct milestones to reflect on the difficulty of sustaining a thought that produces difference from solid and unmodifiable nuclei of identity. Identities as a form of territorialization are key to the debate that inaugurates the problem of alienation. However, we do not encounter forgetting in the celebration of the partial achievements of the "colonized" or Fanon's consciousness where we find a way to forget as a sort of critical amnesia to overcome alienation. The colonial identities that both Memmi and Fanon describe are, in large part, the product of the tragedy of the same regime. However, to assume that a transparency of the representations on identity is assured from these is to think that Fanon, Memmi, and even the rest of us can be converted to a kind of apprentice to Faust in reverse. Let us return to the project when Faust is slipping out of our hands. It would give back to the world the certainty of his historical projects and displace the present as a place where agency of the subject can be manifested. However, the role played by deterritorialized identities on the colonial stage is paradigmatic. (A performative illusion is found in the very image of Albert Memmi as a great example when thinking of the paradoxical, ironic, and tragic situation of his condition in Tunisia.)[8] They reveal the extreme condition of subordination while also offering the strokes by which a sort of "epiphany" of the subject emerges.[9]

The etymology of the word "epiphany" is very interesting as a metaphor for the manifestation of the subject. The Greek word from which it originated, ἐπιφάνεια (*epipháneia*), means to reveal or to manifest. *Epi* means "on, in or toward" and *phaínein* means "to show." It is related to the Indo-European *bhanyo*, which means "to show or place in the light" and the implicit meaning of which is "to make something visible by putting it under the light." The particle *bhā* means "to shine."[10] This etymological reference points to deterritorialization as a form of urgency, of manifestation of the subject even when it is assumed that deterritorialization affects the referential boundaries for the emergence of the subject. Beyond the meaning that Christianity assigns to the word, oriented to a unique and global character without any ambiguity, the implicit meaning deployed here is a metaphor for the process of the subject in the condition in which it appears in the writing of Memmi, Fanon, and others. The "shining light" can refer to the political and cultural intentionality of the authors, which does not "illuminate" in the Enlightenment sense that it clears the weeds that surround and dull a nucleus of truth sustained by an extensive rationality and the plot of their discourses. Memmi's *The Colonizer and the Colonized* and Fanon's *The Wretched of the Earth* offer a way of illuminating, even if this illumination does not mean transparency, because the latter is the privilege of a discourse sustained by faith. They illuminate a subject that manifests itself in the colonial situation and in the critique of colonialism because they present the historicity that inhabits the subject as a history built and lived but not necessarily possessed. Their works contain the elements that fight, such as the dominant being inhabiting this interiority, and from this situation, they offer a subject that cannot think beyond the historical marks that constitute them.

The extreme reality of subaltern and hegemonic situations in the texts of Memmi and Fanon are perhaps the best indication of the impossibility of imagining subjects outside of "incompleteness" or a certain partial condition. But, contrary to the readings on Fanon that I am analyzing here, neither the implicit desires of postmortem ethics nor the Jaspersian historicity that I discussed earlier assure the epiphany of the subject since this epiphany is linked by continuities that, as paradoxical as it may seem, inhabit and condition Fanon's divided figure. The term "epiphany" seems contradictory to that of "continuities," as it recalls the advent of a unique event and reminds us of what Bhabha says in the introduction to the *Location of Culture*: "It is the trope of our times to locate the question of culture in the realm of the beyond. At the century's edge, we are less exercised by annihilation—the death of the author, or epiphany—the birth of the 'subject'" (1). However, the contradiction does not exist if historicity is placed at a register unrelated to salvation. This sort of epiphany of a divided and partial subject is no more nor less than the recognition of its provisions in the complex and often open plots of colonial discourse.

Without repeating the tried and true argument that establishes the multiplicity of the colonial discourse, according to historical scenarios in which it is produced and reproduces, the central point is not its spatial historical variegated forms but its persistence in the imagination of resistance that inevitably crosses ("with the dominant being within it") the anticolonial and postcolonial cultural political discourse. In this imaginary, then, the manifestation of a historical subject will always occur amid a strong tension between drives that order representation, in the sense of stabilizing it, and a set of meanings and drives that try to deposit the configuration of the subject in indeterminate spaces. Zones of no one, intermediate spaces, border situations, interstices. As Bhabha will say, "an exploratory, restless movement caught so well in the French rendition of the words *au-delà*" (1), a beyond, which constitutes the unstable territories by which this subject retracts its total manifestation but concurrently where the manifestation appears. However, it also does not cease to be an epiphany since, despite the subject not separating itself from the historicity that crosses it, the subject expresses a new condition, if not historical, at least theoretical and political, which cannot disguise this historicity. Theoretical condition, understood as reflection that necessarily derives from a "seeing," as Gordon says, is able to deal with the difference within the colonial discourse and outside of it. It is a political condition to the extent that it presents a possible space of representation for the agency of subaltern subjects (in the different versions of the colonized) without abandoning historicity as process and, in turn, without abandoning the present as if it were only one moment of transition to another, thus defining the future in which the realizations of the project in question would be certified and the errors of the past rectified.

The present, or what we imagine as such, can be considered as a time that does not require an extemporaneous justification to validate or justify the practices of subjects. On the contrary, the present can establish the conditions that destabilize a set of representations about culture, politics, or history, and the future that they project in the form of utopia or continuity.[11]

However, this manifestation of the subject is auspicious because it occurs in places that had appeared to have been foreclosed to him (the dual society of colonialism that Fanon imagines and describes or Memmi's intricate network of allegiances in colonial society) and ironic because the promise that emerges from the opening of those enclosed spaces is that of a new displacement.

It is not just Fanon who, from my perspective, can be thought of in this way. The Muslim Indian writer Saadat Hasan Manto expresses a similar situation in the two tales, *"Toba Tek Singh"* and "The Dog of Tithwal," in which the subject finds a possible way of representation in indefinite places and unstable spaces that are offered in the plots of his magnificent tales.[12] Manto narrates with mastery the situation of an asylum in which, after the separation between India and Pakistan, "lunatics" are distributed in a border exchange. An old man, a central character, resists being returned to a place other than Toba Tek Singh, which is otherwise impossible. Another inmate remains above on a tree saying that he wants to live there, paradoxically, in the one place that is territorialized to the extreme.[13] The old man who can never reach Tob Tek Singh dies in a space that has no name, an area between the borders of Pakistani and India. "The Dog of Tithwal," on the other hand, is the story of the misadventures of a dog trapped between the trenches in the battle front. Indians and Pakistanis "accuse" him constantly of being the "other" and, in the struggle to save his life between either trench, he dies. Both stories refer to the tragedy of specific colonial and postcolonial situations and, beyond that, are examples, though tragic, of the way in which identities are thought against discourses that territorialize and fix their attributes. At the same time, they are also examples of the uncertainties that threaten the constitution of historical subjects when we move away from overly integrated conceptions of culture and projects that carry the obligation of their fulfillment. Obviously, the irony and tragedy that inhabit Manto's two tales reflect the consequences of the lack of "home" and the extreme difficulties faced by people trying to find it. It is not, however, the lack of the "home of fiction" since Manto finds that masterfully. The lack mutates to highlight a new impossibility of representing the home and its subject when historicity, not of a Jaspersian form, produced by individuals and societies during colonialism fall upon it.

However, the readings on Fanon that I am discussing do not escape the relegation of control and fixation to a representational space of displacement as another key of modernity. They do not place Fanon widely in the manner of the discourse of the nation, but they do so from two locations that claim authority.[14] First, I refer to the revolutionary tradition of which Zahar speaks from the tradition to which Fanon belongs based on his enunciations. Second, from the allocation of Fanon's writing from an instrumental use, which accounts for two convergent processes: that of the emancipation of the colonial subject and of the emergent stages of a consciousness. It is inevitable that localizing Fanon's writing converts his work in these readings to a thematic question since to represent his work must be linked to previous processes that occurred to the author's consciousness. Thus, the ascending journey is also with respect to a place located before and outside of his writing, the place of the life of Fanon that in its successive displacements from Fort de France to France, World War II, and then Algeria and Túnez[15] among others, constitute a kind of "writing" (or inscription) with each move, prior to the writing of his texts, in which the characteristics of a growing consciousness are profiled. In the face of this, each text corresponds to a context, and each context, despite the increasingly divergent dimensions of his writing, confirms the degree of development of a thematic issue.

Without doubt, Fanon's figure authorizes readings that seem and are at times totally divergent. However, the problem persists with his figure and his writing. If you subtract originality, you run the risk of losing one or more traditions, such as Marxism, blackness, or theories of revolution, in the framework. If granted originality, it is based on strong processes of exclusion like that of the romantic dimension of his figure.

But this problem can be wrongly formulated. If the emphasis is thematic, in the sense that I described earlier, then the analysis enters the sphere of contributions to say, in an order that is external to Fanon's texts to the extent that there is a homologation between the intertextuality that inhabits them and their belonging to different currents of thought and political practices. As we will see later, blackness is conceived as an inherent part of Fanon's texts as they address the problem of the racialization of social relations in the colonial world which, at least for *Black Skin*, becomes added to the grouping of texts from this tradition, closing the space for inquiries or, to use a more precise term, interpellations that come from different temporal, historical, and cultural scenarios.

Intertextuality always relates to the past. Although it is at least at the time of the production of a text, it is not so much when that text enables dialogues that exceed its time frame, particularly toward the future. Thus, this interpellation not only redesigns the scenario of the past that each generation faces but also the priorities of the past and, consequently, the priorities of the present. Bloch's idea, which today may seem obvious, implied that the patterns of temporality are always open. If this is considered, texts should be more than thematic references and spaces of development for any tradition, whether political, methodological, or theoretical. A plot of open temporality shifts the center of the scene of the immediate homologation between intertextuality and referenced thoughts as it relativizes the effects of territorialization. However, the possible stages of Fanonian thought not only refer to the paths of their consciousness and the different contextual situations they face but also to the plot that produces the homologation discussed.

The currents of thought, traditions, and cultural practices concurrent in his texts can be converted with the same logic to a reference or another form of territorialization that subjects Fanon's writing to a set of extremely restricted claims as by Gendzier, Geismar, or Coletti Pichel despite the intentions of those who analyze his work.

Marie Perinbam, in her study on Fanon titled *Holy Violence*, traces a paradoxical journey that allows for reflection on the problems that I point out here. Perinbam indicates that the concept of holy violence and the revolutionary theory in Fanon relate to and are indebted to various traditions:

> Apart from the fact that there is not much to set his theory apart from the revolutionary traditions of Marx, Lenin and Luxemburg, even his specific claim that revolutionary violence can be a uniting, binding, and cleansing force—giving rise to a "New man"—has precedents in seventeenth century revolutionary thought, in the theories of the pre-Marxian utopian socialists, and Russian anarchists. This latter concept even appears in the thought of Mao Tse-Tung. His concept of revolution and holy violence therefore has many precedents and *is not idiosyncratic as his critics suggest*. Not even Sartre acknowledged this in his preface to the first edition of *Les Damnés de la terre* . . . . Fanon's concept of violence, including holy violence, owed much to his own *Critique of Dialectical Reason*. (Perinbam, 107; my italics)

Perinbam confronts Fanon's critics who try to situate his discourse and his political practice as an anomaly. At first glance, this long quotation appears to refer to the type of problems associated with homologation and intertextuality, currents of thought and critical traditions. However, Perinbam's objective shows that although Fanon's work is criticized for a supposed ideological inconsistency and, above all, as it appears to certain critics as a kind of political hallucination, his work is much more than that since it is embedded in the heart of the traditions from which these same critics speak—for example, Marxism and republicanism.

The additional tension exerted by the idea of "idiosyncratic" is directed toward Perinbam's text. If Fanon's staunch critics place his idea of violence as anomalous and territorialization as an idiosyncrasy, then any critical exercise that disavows such statements disallows the idiosyncratic factor at play. The extent of such a factor may ultimately vary according to the reader's greater or lesser sophistication and theoretical and political positions. So, for example, a legitimate question in this context would be: Is not colonialism idiosyncratic in some territory or form? Historians would respond affirmatively to this question because idiosyncrasy has a high coefficient of specificity. However, the problem is not with the specificity of Fanonian writing in the terms of a historiographic question but with the way it is invested with authority. In this sense, Perinbam's treatment of Fanon is no different from the rest.

Territorializing Fanon in the plots of modernity that his writing traverses rescues him from idiosyncrasy. I am not defending idiosyncrasy as a lens for Fanon's writing, but am highlighting that each reading leaves aside, dips, or displaces something to constitute its own authority. Erasing idiosyncrasies implies authorizing Fanonian discourse from the side of its modern intertextuality, even from those places where revolutionary thought increasingly approaches mythological and primordial content. If it has no future, then it will have a past.

However, Perinbam's argument is more complex than what it suggests at first glance. Following Hannah Arendt and Crane Brinton, Perinbam argues that the concrete existence of the revolution itself constitutes Fanon's revolutionary theory a priori as an act of faith (*Holy Violence,* 14). Fanon arrives at that situation because he has made his decisions as a rational man, conscious of "the hideous monstrosity of the a priori violence as the only solution to a problem, on the other hand, insoluble" (ibid). This is a Promethean gesture by Fanon, by means of which he steals the fire from the gods while knowing the consequences (ibid); "When a body of knowledge becomes too complex . . . processes in the mind transfer this knowledge to the level of comprehension where it becomes *gnosis*—or a higher form of knowledge beyond question—which is accordingly accepted as faith" (ibid). In this sense, according to Perinbam, Fanon's language to communicate with the Algerians is that of faith because the "knowledge of the terrible unknowable was better understood by faith" (ibid). Thus, Fanon transforms this "terrible unknowable into *gnosis* and dealt with it as a metaphor" (ibid). This dealing implies that the representation of "holy violence" transforms from an initial paradox to a metaphor, which refers to the representation of the figure of the terrible unknowable but also to "a historical matrix" (115). The metaphor of revolution was associated in its origins with mythological and astrological contents of political mysticism that linked local political acts to universal signs. Perinbam recalls here certain uses of this image in Shakespeare, particularly in *Julius Caesar,* or in the seventeenth century with the association of the metaphor of revolution with the Copernican idea of vertigo and delirium which assured that if utopia is defeated on earth, another would be born in the "compensatory dreams" connected to the "sky." Thus, revolution was linked to the idea of "recurring political change" that contained the logic of "resurrection, reincarnation, and redemption" that would occur with an internal logic of need (115–16).

With these precedents, argues Perinbam, referring both to the Copernican and religious origins, it is no wonder that Fanon's rhetoric would have a metaphor for the revolution "like manna from above" and other examples that suggest the same type of relationship (116). From this perspective, "Fanon's revolutionary theory becomes a metaphor for an unbeatable combination of scientific law and religious faith" (117). Killing the colonial "Lord" is something that seems to be inscribed in a previous way to heaven and earth, which "with faith and good revolutionary works, . . . would come to pass" (ibid). Hence, Fanon's metaphor, according to Perinbam, can be considered "a sacred and invincible fury whose origins descended into profound antiquity" (ibid). Therefore, beyond the communicative effect conveyed to the "masses" of the primordial content of the revolution, "holy violence remained a paradoxical metaphor for the unknown, unthinkable, yet necessarily committable act" (ibid) yet to be fulfilled. Fanon then, in the face of this, remains resolute in "permitting his political imagination to soar generously and permissively on themes of change precious to the revolutionary's soul" (ibid).

Perinbam's analysis of Fanon's writing finds an unsuspected resonance with the readings commented on earlier. There is no separation of the components that seem to refer to the terrain of feelings and representations outside of rationality, even if they are taken from a rational decision as Sartre recognizes in the prologue to *The Wretched*. However, the implicit long duration of the metaphor of revolution in Fanon's texts is not of a historical nature nor developed in his writing as an essentialized place of the past. Fanon's writing, as we shall see, builds the time of his critique from present situations, that is, imagines history as an invention. And, in the process, it preserves the tensions that give rise to the type of reading carried out by Perinbam. Nonetheless, the "theoretical permissiveness" of Fanon's writing occurs in the face of the theoretical and political order that postmortem ethics constructs.

In the face of the political and cultural imagination of his texts, there are readings that demand transparency of communication and precise conceptualization of the processes it describes or analyzes. Perinbam writes in the unstable region in which she agrees with the pressures of a theoretical and political authority while recognizing Fanonian rhetoric as a space of dissemination. Gnosis, which ultimately is that which we cannot know, "The terrible unknowable," and is only experienced, seems to point out the suspected difficulties of writing in relation to representation.

Seen in this way, the idiosyncratic is a problem in Perinbam's reading since it leads to a negative characterization of that which circulates on the edges of the political and cultural traditions of modernity or which cannot find a place or a safe territory or in the alchemy that Fanon's writing produces with the metaphor of holy violence or revolution.

The character of representation seems to pursue the problem of its relationship with the real. In this study, I have spoken about writing and text. This is because the main object of my analysis is Fanon's writing. From that narrow point of departure, many consequences and situations are deduced. If we think of Fanon's writing beyond the duty that he submits to us as readers, we can also consider that it is not necessary to imagine it as a space that must, at all costs, give an account of the real as an external space to writing that is unrepresentable by it. Roland Barthes, in the *Inaugural Lecture of the Chair of Linguistic Semiology of the Collège de France*, writes that one of the forces of literature is that of representation and that, in a certain way, literature is reasoned by an intent to represent something stubbornly known as the real. However, an impossibility exists in that act because there is no correspondence between "a multidimensional order (the real) and a one-dimensional order (language)." Rejecting this situation produces literature. The persistence of this attitude denotes the unrealistic nature of the attempt, in that "it considers sane its desire for the impossible," additionally, its utopian function lies in this desire for the impossible (127–8). This dimension of literature, which we could extend to writing in general, orders the different types of searches in the texts. The utopian functions as inadequacy, which generates, without a doubt, a movement that is not the same as that of the prescriptive. The text knows (by using an extremely subjective figure) that its limits are those of a certain impossibility. But its contents and the homologation between traditions, currents of thought, and intertextuality remain in some way as part of the utopian function, with its commitment to affirm the representation of the real (in newly representing the real) that leaves aside the warning, no longer as a barrier, or as a final point, of the impossibility of such an attempt.

At that point, the text stops circulating through an indeterminate space and concentrates on its duties. It must now respond to those who gave it origin, be it in the form of a tradition, for example, and it must be collated by reason of the scopes and projects derived from the reason for it being originated. That reason for being can come to exist, chronologically speaking, after the text. Postmortem ethics is an example of this. Fanon's writing must answer not only to the utopian questions that emerge from other texts. It must account for different means of correspondence between two types of orders which indicate and consolidate simultaneous denominations of the real. First, in relation to what it describes on colonial society, with the struggles for national independence, the national culture, and with the historical project of an emergent subject. Then, there is a second order that corresponds with what its function prescribes, namely, the inclusion of the text and writing as forms of growing approximations with the real, defined almost from an a priori situation. At that point, the utopian function is not derivative nor does it generate displacement. Barthes will then say that "To persist means to affirm the irreducible of literature, that which resists and survives the typified discourses, the philosophies, sciences, psychologies which surround it" (131). What typified discourses generate for writing is a prescribed utopia.[16] That is to say, a text before the writing of the same, from which the correspondences with what is intended as the real, can be judged. Thus, Fanon's texts can be read from an exigency that seems familiar, by means of signifiers like colonial society, colonialism, colonizers, colonized, racism, national bourgeoisie, and spontaneity, among others. And this familiarity leads to a discussion of the greater or lesser correspondence with a tradition, for that matter, of revolutionary thought from the point of view of the advances achieved in the strategies of analysis of the real.

Another commentary on Fanon, Lucas's *Sociología de la descolonización* (Sociology of Decolonization), is a clear example of this. Lucas thinks of Fanon's rhetoric in terms of something that needs to be surpassed if one wants to see the critical unity of his texts. Thus, the tragic tone expressed by Fanon's rhetoric obscures the "progress" that his texts carry out (17). The idea is that, following Fanonian rhetoric, there is a making of consciousness on the extent of colonialism and post-independence imperialism. Consciousness is taken in the fact that there is no interruption of hegemonic processes, even when their formal structures are defeated (18). But, beyond Lucas's discussion of the theoretical components of Fanon's discourse, the point is that Fanon's writing is placed in the direction of the familiarity of the project of revolutionary traditions that the twentieth century offered. The emergent subject in the colonial situation and the paradoxical epiphany of the same represent, for Lucas, the measure of a progress that we could call prescriptively utopian. The colonial subject seen in Fanon's texts is a mixture of conscious direction and spontaneity. Let us read attentively (with an apology for its length) to understand the articulations of his discourse on Fanon:

> Fanon's will is *disguised* in the empirical and primitive form of a *passionate* fatalism . . . . We have become accustomed to read under a tragic vision, which will never be completely dissipated, the *progress* of a constant search . . . . These developments continue in *The Wretched of the Earth* . . . *We* have talked about fatalism, we have underscored the ethical character of the condemnation that the author directs to the old colonialism . . . . However, *under* this formal "ignorance," under this fatalism and taking advantage of the rise of consciousness that they also express, a critical unit is elaborated. (Lucas, 17–18; my italics)

Fanon's rhetoric is, as in the case of the romanticism of the previous readings, something that must be surpassed to alert readers to the historical force of the rising consciousness that will find itself, regardless, within critical unity and the associated utopian project. This is certainly a critical unity defined by the transparency of his representations of the real. Words are not neutral: "disguise" and "passionate," in Lucas's strategic reading, are symptoms and not causes. Signs of something else. "Progress," "we," "under" point to the correct path of representation in Fanon's reading, that is, in our readings. "Progress" of consciousness emerges despite the enveloping rhetoric. "We" belonging to a majestic us that confirms the place no longer of a collective authorship (at least in the intentions of Lucas) but the authority of the tradition that sanctions what does or does not belong in its discourse.[17] "Under" signals that the surface of the discourse conceals something. Moreover, "under" reasons judgment on Fanon's writing, no longer on its formal aspects but, to paraphrase Hayden White, in the content of the form. The real of the process lies underneath. In other words, layered fiction's prescriptive games.

From this point of view, Fanon's writing is always displaced to regions of meaning located in the depth of the surface of his writing. It is not, however, displacement by association, irony (as in the case that Sartre disputes, which I will analyze later), or as a point of departure. It exists and is always defined in relation to something that prescribes it from the exterior. The divided subject of the colonial condition is manifested and linked to a historical project that, in short, is no other than that of modernity in a broad sense. However, its legitimacy is found in the projected accounts of utopian desire in a tradition of thought and not in this almost inevitable project of contemporary historical experiences. It establishes as a frame of reference a measurement of approximation to the real in Fanon's writing and to what his writing hides. Not a secret plot, evoking conspiracy writing, but the inevitable representational failure of all writing reminiscent of Derrida's analysis of Jean-Jacques Rousseau's and Claude Levi-Strauss's texts in *Of Grammatology*. But it is a contradictory measure because it claims legitimacy from the place where meanings hide behind the rhetoric of tragedy linked to what theoretical revolutionary tradition has defined as writing or, rather, the inscription (ultimately a script) of a utopian project and its conceptual and explanatory forms of historicity:

> The historical subject of *The Wretched of the Earth* is known in the search for balance between conscious direction and spontaneity. He is known in the double movement whereby imperialist relations and the "bourgeois classes" are unable to order the praxis of the masses, oppose the futility of historical action and the curse of independence: "Since you want independence, take it . . . " But the historical subject is also known in the denial of the curse, negation whose *necessity* and *possibility* Fanon attests in all his work, ultimately in the necessity and possibility of a rise of consciousness of a social class whose historical reality Fanon implies when he speaks about the *possible* and *necessary* movement of the "intellectuals" of the dominated societies. (Lucas, 37; my italics)

Once again, the historical subject of *The Wretched* is known in relation to something else and that is not always the sociological historical explanation but precisely the device that contains it.

If we return to the concern for displacements and deterritorializations, it can be said that Fanon's writing is not decentered—it is forgotten by reason of its duties. The demands of a postmortem ethics impose these duties. In this logic, if the relentless and tragic tone in many of its pages has some role, it is for its readers to find themselves in what it holds beyond it. But this beyond, as I said above, is not conditioned by displacement or deterritorialization. On the contrary, the code and format of the prescribed utopia domesticates the Fanonian impulse and his writing.

Barthes concept of utopia in literature, which we could extend to writing in general, moves away from Fanon's texts. The subject that Lucas sees in *The Wretched* is the result of a series of cause–effect operations provided by the format of his speech, which obliges him to exorcise any trace of representation in Fanon's texts that does not strictly abide to the real. In other words, language, but more precisely Fanon's writing, becomes an obstacle that must be sorted out more than integrated in the analysis. His tragic tones and his fiery rhetoric, ultimately, must accommodate the dimensions of "need" and "possibility," the undisputed progress of a "consciousness-raising," as sort of successive illuminations and transparencies that ensure a sound course for the predictions he has prescribed to utopian reason and (in this case, it is possible to speak) of a theoretical political tradition. Seeing from an opposite perspective, however, could lead to recognizing that Lucas's reading of Fanon's texts decenters them from the rhetoric of Fanon's writing, a rhetoric that shows, as David Caute points out, the direct connections that Fanon makes between the individual man and the totalizing categories of Hegelian philosophy (Caute, 15). However, this displacement is not synonymous with deterritorialization or, if one wishes, a drift which propels representation to move across distant territories to the authority of tradition or currents of thought. It is a decentering that, through its omission, highlights the representational "failures" of Fanon's writing. It omits the surface of his discourse because of what it supposedly represents in a twofold direction: on the one hand, the history of colonial society and, on the other, the theoretical revolutionary tradition of which his discourse is part. This representation is found in the depth of his text in what is situated at a distance from the surface, which, in the same procedure, is ultimately transformed into a secondary effect.

Caute points to the problem of Fanon's rhetoric which differs from Lucas's but is close to that of Perinbam. The exaggerations to the psychology of the white mask between the Antilleans and its reversion in 1955 by Fanon respond to a didactic interest in his writing, focused on the search for the project of a type of subjectivity and the world in the process of change (15). The proximity to Perinbam lies precisely in the discourse for the masses. The millenarianism which Perinbam perceives is an act, ultimately, linked to the communication with the "masses" on the part of Fanon, that is, also a didactic function. In that sense, Caute points out that Fanon's task in having seen the revolutionary break of Algeria and the rising consciousness of the independence movements in the black colonies became that of a political militant. His interest focused on exploring the historical roots of the emergence of a black political ideology, and his method was "to merge the descriptive and normative to put the 'as is' to the service of 'as it must be'" (ibid). Therefore, the texts show a rhetoric of his political will. An interesting point of this argument signals the dimension of the political and moral urgencies that are at stake in Fanon's texts without pretending to expose them ex post facto to a sort of critical ordeal.

Undoubtedly, the "as it must be" is the basis of the extensive political fiction of his texts where he can deploy the rhetoric of racialized relations in colonial society and the emergence of a divided subject but in transit toward a "cure" for alienation, a cure, by the way, that is always postponed or deferred. However, beyond the prescriptive sense that one can find in this dimension of Fanon's will (do not forget the characteristics of the romantic hero facing history), considering his texts from this perspective positions readings which should not account for his affiliations (in terms of homologation between currents of thought and intertextuality) while enabling his writing to emerge as the object of a utopian desire. That is, if Fanon's political will leads to, or is intertwined with, his texts' powerful fictions, it is because of a utopian desire that extends from the prescriptive intent from the outside. In this sense, Jaspersian historicity is as useless as any model of historicity that does not align with the zones that manifest his own ambivalence.

Thus, historicity is reestablished in a highly provocative way: in relation to the present. In relation to the possibility of finding and establishing the spaces where the agency of subordinated subjects can express themselves in a temporality marked by moral and political urgencies. This possibility of history is not a novelty in thoughts of modernity nor for the pretensions of history as a discipline, at least in the twentieth century. However, pushing it into a region where political and cultural fiction is acceptable generates a hiatus, an intermediate space, in which prescriptions become uncertainty, sometimes stated and sometimes not.

Therefore, if any centrality of discourse can be imagined, it is to show an encompassing character—such as the leap between an individual man and Hegelian categories—and, paradoxically, the absolute referral of each content to a particular form of historicity. This undoubtedly produces paradoxical misalignments in Fanon's writing.

As we will see later with Ella Shohat, the inscription of a history of resistance acquires at times a homogeneous character. For that reason, we always find Fanon between difficult positions that should not be seen necessarily as an authorized perspective that does not recognize the "dominant being" in the discursive practices within each of them. On the contrary, therein lies one of the reasons why Fanon's writing always eludes any attempt to define or confine it as a utopian prescriptive project. The spaces in which his writing unfolds are almost always spaces of instability, not only of the meanings so emphasized by the postmortem critique but also of the textual surface, say of the phenomenon of writing. This surface is not synonymous with superficiality but is a place where discrepancy and the commitment to centripetal forces are manifested. Paradoxical, these concur in Fanon's writing and pressure it at different levels. Fanon thinks of a history of the colonial subject and of the alienation which is concomitant to it. (I am referring to the general character of his texts without distinguishing here the fact of a greater emphasis, or not, in history as a central concern.) If historicity is something to be lived, experienced, resisted, and even denied in terms of a dialectical reason, then it is a history where the desire to surpass alienation intertwines in the inevitable presence of it. In fact, the problem of essentialisms can be easily deduced from the evidence that Fanon's texts offer. It is not enough to remain in the frame of basic oppositions that delineates, for example, *The Wretched of the Earth* and cautions of the central figures that traverse his analysis as overdetermined in Althusserian/Lacanian terms. If the processes that produce and manifest complex subjects is understood as historicity, where difference is always a problem of a temporal, spatial, and cultural order, then this could be the reason Fanon authorizes the deployment of Manichean categories to think of a problem that is more complex and to criticize the space of historicity. However, essentialisms represent a problem for our contemporary analysis because they ultimately evoke the hard nuclei of the politics of identity and the representation of culture. They constitute, contrary to what Stuart Hall says (Hall 1997, 112), a matter of being and not of becoming. At the theoretical level or in disciplines accustomed to agreeing with notions of temporality that are constitutive of their discursive practices (I think here of historiography, for example), a notion of essence is uncomfortable and theoretically represents an impossible notion, unless it is historically read, bounded to a specific historical process, or to some determined discursive practice.[18] In other words, unless it is integrated into a set of temporal rhythms which explain and justify it.

Perhaps there is another possibility for essentialisms, which are not the ones that offer the discourses of exclusion and are, however, the ones that threaten the practice of historicity. Benedict Anderson's reflections in *Imagined Communities* regarding the idea of nation are an extensive warning of what happens in the practice of historicity when some of our historical inventions acquire the rank of a suprahistorical entity. Despite the limited vision of Latin American historical processes, Anderson's text offers what we might call a conscious attitude toward the historical character of essentialisms, which does not mean that they are read or, in a hermeneutical dimension, that they might not possess external phenomena to historicity. Anderson warns against the construction of this character as a political and cultural strategy to situate himself in the difficult cornice of treating essentialisms while, at the same time, separating from them. This is an attitude in historiography that does not confuse the dimension of analysis, epistemological positions, and theoretical subjects with the object of study. But, beyond this question and central also to Shohat's warning is the understanding that a certain group or society can adopt homogenizing visions of the past. It resonates in the field of what could be called theoretical political strategies in relation to essentialisms. At stake in Fanon's texts then is not the simple deduction offered by its dichotomous categories, or to extend the case, what Albert Memmi's texts offer, but a strategic question in its use, implying that the limits on the essentialisms must be present.

Gayatri Spivak, who is known mainly for her feminist critique in essays that combine Derridean deconstruction[19] with a broad theoretical spectrum that includes Marxism and readings of Lacan and for being one of the central figures of the initial project of the Subaltern Studies Group,[20] has pointed out this problem of essentialisms with notable insight. In the interview book titled *The Post-colonial Critic: Interviews, Strategies, Dialogues*, Spivak replies to the question of whether there are essentialisms at play when we discuss binary oppositions, such as book-author or individual-history, that the first opposition has had a double use to exculpate the author or to fix his transcendence of history. As for the second, she says that it has been used to affirm the forming role of the individual with a homogeneous consciousness or to separate that consciousness as if it were a text. Thus, the use that makes these oppositions is strategic,[21] in the sense that "she" knows that several problems linked to essentialisms emerge when binary schemes are evoked. At the same time, it is impossible always to escape from essentializing within the discourse. The point is that Spivak looks strategically at essentialisms, "not as descriptions of what things are, but as something one must adopt to produce a critique of anything" (50–51). Spivak's reasoning, and according to the practice that Derridean deconstruction inaugurated, is that the interest is not so much in elucidating or offering final explanations but in "a persistent critical practice [that] once recognizing the totalizing impulses, may cease to privilege its own disciplinary practice" (53).

Strategic essentialism, as Spivak calls it in *Outside in the Teaching Machine*, moves in the region where what has been pushed to the margins returns as a reminder not of the repressed but always in a struggle for meaning. The inscription that Shohat views necessary in certain past communities is ultimately the same necessary inscription for theory of historicity. The essentialism of the Other is no less, after all, than the possibility of forcing to its limits the historical operation that has been developed over that Other. Thus, strategy implies the conscious adoption of an essentialist mode of enunciation that reveals precisely the nonessential character of the histories of difference. Eduardo Grüner clearly explains that the emergence of a boundary results in an intermediate place, a place of unspeakability (evoking the orientalism of Said and the strategic essentialism of Spivak) that allows us to appreciate that there is no natural or original constitution in historical and cultural practices. Rather, what we have before us is the place where the struggles to assign attributes to identities, languages, and so on are resolved (261).

The strategy, or the idea of its use, returns to the theory that holds the character of a calculated movement of thought. If the operation of the discourse which makes them appear as natural constitute zones of struggle for meaning, then the notion of strategy allows us to see this naturalization and its use as a historical tool. It requires one to think against Foucault as a different step. For example, it is not a question of identifying only the ways in which colonial subjectivities are constituted in colonial discourses, but to make "use" of those modes that, when thought past their limits (we will see later the "use" of Fanon on blackness), reveal the difference that operates on them, which is converted into the critical control of the intent.

Thus, when Fanon's writing evokes an essentialist sense due to the use of binary categories, he does so to warn simultaneously of the limits that they represent for the critical task. This is, as we will see, one of the possible readings of his critique of Sartre's *Orphée Noire*.[22] The same happens in his texts with alienation, which is raised as a problem to overcome. However, alienation holds a mirror that reveals its counterface (or opposition in binary terms) of the unrealized desire to surmount it. By its nature, only a totalizing act can begin the task of his critique found in the absolute desire to overcome alienation. Beyond these two extreme dimensions of the problem, Fanon reclaims in his texts a strategic essentialist action, resolving the historicity of the subject at the crossroads of alienation. However, the essentialist response associated with political and moral urgencies does not solidify a canon from which any historical development will be assessed, and rather, as Benita Parry would say, signifies the critical control of the "impulse" itself.

Thus, one could think preliminarily that the role of essentialisms in Fanon is no other than that of defying the plot of his own writing. Its use is not diagnostic but rather therapeutic for his own rhetoric, an aspect that we will see focused on blackness. The differences with readings like that of Benedict Anderson are many, because the objectives are also different. However, Anderson's position freezes the possibility of the author, from his position, posing an essentialist strategy to consider the nation's discourse and its practice. In his case, his writing assumes the characteristic of diagnosis, which, besides providing a series of interesting elements to analyze the forms and processes that establish "imagined communities," places the reader and author as subjects of a new community capable of separating from the dangers that an extensive adherence to essentialisms entails. The paradox lies precisely in the mechanism that allows such externality. It is also an exteriority on which disciplinary discourses have traveled extensively. Historiography, for example, is built on the premise of a foundational exteriority. The procedure of bringing the past closer to the concerns of the present generates along the way what we might call a colonizing effect on the past. This effect implies a return to familiar territory which is unfamiliar in the eyes of contemporary readers of historians. It is also obvious that such a procedure has a certain inevitable condition: the treatment of different orders of temporality.

However, exteriority is a foundation that exercises and offers the possibilities of separation because its discourse concentrates on methods. What it reveals in the manifestation of its intentions is not so much a fusion of levels between the one who writes, the subject matter, and the readers but rather the possibility of distance and separation of what has become the object of investigation. The professional writing of history can offer explanations of the past without a consideration that a transfer of the process that is explained is occurring to the practice of the readers. This procedure, which is not inherently objectionable, in terms of writing, always implies a form of representation that becomes problematic when the historiographic discourse accepts, as given, the act of representation as the representation of the real. It is no longer the utopian pretension of literature that Barthes identifies, but the homologation of a method of investigation and of a writing associated, in terms of efficacy, with the measurement of what is considered real. If we look at it carefully, there is a sort of essentialist belief in the power of writing. The point is, again, in the way that such essentialism is thought. A reading of a book like *The Cheese and The Worms* by Carlo Ginzburg serves to highlight the complex character of a strategy that posits the explanatory confidence in a single case. Michel de Certeau's *The Writing of History* warns that any illusion of redemption of the real in its historiographic project must pass through the sieve of writing and by the rules that it establishes for representation.

Returning to Fanon and his readers, the essentialism in his texts are complex since he repeatedly evokes the figures of difference in a categorical and often reductive way, which may offend our current sensitivities. However, the "how it must be" that Caute points out is then much more than a futile desire. It is the exercise of a literary political imagination in which the utopian component of Fanon's writing does not refer to the abolition of the present according to the project nor does it unfold as the definitive capture of the real because the exercise is in the present where any form of construction of the subject is debated, stressed, and articulated. It is a construction, as I have pointed out, inhabited by profound paradoxes.

However, Caute's observation of Fanon must be extended to deepen the argument on essentialisms. The claim that Fanon must be ignorant of the realities of the rest of Africa if he participates in the cultural environment of Négritude can only be valid if we agree in advance to renounce his writing on this question. In this sense, Fanon follows a schema in *The Wretched of the Earth* based on three levels of native writing. In the first stage that deals with assimilating the culture of the occupier, in Fanon's example, intellectuals embrace the culture of surrealist poets and French symbolism. In the second stage or moment, due to its European formation, the colonized intellectual exaggerates the traits of what he considers the local culture in a retreat to seek authenticity. The third stage is that of the literature of struggle as the colonized intellectual learns from the people with whom he comes in contact. This scheme, says Caute, contains a persistent appeal to the human spirit; however, in Fanon's case, he notes that his Antillean background and his essentialist and rationalist philosophical inheritance produce an overly abstract look that is unaware of the diversity of African development (30). These observations have an undoubtedly valid character if Fanon's texts are used to understand specific decolonization processes in Africa, beyond the Algerian case. But if we understand that Fanon's writing is not debated as much in the field of particular case studies nor in relation to a specific contribution to a particular field of knowledge (the way that postmortem ethics tries to integrate it into practical theoretical knowledge of revolutionary theory), then we can better understand the character of generalizations often associated with the essentialisms in his texts and their strategic uses.

Caute does not assign Fanon's ignorance of African diversity to the fact of his generalizations but to a formative difference and to Antillean cultural antecedents. Regardless of this, his observation covers the negative judgment regarding the extension of Fanon's texts to regions of knowledge that seem not to have been mastered. Thus, generalizations are presented in the scenario of this reading that report on a double problem. First, they do not contain the necessary discrimination (in the sense of distinguishing) demanded by disciplinary thought. Second, when this occurs, generalizations become essentialist forms that reduce the perspective of analysis and, in this case, the variety of cultural history. The point to reflect upon is whether what is seen as the generalization belongs more to a mode of writing linked to the essay that, in Fanon, varies from the psychological, cultural, and historical in *Black Skin, White Masks* to the essay of political historical imagination characteristic of *The Wretched of the Earth*. However, if the essay possibly territorializes a discussion of Fanon's texts, we should say that these resist traditional forms of disciplinary knowledge. Fanon can use concepts that come from disciplines, but this does not mean that his uses are accountable to a specific tradition or a premise directed toward disciplinary knowledge. That's a part of the problem. However, generalizations that derive from writings that are, at times, totalizing also point to a question in the order of culture. Let's explore this in more detail.

What is perceived as problematic is that generalizations and concomitant essentialisms leave out many things and, in turn, they are used to interpret many other phenomena in unambiguous and homogeneous ways. If we think that much of the critical effort of this century has been against generalizations (we already know what many of them have led to), then it is difficult to imagine a space in which they can appear and represent an alternative. But there is also another dimension when one thinks of the strategic use of essentialisms, not so much in matters of political and moral urgency but in an ethic that tries to respond to the monstrosity of certain historical, cultural, and social projects. Fanon's writing, in the exaggerated tone that many of his critics emphasize, could be placed at that crossroads that is not necessarily the privilege of anticolonial discourses. It suffices to recall the case of the famous statement by Theodor Adorno on the inability to write poetry after Auschwitz. Adorno marked a kind of double impossibility in the face of the horror of Nazi history: the impossibility of celebrating the world after Auschwitz against the concrete impossibility of not continuing to write after it.[23] Either end of the argument is directed toward the essentialisms that inhabit almost any ethical formation. But its paradoxical situation, the double impossibility, allows thinking of them as a strategy to face the memory of the horror of those years. One more possibility, among many others, is of referring to essentialisms as what a certain practice has consecrated. The essential word refers to the contents that are indispensable for differentiating or attributing identity to a specific phenomenon or process. The idea of the essential is a kind of phenomenological reduction in the sense of the metaphysical reduction of Husserl.[24] However, it is also possible to consider that essences refer to what has historically been considered as a form of distinction or difference in some irreducible way. Teresa de Lauretis, exploring this problem for feminism, points out that the situation of essentialisms should be discussed in the field of different conceptions and not intrinsic natures prior to any historicity (78). Thus, she adds one more dimension to the debate that in some way Spivak proposes on the subject, saying that essentialisms can be thought, strategically and historically, as forms of differentiation rather than as concepts that reveal the nature of the things:

> For the great majority of feminists the "essence" of women is more like the essence of the triangle than as the essence of the thing-in-itself: it is the specific properties (e.g. female-sexed body), qualities (a disposition to nurturance, a certain relation to the body, etc.), or necessary attributes (e.g. the experience of femaleness, of living in the world as female) that women have developed or have been bound to historically, in their differently patriarchal sociocultural contexts, which makes them women, and not men. (Lauretis, originally cited, 81; in *The Essential Difference*, 4)

From this point of view, the assignment to Fanon of an essentialist imagination includes one more characteristic. Namely, that the type of reduction that Fanon carries out in his large categories, like those of colonized and colonizer, can answer the problem of the historical practices that reveal the individuals that are explained by these. In this context, it is pertinent to think that he establishes, as with the rest of his writing, a relationship that fluctuates between universalizing dimensions constituted by colonial discourse, which have representational efficacy while thinking of social and cultural hierarchy; the need for transcendence, not in ontological but cultural terms, of the notion of "fait accompli" established by colonial society and, therefore, the cultural political imagination of difference from a distinct basis from that being offered, the historicization of representation offered by the colonial discourse; the conceptually limited use of certain essentialisms, for example, that of blackness to confront a form of essentializing of historical processes by the Hegelian dialectic, as does Sartre in "Black Orpheus." At the same time, Fanon establishes the paradoxical need to have a discourse of universal scope or appeal, as is the idea of the founding of a new humanism that unfolds through historical practice.

III

Histories of Ambivalence

Fortune is ours. I agree with Calafate: Let's be irresponsible, unpredictable. They don't even realize that all of this can be stopped at any time. I do not think we should define ourselves. Let's fluctuate. —I'm a sponge. —Let's be sponges. We don't need to possess the whole truth.

—M. Eckhardt, *Ya Fue*

I say Hurrah! The old negritude progressively cadavers itself, the horizon breaks, recedes and expands and here among the tearing of clouds the overpowering of a sign.

—Aimé Césaire, *Journal of a Homecoming*

Imagining "Fanonian spaces," Stephan Feuchtwang wrote that the European discourses of the seventeenth and eighteenth centuries built a project of humanity and government based on the idea of the individual who gathered in himself a unifying will and universal capacities. This also meant the start of a natural history of "man." With this principle, which was an instrument of moral judgment and empirical research, the enormous diversity of societies, cultures, and groups was thought of according to the signs that manifestly marked their differences.

The colonial occupation was an enterprise linked to these types of valuations. The colonized societies possessed a history that needed to confirm the reason for the utopian principle of the government of this natural history of "man." But the European occupation and their categories for people, together with the idea of a universalizing history of humanity, created a rupture due to forced occupation. Feuchtwang reminds us that Fanon analyzed this process as one of negation, which combined Freud's psychology, the French Freudians, and the phenomenology of Sartre (125–6).

This general appraisal of Feuchtwang is useful to begin to explore the itineraries that *Black Skin, White Masks initiates*. These are itineraries that undoubtedly compromise the discussion of the subject and the various dispositions that Fanon makes. Let us remember now the representation in triple person that announces the lived experience of Black people, another possible Fanonian space that signals the impossibility of a stable representation for the colonial subject. Or, rather, the one that assures the stability of representation for the colonial subject but outside any space of historicization where it is possible to distinguish it from a horizon of events that permanently situates him in a double territory: that of extreme identification "Mama, see a Negro!" (originally cited, 103; 109) and in the extreme disappearance represented in the triple person.

> As long as the black man is among his own, he will have no occasion, except in minor internal conflicts, to experience his being through others. There is of course the moment of "being for others," of which Hegel speaks, but every ontology is made unattainable in a colonized and civilized society . . . .In the Weltanschauung of a colonized people there is an impurity, a flaw that outlaws any ontological explanation . . . . Ontology—once it is finally admitted as leaving existence by the wayside—does not permit us to understand the being of the black man. For not only must the black man be black; he must be black in relation to the white man. (*Black Skin*, originally cited, 101; 109–10)

> The black man has no ontological resistance in the eyes of the white man . . . . The black man among his own in the twentieth century does not know at what moment his inferiority comes into being through the other. (*Black Skin*, originally cited, 102; 110)

The lack of an ontology travels a long journey from Fanon's theoretical proximity to the construction of his cultural critique.[1] The impossibility of a self-representation signals the presence of "some Being." This impossibility is in Fanon's summary of his reading of Sartre, which links a "certain Being" with the external determination: "Look, a Negro!" (103; 109). The "ontological resistance" which presupposes a nucleus in some untranslatable way is not found in Fanon's black or colonized person because they cannot be thought of outside the history that has constructed them as such.

From my perspective, Fanon's proximity to existentialism comes more from his position of cultural critic, what he "sees," as Gordon would say, rather than a previous rejection of any metaphysics. In fact, Fanon "sees" the impossibility of all metaphysics. For that reason, the starting point in his work is that of the colonized (almost an oxymoron), who is the partial result of a process defined historically by means of imperialism and colonization. The subjects that Fanon finds cannot enter any image or idea of being, in that they are "not for others" as a result of the discovery of an emerging inner freedom but are for others in a relation of subordination where alienation plays the central role. However, Fanon believes in the possibility of such subjects moving by means of an exercise of historicity of that zone where external overdetermination and alienation conjugate. Every form of existence begins in this text with a strong anchorage in historicity.

> The architecture of this work is rooted in the temporal. Every human problem must be considered from the standpoint of time. Ideally, the present will always contribute to the building of the future. And this future is not the future of the cosmos, but rather the future of my century, my country, my existence. In no fashion should I undertake to prepare the world that will come later. I belong irreducibly to my time. (*Black Skin*, originally cited, 18; 12–13)[2]

This is not a historicity that is restricted by its own results, but a displaced historicity. In more than one sense, it is contingent because it allows endless figures of difference in a tragic and ironic process that at the same time conjugates a partial response to the tragedy[3] on the path of existentialism and finding the irony[4] of the illusions which, for a moment, assume the transparency of self-representation. The catharsis ends:

> Out of the necessities of my struggle, I had chosen the method of regression, but the fact remained that it was an unfamiliar weapon; here I am at home; I am made of the irrational; I wade in the irrational. Up to the neck in the irritational. And now how my voice vibrates! (*Black Skin*, originally cited, 113; 123)

But where does it vibrate? The problem of being for others is found here. The voice vibrates, but Fanon leaves questions, by means of irony, that ask: Is the voice heard by someone? Is a dialogue opened? The vivid experience of the black man returns by means of difference to the image of a dispossession that does not offer belonging. There is a belonging, if he is not questioned from the outside, pending there is no enunciation to make him relative. What is tragic? It is to lose a "consciousness of existence" that should not be subjected to any dialectic, to any form of historicity founded on negation. Because, perhaps at the most Hegelian moment of his text, the "existence" becomes constituted as an affirmation of an absolute consciousness. Here is a contrast with or, let us say, an intentional hiatus from the existence linked to the contingent but resolved in the direction of the substitute. It is the supplement because what was thought as consciousness we now remember returns as a historical form, a passage, a construction, which has the traces of temporality and, therefore, its tempo; the irony is this: It is the voice of Sartre, which in the "lived experience of the black," is articulated as a factor that removes Fanon from oblivion. In this figuration, Fanon's at the fore but uses Sartre's voice to dramatically contrast the "irrationality" in which he has been immersed. He does not allow himself to be lost at the end of the catachresis because there is no such end when the names do not appear and it is impossible to name an experience it-supposedly-is. It can only be named for what it-supposedly-becomes. To use the image of Stuart Hall, "Cultural identity [. . .] is a matter of 'becoming' as well as of 'being'" (1997: 112).

The consciousness Fanon alludes to has a double content. It is political action and it is also ideological dimension. Fanon highlights that the ideological dimension is limited by its very description but links the strongest potential to political action.

Benita Parry believes that the echoes of a nativism are intense even in Fanon and Césaire's theories of liberation beyond which these authors propose, a new post-European humanism as the goal. Négritude for these theorists, for example, gained a space in the debate before the nationalist movements in Africa and the Caribbean and after the Marxist criticisms and analysis were developed in the struggles for Indian independence (Parry, 92). Parry considers blackness as a structure of feeling that developed in a relatively long and divergent process from the Haitian literary movements of the nineteenth century, through to the Back to Africa movements in the United States to the Pan-Africanism of Du Bois.[5] All these antecedents are finally articulated by the students, intellectuals, and writers of the French colonies. The role played by *Présence Africaine* gives a corollary to this process.[6] In this context, then, the idea of blackness for Caribbean writers is an answer related to a construction of Africa that would allow for the creation of a notion of community beyond the geographical space that the word designates, *a country of the mind*, says Parry, a country discovered in poetry for Sartre ("Black Orpheus," 26), where black identity is founded on creolization and dislocation (Parry, 93).

Parry interestingly proposes an analysis of blackness that does not close in on one or two more or less current answers, but emphasizes the fact of multivalence, which resists any futile attempt to close or fix it and is converted into a tool available to analyze other modes of oppression (96). This is an interesting attitude since Parry tries to look at so-called "nativism" without applying the judgment that they are an epistemological error that ultimately reproduces the logic of what they oppose (88). Thus, her analysis attempts to see the effects that reinforce the construction of a coherent identity, which differ from situating these effects in the field of reviving the precolonial past (91). As I already mentioned, Ella Shohat deals with a similar problem. Speaking of a certain anti-essentialist emphasis in her postcolonial analysis, for example, she states that sometimes one loses sight that, in a certain way, it is necessary to have some openness toward searches that point to community attributes and not censure them immediately in the name of hybridity. Shohat also wonders if collective resistance is possible without inscribing a homogeneous past to a community (109). This road leads Parry to discuss blackness and ways to build a black identity in Fanon. A preliminary answer emerges by instead of through proposing that Fanon's ambivalence becomes an area where "critical language is permanently interrupted with articulations of empathy with impulse" (Parry, 98), and the impulse is ascription "visceral to the powerful fiction of black identity" (ibid). However, Fanon settles in an area of undefined meaning, a point of tension, she calls it, between cultural nationalism and an idea of transnationality without solving the contradiction nor ascribing to any side (97). Parry's discussion builds a Fanon within the tradition in its moments of rupture but which does not resolve the tensions which his own writing generates. Howeve, something more to consider is the fact that Fanon juxtaposes the voices and people in the anecdotes as a critical "narrative" and, in doing so, positions, attitudes, and, as I pointed out earlier, irony that remain in profusion. The pertinent question here is why irony and ambivalence since his texts are also crossed by political and moral urgency and not only by the fact of being a tributary of certain traditions like blackness,[7] Marxism, psychoanalysis, and existentialism. The irony is expressed at times as part of an ambivalence and the profusion of people, apparently decentered by Fanon's voice, are willing to be narrative objects, as people that often evoke an elusive ethos of community, counterbalance to the seduction of a final formula to build figures of resistance and opposition.

This counterbalance of possible ways of imagining the postcolonial community must necessarily be contrasted with some remarks on the questions of gender present in Fanon's texts. For example, Rey Chow addresses the problem of admission to a community linked to the question of black identity when discussing the role played in *Black Skin* by black women. Her discussion is relevant since what is at stake are the forms of exclusion that a policy of admission to the community entails (69). Ambivalence from the postcolonial readings, in which I include mine, has, for Chow, the character of privilege (67).[8] In a sense, as she indicates, ambivalence generates the impossibility of choice, in the case of Fanon's colonized man, between the world of whites or blacks, which frees the colonized man from an agency subject to a concrete, conscious or subconscious, definition. Thus, the demands that must be fulfilled by the black man are more open than those that Fanon places on women in defining the limits of admission to the postcolonial community. Chow writes that "whereas the women of color are made to stay completely within the boundaries, the black man is allowed to waiver between psychic states, and ethnic communities, to be 'borderline'" (67-8). Women's agency is, in this case, a factor external to them.[9] Chow shows the tension or the contradiction between the conscious or subconscious desire of women for interracial relations (which Fanon critically assigns to black Antillean women in the fictional works by Mayotte Capécia)[10] and an attempt of intellectual men, conscious of the problem of race, to put an end to the compartmentalization that colonial discourse and practice provoke. One way or another, the Manichean division of the colonial world is broken.

This tension implies that Fanon's own discourse regarding black women enters an area of ambivalence or instability. His discourse, which claims a new humanism, traps women in an unstable manner in his attempt to define their agency. However, the second and third chapters of *Black Skin, White Masks*, "The Woman of Color and the White Man" and "The Man of Color and the White Woman," have elements that allow Chow's assessment to be nuanced when the problem of alienation is considered from a negative perspective. There is no such privilege of ambivalence when discussing the problem of subordination and alienation which links a mode of representation to a definitive image of the world: "The Negro enslaved by his inferiority, the white man enslaved by his superiority alike, behave in accordance with a neurotic orientation" (*Black Skin*, original and translation, 60). However, Fanon's acknowledgment of an agency of the black man and woman who are always constructed from alienation does not celebrate the kind of ambivalence that Chow suggests: "In the man of color there is a constant effort to run away from his own individuality, to annihilate his own presence. Whenever a man of color rebukes, there is alienation" (60). Let's read the final paragraph of the chapter "The Man of Color and The White Woman":

> Just as there was a touch of fraud in trying to deduce from the behavior of Nini and Mayotte Capécia a general law of the behavior of the black woman with the white man, there would be a similar lack of objectivity, I believe, in trying to extend the attitude of Veneuse to the man of color as such. And I should like to think that I have discouraged any endeavors to connect the defeats of Jean Veneuse with the greater or lesser concentration of melanin in his epidermis. The sexual myth—the quest for white flesh—perpetuated by alienated psyches, must no longer be allowed to impede active understanding. (*Black Skin*, originally cited 78; 81)

These last words of the chapter dedicated to Jean Veneuse sound of late recognition (in the text) that a kind of double discourse has been generated in relation to women and men. As Lola Young points out, this can be understood as a textual strategy by Fanon to provoke (91), but disequilibrium emerges between black men and women in Fanon's analysis of them as literary characters. While the phenomenon of alienation (in terms of the desire to be white) circumscribes Jean Veneuse's approach, it is also a political adventure. The case of Capécia and Niní, characters of a text written by a man, entails the dissolution of racial and cultural heritage (93–4). In this imbalance, Fanon recognizes that the sexual myth fixes the subjects in a sort of agency determined from the outside, be it men or women. Nonetheless, Chow's claim that I quoted earlier is more than a retrospective accusation regarding Fanon's texts. It is a challenge to the policies of admission in discursive communities that are defined among postcolonial critics who consciously decide to overlook themes of gender and sexuality in Fanon.[11] Chow remarks that these issues are dismissed because of the supposedly more urgent issues of racism and colonialism (72).

Perhaps the point of this discussion can be established from a new displacement, to thinking of Fanon from the crossroads of "homophily" and at the crossroads of a discourse that, along with articulations that confine and define female agency from a dissected place, also open extensive possibility of its criticism from its same political theoretical affirmations. bell hooks points this out with great clarity:

> More than any other thinker, he provided me with a model for insurgent black intellectual life that has shaped my work. He taught me the importance of vigilant interrogation. Certainly, I took him at his word when he passionately declared, "Was my freedom not given to me then in order to build the world of the You? At the conclusion of this study, I want the world to recognize with me, the open door of every consciousness. My final prayer: Oh, my body, make me always a man who questions." In becoming a woman who questions, I found feminist thinking transformed my understanding of Fanon's work. (hooks, 85)

hooks's statement is more than what, in English, is called "wishful thinking." It is to think that the inheritance of Fanon's theories do not not necessarily have to be recovered in his normative spaces, in the dimensions of his project that refer to prescription. Nor does it mean, as Chow clearly states, that we should look away from the politics of sexuality that close the critical spaces of his texts, especially when it comes to thinking about the complexity of the colonial and postcolonial subject. In that sense, one can recognize that, when Fanon speaks of the colonized, he clearly distinguishes the figure of women. The colonized is a man and his writing is oriented, when he speaks of a generic subject, in agreement with the signifier "man." This generic "man" ceases to be so when, thanks to the readings of Mercer, Chow, and hooks, among others, the rhetorical dimension advances in the fields of politics of identity, sexuality, and subordination in discussions of discourses and practices of opposition. This implies that even in writings that we might think of as less normative with reference to culture, history, and its subjects, a schema repeats that neither the critique of colonialism nor the postcolonial imagination can easily settle.

Moreover, hooks's reading opens the possibility, as I try to carry out in this study, of putting Fanon's texts in conversation with other texts and traditions. If the final claim found in the phrase that hooks rescues (which I presume each reader of Fanon rescues) allows her to rethink the place that Fanon occupies in his critical formation while allowing her to distance herself critically from him, then it is possible that we may not necessarily have to forget, for example, the Fanon that is in conversation with Sartre.

I am not referring specifically to the dispute over the representation of blackness nor to the absence of Sartre when Fanon's texts are read, but to the implicit proposal to set Sartrean existentialism aside, even if it is one of the most important theoretical and political resources in his texts. To a large extent, as hooks's quote suggests, it illustrates that much of Fanon's critical work contains its own reversibility. Examples abound on this point. As I have already said here in multiple ways, the paradoxical situation that inhabits his texts allows reversibility, even of those statements more resistant to it. This condition is part of the enunciative dimension of his writing, which, beyond an apparent affirmative attitude, always opens up the space for doubt, instability, uncertainty, for the liminal: "The Negro is not. Any more than the white man" (*Black Skin*, originally cited 204; 231). "Before it can acquire a positive voice, freedom requires an effort at disalienation" (ibid). Reversibility is not, as you can imagine, the space to say the same from the unsustainable territory of a Manichean structure: "Now I say what you said but from the opposite place." Reversibility is the face of the subject that Emmanuel Levinas has considered. To make something reversible is to make it change, to transform it, to make it variable.

If we accept this, then the face of the postcolonial subject is an enlarged metaphor for Fanon's writing. It no longer simply faces a methodological or sociological question, but a significance that we might call "ethics." The critique of dualisms includes not only the critique of the colonized, the colonizer, and the complex figures of difference, dualisms' ubiquity, its place, and representation but also the possibility of imagining subjects in such a way that makes it impossible to place them in a horizon of events in which there is no distinction. The face, thinking with Levinas in his most Kantian moments, hinders the temptation of total denial because it resists the significance of one more among others. It is the inability to literally and metaphorically kill. Its discourse is in the same situation (Levinas, 1993: 21–2). It cannot establish itself as a place of erasure. This condition of reversibility is nothing other than that of the displacement which produces an effort in negation—seen in Fanon's readings of Hegel, but above all of those of Sartre—before any positive celebration against the same alienation, as Irele and Bjorson represent it.[12]

Reversibility challenges dualistic thoughts, in that it is not exactly the opposite of a specific state but is the condition of its existence. It does not show the starting point for a thought, as could be deduced from hooks's quotation. It is the impossibility of not recognizing the dimensions and characteristics of the phenomenon that binds it irremediably to what it represses. Not to a hidden side since, as I said, the colonized for Fanon is man and this is very clear, but to what clearly remains equally distant and fundamental. Alienation is not hidden in the plots of his texts but is shown both in the explicit recognition of its existence and in the regions less controlled by Fanon's authorial authority. Alienation, as such, is not the object of a contrary response but the condition of it. But for this to happen, it must be reversible in several directions. First, in the direction of what it represses and converts into the mechanical procedure of representation, such as the case of the experience that Fanon describes and argues for Niní, Capécia, and Veneuse: "Mama, see the Negro!" or representation in the "triple-person." Second, alienation assumes the direction, as in these tragic cases, of displacement, but now resignified as the possibility of establishing a critique of the conditions that bind subjects to fixed attributes of identity. In this direction, it reveals the face of the subject, which can no longer exist in the undifferentiated horizon in which differences are erased by reason of "Difference" that, disguised as ontological, intends to appear as the final explanation of the world and as the end of its hermeneutics.

Finally, from the revelation of the face and of complex figures and practices of difference, alienation imposes on the subject the theoretical (and often practical) role of "becoming Other," an impossible task, by the way, but one that offers critical reassurance against the narcissistic seduction and, at times, totalitarian reason that can only consider its mode of representation from a clean slate in front of which the world is an indefinite set of elements arranged for the gaze of a subject that stops one's being in its path:

> In the course of this *essay* we shall observe the development of an effort to understand the *black-white* relation. The *white* man is sealed in his whiteness. The *black* man in his blackness. (*Black Skin*, my italics, originally cited, 15; 9)

> As long as the black man is among his own, he will have no occasion, except in minor internal conflicts, to experience his being through others. (Originally cited, 101; 109)

Hence, the debate at play is the role of places. Alienation is, at the same time, topos and a-topos. If blackness is, like "whiteness," a place of confinement, then the alienation that occurs in the world of "mystifications" and "mystifiers" holds double meaning: at the same time that it situates, locates, and territorializes the place of representation, it also defines its limits and offers displacement because to situate, to locate, and to fix, necessitates to first move the subjects from the places that they occupied or created.[13] That is why, paradoxically, the "site" of "blacks" becomes the displacement of "blacks."

In other words, there is a kind of descent from essentialism to historicity. The starting point, if one can consider such a thing, contains its own denial. The displacement that produces alienation also allows Fanon to think critically about how to "experience his being for others." Hence, the alienation in the discourses and practices of opposition represents a much more complex operation since one must consider that it is not something to overcome only with the figure of desire or, to be more precise, with the figure of utopian desire. Rather, while maintaining the positive desire for emancipation, alienation points to the inability to dispense with the elements as a process of negative criticism and displacement. That is the function of the "essay."

As I said earlier, the form of the essay offers Fanon's writing the possibility of a more open experience when considering all the factors with which it deals.

Let us now return to the problem of discourses on identity and what Fanon does with them. From my perspective, the problem is not only of discussing the reinforcing effect of Fanon's attempts to construct coherent discourses of "identity" (also a fundamental task) but of displacing such discourses through a critique that problematizes their use by situating them in the impossible terrain of comparing the differences between historical and theoretical postcolonial processes and an imagination critical of colonialism.[14] This positions a judgment on Fanon's ambivalence after knowing the outcomes of history—as if that were possible—even more so when we have not renounced representation.

Fanon puts any illusion about identity in parentheses. This is not to reject the image of a coherent and relatively homogeneous identity but to avoid becoming trapped in the possible terminal logic of a figure of that type. In other words, unlike what Parry sees as a visceral attachment to the discourse of blackness, I think it is rather that a historicization of identity processes occurs, among which blackness is, as conceived by Césaire, a form of cultural and historical practice, and that this is very appropriate for the political and moral urgency I mentioned earlier. Parry recognizes this point when she places many of the Marxist intellectuals among the defenders of Négritude.

It is by way of historicity that Fanon reencounters images of identity that seem to turn toward essentialisms, but it is precisely in the rejection of an ontological dimension, in the warning that the history of colonization constitutes the plot of alienation where, from my perspective, they dissipate in the random character of ambivalence. Fanon's search for a coherent identity reveals a tension and fundamentally a strategy, namely, to think of identities from various combinations: historical, existential, essentialist.

In that sense, two key elements are combined. On the one hand, the aporia, as the process by which Fanon establishes a boundary, a problem that cannot be drawn from the claim that appeals to identities constructed from "nativism" and, hence, as a reflection with an almost "false" result. This "falsehood" presses on the limits of nativism as a recourse and its representation of black women. On the other hand, irony, which allows the placement of the text in a critical context. These limits permit Fanon to experiment with different figures of identity (ultimately as nativism) to abandon or to preserve them, to paraphrase Fanon, as long as they are not mummified.

I am not arguing that Fanon makes instrumental uses of blackness, but I do propose that his uses are linked to the need to find answers to the problem of colonial silence. It is a silence that does not only occur because of the erasure of subaltern voices. It is fundamentally silence by a mode of representation that prevents evocation of any oppositional figure outside the domain of this silence. We will return to this point when we discuss Gayatri Spivak's famous question: "Can the subaltern speak?" What interests me now is the tension that Parry identifies. From my perspective, Fanon's political text calls for certain places of enunciation that recognize the moral and political urgency but that, nonetheless, must place the "impulse" in a less affirmative region.

> This book should have been written three years ago. . . . But these truths were a fire in me then. Now I can tell them without being burned. These truths do not have to be hurled in men's faces. They are not intended to ignite fervor. I do not trust fervor. (*Black Skin*, originally cited, 15; 9)

This strategy is instrumental in Fanon's text. It allows ambivalences and tensions to be read as an effort to tame the seduction of analyzing colonialism as an aporia. However, there are aporia when Fanon forces the reading from a single point of reference, for example from blackness, though its role is relative when its (enunciated) traits carry a risk for the historicity being developed. Nevertheless, the dialogue with Sartre has more complex facets than that of having reintroduced blackness within the history imagined from a strong teleology. Although that teleology that Ross Posnock and I too recognize in Sartre is important, it responds to a moment of this philosopher's work and does not represent the nucleus of Fanon's reading of him. One facet is the resistance to accept, as Posnock says, "Sartre's Hegelian invitation" while also preserving, "the interplay of the universal and the particular rather than liquidating them in an optimistic teleology" (329). Despite this, the limits for this action are diffuse and complex because, as Posnock points out, blackness should not be understood as an endpoint of identity but "rather moments, critical stages, to be worked through to reach a telos of the universal" (ibid). This also fits a reading of *Black Orpheus*. However, Posnock would disagree, because for him, a point of controversy is that Sartre imagines blackness as a moment of negativity of a dialectic which will synthesize its thesis in a universal society without racism ("Black Orpheus," 60) while Fanon intends to preserve dimensions of particularism and a memory of the experience of racism (Posnock, 329). Beyond that, *Black Orpheus* can be read with the same key, and this situation designates one of the uses of irony in Fanon. While Fanon can be read in agreement with Sartre on existential phenomenological grounds, these can be differentiated from their historical vision or, at least, put it in question, while mitigating the effects of an understanding of blackness linked with essences and so-called nativisms.

This critique of Fanon, as opposed to Sartre, positions a "complaint" that reveals a subtle disagreement with a Sartrean conception of historicity. While Sartre's historicity advances embracing the dialectic and the action of the subject by means of freedom of choice, Fanon must discuss the telos that this dialectic has incorporated. The disagreement appears when Sartre's text seems to reduce freedom of choice to the stage of a "prewritten" sense of history to which Fanon responds with a double movement: with the freedom of choice that the subject who interrogates the world has and with the political urgency of that interrogation, which, in this case, embodies the subject who discovers a place in the world affirmed in blackness.

Benetta Jules-Rosette claims that Frantz Fanon and Alioune Diop regarded Sartre's views as distorting and relativistic. Fanon, in a way, saw in Sartre's proposal that what the latter considered as a means in the dialectic process (the affirmation of blackness), for him represented a "motivation and the final point in a long struggle for self-realization" (28). For the French intellectuals who supported the views or spirit that was coined in the magazine *Présence Africaine*, blackness and the existence of a country of the mind called Africa, as Parry says, involved thinking about the dimensions of a constitutive Otherness.

SARTREAN ROUTES, FANONIAN STRATEGIES

Fanon's closeness to Sartre can be traced in different ways but, for this discussion, I am interested in concentrating on how Sartre articulates the problem of freedom in *Being and Nothingness*.[15] For Sartre, every action is intentional. This idea of the intentional comes from the phenomenology of Husserl. Action, for him, is not linked to facts and events that occur without conscious intervention. Just the opposite. There must be, after every action, a desideratum, an objective lack, or, as he mentions it, a negativity. This means that, after the action, there is always a lack, the central characteristic of which, or essence, is the fact of being a desired potentiality that is not realized. This dimension of the "lack" orients action and determines it because it has created an intentional separation of consciousness with what it is in-itself.[16] What is this process? The concept of the act exists beyond the conditions in which things are presented. To do so, "consciousness has been able to withdraw itself from the full world of which it is consciousness and to leave the level of being in order frankly to approach that of non-being" (*Being and Nothingness*, 434). And to imagine "what is not" it is necessary to leave a terrain of the affirmative (ibid). Sartre gives several examples of this, but that of the French workmen of 1830 is interesting. He points out that workers rebel when wages are lowered because they can quickly imagine what the living conditions would be in that case, but their existing sufferings do not seem intolerable because they do not represent them as such. Instead "he adapts himself to them not through resignation but because he lacks the education and *reflection* [my italics] necessary for him to conceive of a social state in which these sufferings would not exist. Consequently, *he does not act*" (original italics, 435).

Since what is being discussed is freedom, no situation can determine consciousness that he defines as "lack" because any determination is negation (436). The problem, then, is that all action should not only discover a condition as "lack" but also and, before it, must form a system isolated from the state of things in question. For example, the for-itself (the sphere of the subjective), as a force linked to consciousness and action, is the one that ultimately defines what we affirmatively call a "state of things" because consciousness, as Sartre says verbatim, "is invested by being, as it simply suffers from what it is" and therefore must be enshrined in the Self (436).

Thus then, the state of things (the "worker-finding-his-suffering-natural") (436) becomes the "object of a contemplation which must be surmounted and denied" of such a state of things, which entails a "wrenching away from himself" by part of consciousness and a separation with respect to the past by means of denial, which constitutes the non-being that will allow "to confer on it the meaning which *it has* in terms of the project of a meaning which it *does not have*" (italics in the original, 436). Consciousness produces a denial of the state of things to become an end and motive at the same time. It is by the procedure of the action, which by definition is intentional, that these ends and motives are constituted. The past then is not the object of any recovery but is assigned a sense of the future and the action of the present. Freedom is assimilated to an autonomy of options in the face of this capacity of negation that possesses consciousness and nihilation as indivisible parts of positioning an end. The fact that any action is conceived as intentional means that any action has an end, and it invariably refers to a motive (436). For that reason, Sartre will say that this means "the unity of the three temporal ekstases; the end or temporalization of my future implies a cause (or motive); that is, it points toward my past, and the present is the upsurge of the act" (436–7). Despite this apparent primacy of consciousness of "in-itself" (the objective), it seems that the inverse is at stake. Sartre points out that "the resistance which freedom reveals in the existent, far from being a danger to freedom, results only in training it to arise as freedom" (Sartre, quoted by Dobson, 27). Hence, in a certain way, the in-itself is established with an ontological primacy against for-itself (ibid). But the point is that Sartre never sees in-itself as given but as the result of an operation of consciousness, ultimately the project that it generates on the given (ibid). Hence, my freedom can always be stipulated when I have the freedom to change the project and the relationship with the given (27–8).

The problem here would be that freedom is a matter of options and situations and not something given, existing beyond any situation, or nearer of any situation, in the sense that freedom is something that is present as essence and that can be attacked, restricted, or narrowed, but never disappeared. As Dobson points out, freedom for Sartre is a question of autonomy of options (28), although it is necessary to emphasize that this autonomy of options is that which allows negation to be established and the critique of the (historically) given, of the state of things. In this field, Sartre's freedom, as Dobson says, is less a freedom for political action than a freedom of choice (ibid). However, the other aspect that is very important in this discussion about freedom in Sartre is the problem of the Other and the sphere of the role of community. This point is important as the problem of the postcolonial community recurs in my study and is one of the most controversial aspects of Fanon's texts.

So far it is clear that my reading indicates that Fanon is a reader of Sartre but that, additionally, his reading is articulated deeply with it. However, before returning to the point of the nativism in Fanon and its relation and difference with the reading of Sartre, I will make some brief comments on the way Sartre conceives the problem of the Other.[17] Sartre identifies two fields which express the idea of the "we." First is the idea that the "we" is constituted from the perspective of a third party directing its look to it. I am observed by others whose look from the outside integrates me into a notion of community. But this integration into community produces a we-as-object that has been defined at by the third party, the one that looks at us, who constitutes a they-as-objects. From here, Sartre points out that the moment when the "we" emerges, it is simultaneously the moment in which every action of knowledge is lost, since it is a "we" conceived from "my-our" alienation. This idea of community defined from the outside is present in the pages of *Reflections on the Jewish Question* when Sartre affirms that the anti-Semite constructs the Jew (83–4). However, his analysis privileges this relationship, even when he analyzes class consciousness as an experience of the "we" that always requires the look of a third party. The other possibility, that of the "we-subjects," is summarized in a way of experiencing an undifferentiated transcendence in objects and in front of which I behave within relatively expected ways. Sartre dismisses this condition as part of an ontology and held in the field of psychological experiences (426–30). However, the origin of this idea of the we-subject comes from the fact that I can experience myself existing for the Other (Dobson, 32). But before the successive ways in which the "I, you, and he" begin to form the structure of "we," at stake in the process in which the transcendence of the Other is asserted on mine is the fact that to become an object of transcendence, the Other must first recognize my subjectivity, that is, my status as subject.

When that happens, then, we are on the ground of the Hegelian dialectic of the master and slave, to which we will return later, imparted in Fanon's texts, especially in *The Wretched*. Beyond considering the political effectiveness of Sartre's narrative of freedom, the point is that it is both functional and essential to Fanon's project.[18] It is functional, in that it allows him to "change" the project to discuss the teleology that it has incorporated. However, Fanon does not change the project; he disputes it within the logic that Sartre's own construction of freedom of choice proposes. Against a type of historical determination, what Fanon "sees" resumes the place of political and cultural imagination. Nor is it skewed, from my perspective, or from a naive recourse of "nativism," but from a dispute over representations because Fanon "must" ascribe political and cultural efficacy to autonomy. The fact of recognition is not enough by itself since it does not inaugurate any history of emancipation. Blackness for Fanon has the possibility of reintroducing history in lowercase in the place where Sartre introduces it with a capital letter.

If a permanent instability can be inferred from Sartre's narrative of freedom, the same instability appears in Fanon's writing when he discusses how Sartre objectifies blackness. Fanon disputes the transcendence, in the Sartrean sense, of an interpretation of history which situates the particular in the movement of an ascending dialectic. But the argument is established in the circular terrain of transcendence, that is, in the terrain that produces the objectifications of freedom of choice. Thus, Fanon's "complaint" against Sartre, which is organized ironically, and advances beyond the rhetorical process, manifests in phrases like:

> In opposition to historical becoming, there had always been the unforeseeable. I needed to lose myself completely in negritude. One day, perhaps, in the depths of that *unhappy romanticism*. (*Black Skin*, my italics, originally cited, 123; 135)

What is stated as "unhappy romanticism" disputes an interpretation of history, which paradoxically affirms Sartre's "freedom of choice." No unpredictability exists in the fact of blackness, but rather a disposition to read it without confinement, although Fanon repeats the word "absolute" as a litany. "Black Orpheus" attempts it on several occasions, as we will see, but it will not be contingent on it in historical terms and in terms of it as a reading, which is its main feature.

However, the central problem continues both for *Black Skin* and *The Wretched* on whether Fanon presents a racialist perspective of colonial society when he approaches blackness in this way. First, the scope of the notion of contingency that I am using needs to be specified. A possible reading is one which Fanon, evoking Simone de Beauvoir's influential essay *The Ethics of Ambiguity*, attributes to the situation of a consciousness which cannot yet separate with respect to the world, a separation in terms of a critical consciousness: "The tragedy of man is that he was once a child" (*Black Skin*, originally cited, 204; 231). But this is one of the modes of contingency reminiscent of Nietzsche's "Untimely Meditations" (53–101), which rejects the weight of a historiography that has turned the subjects of the present into followers of the past.

Fanon assigns a meaning to "childhood" that refers to the idea of the past *tout court*. It is a past that is nothing but the framework of the colonial histories that produce a bound subject, split regarding the possibility of representing its Being in the plot of existence. It is no coincidence that *Black Skin*, at the moment of greater "reconciliation" with Sartrean existentialism, prepares the territory in which this subject is bound and splintered, separated from childhood, in one of the most powerful political fictions of our time, the chapter on violence in *The*

Wretched. I say "political fiction" with all intentionality to accentuate the original character of Fanon's thought in the tension between the local and the universal. If the political fiction of *The Wretched* has its foundation in the solid base of the context of colonial society, defined in more than one place by the racialization of human relations, then the emerging fiction must also show that tension while ensuring a cultural, historical, and political agenda. Therefore, I do not agree with Ato Sekyi-Otu, who sees, toward the end of *Black Skin*, a kind of appeasement of Sartre after having established a strong dispute with him on the question of black lived experience in chapter V. For Sekyi-Otu, Fanon attenuates the effect of his defense of blackness and adopts a kind of apology for the freedom of the subject.[19]

I believe that, notwithstanding the contrast of the latter part of the book with chapter V, as pointed out by Parry, Fanon's writing again reveals his counterpoint processes (we could use Sekyi-Otu's phrase "dialectic narrative") that leave in uncertainty what seemed affirmed two lines before. The theoretical and political consequences of this are not minor. They compromise the general stability of the text or, in other words, his project. In turn, the instabilities that emerge are those that begin to delimit the space of historical invention that Fanon develops when he has to imagine the itineraries of a consciousness that since "childhood" traces back to his relationship with the world and becomes a consciousness that brings agency.

IV
Historicity and Contingency

Only the present is here. Memory erects time. Succession and deception are the routine of the clock. The year is no less vain than vain history. Between dawn and night there is an abyss of agonies, of lights, of concerns; the face that looks at itself in the expended mirrors of the night is not the same. The fleeting today is tenuous and eternal; do not wait for another heaven, nor another hell.

—J. L. Borges, *El Instante* [The Instant]

Important nuances emerge from the notion of contingency in the context of a consciousness that bears agency. Represented in an undifferentiated space, the contingent is presumed to be near the unforeseen, to that which cannot be strategically dominated, in other words, to that which resists the imprint of an assigned meaning. In "Spontaneity: Its Strengths and Weaknesses," Fanon states:

> The settler is not simply the man who must be killed. Many members of the mass of colonialists reveal themselves to be much, much nearer to the national struggle than certain sons of the nation. The barriers of blood and race-prejudice are broken down on both sides. In the same way, not every Negro or Muslim is issued automatically a hallmark of genuineness; and the gun or the knife is not inevitably reached for when a settler makes his appearance. Consciousness slowly dawns upon truths that are only partial, limited, and unstable. (*The Wretched*, originally cited 134; 146)

The partial, limited, and unstable truths that consciousness discovers point out that historicity's terrain differs from that of absolute affirmation. It is not to say that Fanon does not make absolute claims but to think about these in terms of the type of historicity that contingency proposes. Homi Bhabha has pointed out that Fanon tries to distinguish, particularly in this chapter, between what he calls "the historical law" and his sense of the exercise of politics in the day-to-day. "The contingency of historical temporality and causality" ("Day by Day . . . with Frantz Fanon," 188) represent the type of partial truths that refer to Fanon's paragraph quoted above. Bhabha calls this historical temporality the *"emergency of the (insurgent) everyday"* where Fanon thinks of subjects positioned "outside of the 'official' discourses of the nationalist struggle" (188). Such temporality of the day-to-day, that Bhabha identifies in Fanon's texts, arrives from "what Fanon calls the 'knowledge of the practice of action'" (188).

Bhabha quotes the paragraph in *The Wretched* where Fanon points to the shift from a nationalist consciousness to a socioeconomic one to posit the construction of the subaltern consciousness in which three forms stand out. The first, where the day-to-day articulates the struggle and, as it occurs, takes advantage of the situation by going into a temporality of transience that attempts to reformulate the knowledge of strategic political action. The second form relates to the heterogeneity that constitutes the liminal subject or to the body of colonized people in the very act of insurgency. This heterogeneity contains all the race, gender, and class conditions of economic, ethical, and generational oppression. This form of consciousness holds the least relationship with the Manichean description of the colonial world. Third, Bhabha assigns to the subaltern consciousness that develops in Fanon's texts the condition of what he calls the "emergent everyday," which confronts and disarticulates any utopian or essentialist idea implicit in the linear time of going from colonized subject to self-governing citizen ("Day by day . . . ", 189). Bhabha proposes that the "(dis) illusion" of that type of transformation is explicit in Fanon's gaze when he refers to how the colonized continue to admire the immediacy with which their muscles appeared to transform the colonial situation, referring to their ability to attack the colonial world but to execute "no real progress along the road to knowledge" (*The Wretched*, originally cited, 127; 138). Thus, Fanon "insists on a moment of caesura or negation in the recognition of historical freedom that cannot be sublated in emancipatory ardor" (189).

Bhabha observes discontinuity in this type of subaltern consciousness from the homogeneity of the discourse on colonialism which he also observes in the chapter on spontaneity of *The Wretched* as a discontinuity from the discourse of the nation.

In thinking about the discontinuity that this subaltern consciousness proposes, unstable and contradictory modes of configuring social, historical, and cultural space emerge.[1] The idea of struggle is constituted in Fanon from the instability of time in the present and radically quotidian as they confront the dimension of continuity in the affirmation of a historically defined path (in terms of a discourse on the sense of history and substitutes, such as a homogeneous discourse of the nation or of historical becoming). Hence, historicity in Fanon becomes something that must be an object of reflection to be questioned from every interstice of the subaltern consciousness. Perhaps Edward Said expresses this key idea best in *Culture and Imperialism* in his discussion of the problem of contingency and the reformulation of historicity in Fanon as a cultural discontinuity that exists between the idea of liberation and that of national independence (277). Such discontinuity implies that the practices of the colonial subject or, rather, its definition is not found in the reconstruction of some mythical past of colonial societies, but in daily life, in the day-to-day that Bhabha proposes in considering Fanon.

Therefore, the contingent synonymously emerges alongside a historicity that is built toward the same direction. That movement implies the kind of discontinuities that Bhabha sees in the consciousness of the Fanonian subaltern. Given the possibility of reinforcing, not strategically as we have seen, the discourse of blackness or the values of an African culture presented from the perspective of the racialization of those values, Fanon proposes a national culture as an unstable space in which a mode of open, contingent, and emergent historicity can be represented.

> A national culture is not a folklore, nor an abstract populism that believes it can discover the people's true nature. It is not made up of the inert dregs of gratuitous actions, that is to say actions which are less and less attached to the *ever-present* reality of the people. A national culture is the whole body of efforts made by a people in the sphere of thought to describe, justify, and praise the action through which that people has created itself and keeps itself in existence. (*The Wretched*, my italics, originally cited, 214; 233)

Regarding racialization and national culture:

> Men of African culture who are still struggling in the name of African-Negro culture, who have called many congresses in the name of the unity of that culture, should today realize that all their efforts amount to is to make comparisons between coins and sarcophagi. (Originally cited, 214; 233–4)

> For culture is first the expression of a nation, the expression of its preferences, of its taboos and of its patterns. It is at every stage of the whole society that other taboos, values, and patterns are formed. A national culture is the sum total of all these assessments; it is the result of internal and external tensions exerted over society as a whole and also at every level of that society.... The nation is not only the condition of culture, its *fruitfulness*, its *continuous renewal*, and its deepening. (Originally cited, 224; 244; my italics)

The process of the nation itself produces the transference of a model of a semi-individual identity to a collective one. Nation also results in a process in which the present and its continuous renewal are constitutive of contingency, or what Bhabha calls the "emergent insurgent," that produces a subaltern consciousness always open to discontinuity. Therefore, Fanon also defends the type of continuity that affirms an identity, which can be called national, which constantly presses against cultural meaning, the modes of representation, and practices. This idea takes a contradictory path in Fanon. If a "national culture is the sum total of all these assessments" the result is not exactly additive. Thus, the space of cultural representation that results from his way of conceiving of national culture is contingent, and thus open to a process of negation in which subjects are constantly redefined. The concept of Fanonian national culture enacts a process which distributes difference by reason of mobility and the present, rather than in relation to a catalog of defined characteristics of an identity. Thus, it remains open ended. Notwithstanding the apparent openness of his discourse on national culture and the relatively clear manifestation of the emergent in the agency of the colonized, it should be noted that the result of this reading would be otherwise if we project Fanon's statements on so-called field studies on the survival of precolonial cultural practices. Neil Lazarus, in a provocative essay, firmly discusses the readings of Fanon's texts by several contemporary authors, among whom are Christopher Miller and

Bhabha. What interests me to highlight is that he recognizes in Fanon's writing places that criticize a mode of nationalism but not necessarily outside a nationalist matrix (Lazarus, 162) and that Fanon's theoretical error is not to distinguish dominance from hegemony when it refers to the problem of cultural survival of precolonial history in the colonial and postcolonial present.

Lazarus accepts Guha's perspective on the two terms while, for the latter, colonialism was experienced in many regions far removed from administrative and bureaucratic power as domination, that is, as conquest, tax enforcement, forced labor. This resulted in the subaltern classes being able to participate in these spheres but did not necessarily transform meaning, in a hegemonic sense, in the sense of sharing the values and visions of the world of the dominators. Thus, the permanence of the precolonial past in the practices of these sectors is clearer than it appears (172–3). Regarding the first aspect, Lazarus positions Fanon as a participant in the movements of national liberation. Therefore, Lazarus is able to criticize those who try to locate Fanon's writing outside the claims of nation, as is the case of certain poststructuralist readings, especially that of Bhabha.

According to Lazarus, Bhabha moves beyond reading Fanon in the direction of his enunciations and nationalistic belongings; rather he solves the problem of nationalism annexed to its theory, stating the perspective that Fanon's position "does not allow any 'unisonance' in the imagined community of the future" (Bhabha, "A Question of . . . ," 102). Lazarus argues that this unisonant perspective for the decolonized state allows Fanon to distinguish between "bourgeois nationalism and another would-be hegemonic form of national consciousness from a liberationist, anti- imperialist, nationalist internationalism" (162–3).[2]

Despite widely defending and sustaining the argument with passages from Fanon's texts, especially from *The Wretched of the Earth* (which is not incidental), a different problem arises. First, it must be said that if we do not value the ambivalence in Fanon's texts and the role of alienation in their theoretical and rhetorical development, we run the risk as readers, even if minor, of ordering the projections of the Fanonian postcolonial community in an unambiguous direction, namely, that of a project that necessarily obstructs and hinders difference. Second, if we accept that the contingent or the emergent of the day-to-day, in Bhabha's terms, has some political and poetic efficacy in Fanon's texts, we can also accept that they are more, in terms of the apparent political project, than a unisonant voice. In other words, the uncertainties of the construction of historicity in day-to-day life imply a challenge for any discourse or discursive practice that attempts to represent culture from a unique and hegemonic perspective.

Tragic historicity, in more than one sense, which introduces alienation as a historical product in Fanon's texts, does not resist being simply obviated by an act of political desire. Nor, despite the manifest desire of Fanon and other writers, such as Albert Memmi, to overcome it, does it mean that it does not play a role that goes beyond the recognition of its existence. It articulates Fanon's historical visions, but not only in terms of a conceptual and theoretical instrument with which he describes the world and, precisely, the postcolonial national culture but also, and fundamentally, in terms of the difficulties of imagining a historical subject and an agency of the same oriented toward emancipation. This is not a minor problem. This is an imagination, by the way, that dwells in the folds of postcolonial critical thought. Let us look at this point from another angle. There is, in addition to the theoretical and methodological implication and disciplinary contents involved in Fanon's texts, an aspect that should not be forgotten, namely, that they are above all specific modes of responses to a political and moral urgency. For that reason, they not only appear within the postcolonial imagination in terms of a politics but also of a poetics. At both levels, it is necessary to consider the allegorical modes that traverse Fanon's politics and poetics escape the conceptual precision that many of their readers require.

Understood in this way, the argumentative mode and the plot of his texts become the most interesting for my analysis. I am not referring here to extreme textualist perspectives but to the fact that the argumentative modes and the plots of the text reveal a politics and a poetics. In the case of *The Wretched of the Earth*, for example, the process that Fanon describes from beginning to end is that of the development of an emergent consciousness which must permanently agree with its historicity. Accepting this dimension of a subject—that is difficult to apprehend (as consciousness even if the contrary is opined)—means accepting the limits of the text in terms of its categories and concepts. This means that neither Fanon's colonized nor colonizer are figures strictly derived from an empirical analysis, but they are historical figures drawn from his way of imagining them. And this way of imagining them, which does not mean a conscious way, becomes useful to the type of assimilation that

Bhabha produces with Fanon's texts for the benefit of his theory or the type of assimilation, which, ultimately, I am carrying out in this study. I do not direct these annotations entirely to Lazarus's arguments, but to a kind of doubt that remains, unsettled around knowledge and the role of the same in the context of the disciplines. In the earlier pages of my study, where I refer to the ethics of postmortem, I stated that what the discourse of revolutionary theory could not capture was left free to the disciplines as significant forms for territorialization. The problem persists. If the contingent, or the emergent insurgent as Bhabha calls it, has some meaning in Fanon's readings, it is precisely from our political and moral urgencies. The suspicion of the existence of an ambivalence, not necessarily in the privileged mode assigned to him by Chow, or of an uncertainty in Fanon's texts, is also the product of the direction assumed by certain readings. This does not mean that the elements to authorize such readings are not present in Fanon's writing. They are present in an explicit way in different passages. "Partial truths" are just that. The guidance I give to a way of thinking of postcoloniality, with an apology for the neologism, depends on our historical contingencies, our day-to-day. However, this dependence on our contemporariness also becomes the source of questioning the assumptions regarding the discourses of identity, be they of any kind, and of the pretensions of our theoretical projects (when these are present). In this direction, Fanon's texts exemplify more of what happens when problems are linked to historicity than to a conceptual source for designated disciplinary development. This does not mean that his texts are not used as sources for study, let us say of nationalism and liberation movements, or of the role of the intellectuals in postcolonial societies, as in the essay by Lazarus. Such use is perfectly legitimate and can offer the kind of meaning that Lazarus suggests regarding the consideration of the precolonial past in Fanon or the lack of distinction between domination and hegemony.

However, as I said above, the notion of contingency holds nuances. The first, linked to the idea of changing historicity and the second, absolutely related to it, which manifests itself in the instability of the representations of culture as an act through which we try to trace our relationship with the world and produce through it a consciousness of historicity, that is, the deployment of the agency of the colonized in the interstices of a discourse he faces daily. This nuance could be characterized as a type of contingency that results from a freedom that reveals itself in negative form, like negativity. That is the contingency of dialectics. It is possible to recognize in dialectics the historical project that has been stated, precisely, in something that is inexistent such as, when I argued earlier, in the dimension of consciousness that "discovers" its place in the world that denies him. The project delimits the ways in which each temporal ek-tasis will be read, but it is also open to what may seem heterogeneous or even "aberrant" in that process. In that moment, one could criticize Fanon's ambivalence between an extensive relativism and a determined rationalism, but, before doing so, it becomes necessary to acknowledge that it is precisely in the field of a Fanonian Hegelian dialectic that ambivalence is constitutive. Therefore, I observe an error in considering Fanon's statements absolute as this implies confusing the place of an affirmation with the intentions of the author or, even worse, a belief that Fanon's texts construct a homogeneous sense and that every rhetorical articulation serves as evidence of such a sense.

Sekyi-Otu has highlighted this problem by describing Christopher Miller's position regarding Fanon, where Miller believes that Fanon's texts do not indicate that meaning is being negotiated in the way dialectics implicitly does because Fanon persists in sustaining transcendental truths (33). For Sekyi-Otu, Fanon's texts should be considered a "dialectical narrative" (32) which implies considering the texts as organized around a principle that we might call foundational. In the case of *The Wretched,* this principle is the situation of the colonized subject by means of an abrupt event like that of colonization and the history of emancipation that this subject will go through and build at the same time by means of a dialectical procedure with the world that has made him a colonized man. The dialectic traverses its own ordeal since we find it threatened at the moment when no form of dialogue is possible between colonizers and colonized (dialogue here also connotes conflict) until its triumphant comeback but also open at the time when Fanon strives to imagine the space of national culture and a humanism that surpasses racialized forms of culture. As Fanon states:

> Decolonization is quite simply the replacing of a certain "species" of men by another "species" of men. Without transition, there is a total, complete, and absolute substitution. . . . But we have precisely chosen to speak of that kind of tabula rasa which characterizes at the outset all decolonization. (*The Wretched*, originally cited, 30; 35)

And further on,

But it cannot come as a result of magical practices, nor of a natural shock, nor of a friendly understanding. Decolonization, as we know, is a historical process: that is to say that it cannot be understood, it cannot become intelligible nor clear to itself except in the exact measure that we can discern the movements which give it historical form and content. (Originally cited, 30–31; 35–6)

Decolonization is, then, a historical process that enunciates the possibility of a dialectic but, at the same time of its initiation, is the negation of it. What, in the first instance, may seem like a paradox or, in the worst case, an incorrect approach on my part, becomes, in Fanon's text, a double process of historical invention. The species of men that must replace the other species of men is not yet the decolonized subject or, to be current with the times, the postcolonial subject, who recognizes the plots of identities in an extremely imbricated process from which he cannot distance himself unless he exerts violence on any of the narratives that constitute those identities. No, on the contrary, the subject at the beginning of this historical process is the one who must enunciate himself as an absolute, as a concrete incarnation of the opposite of colonial society, even when it was a colonial society that constituted him in the "historicizing movement." One can perceive the action of the dialectic in this movement that abolishes itself in situating a "beginning" that appears as a kind of zero sum.

For this reason, the men of different species are not the postcolonial or decolonized subjects but the colonized who conceive the world as a situation represented by a similar substitution. The narrative structure resonates with meaning when Fanon asserts that the colonial world is a split world with an exclusionary logic:

> The zone where the natives live is not complementary to the zone inhabited by the settlers. The two zones are opposed, but not in the service of a higher unity. Obedient to the rules of pure Aristotelian logic, they both follow the principal of reciprocal exclusivity. No conciliation is possible, for of the two terms, one is superfluous. (*The Wretched*, originally cited, 33; 38–9)

However, despite Fanon's ascending narrative, particularly in this chapter of *The Wretched*, it must be kept in mind that these passages have a descriptive motive. The trajectories that traverse his discourse of opposition incorporate a subject who, in their being, become a critical expression to the colonial regime. Yet, it is an incomplete subject, in a certain way inhabited by a lack or, we could say, by an absence. The logic of reciprocal exclusion entails difficulties for recognition because, unlike the Hegelian dialectic of the master and slave, where the slave is always a slave when the master recognizes him as a subject and, from there, "objectifies" him, Fanon does not see that dimension in the case of colonial society. The colonized remains, as he expounds, outside the logic of recognition, in Hegelian terms, because the colonizer cannot generate recognition under any instance. They inhabit parallel worlds. In this context, the colonized has a double task: to discover the world around him and to discover himself in the process. Each of the moments of this discovery refers to the stages of alienation mapped out in *Black Skin*. It is through a critique of alienation that this subject-in-formation will find his place in the world.

However, the question that remains at stake and which again refers to the problem of contingencies is: What direction does disalienation assume in Fanon? A quick response is that the direction of consciousness establishes a critical relationship with the world. But this response poorly characterizes the process through which Fanon's ascending narrative mutates into uncertainty and ambivalence. Thus, certainty exists in the diagnosis and ambivalence in how Fanon constitutes a subject subjected to a permanent lack, because the subject of *Black Skin* and *The Wretched* is a divided subject, splintered or at least still in the process of formation. The struggle for recognition implies that the beginning of this dialectics (I apologize for the paradox) is a subject that cannot in any way be placed outside the contradiction of his own history, that is, the history of colonial society. Hence, contingency acquires the dimension of a moral and political urgency and of a historical understanding. However, Fanon's oppositional discourse relates to "the modern" (ultimately the subject that emerges from *The Wretched* is much like the idea of a rational subject) search for spaces to represent new modes of consciousness. The new modes of consciousnesses locate and sustain a profound image of ambivalence which cannot be other than unstable spaces. For this reason, the instability of the decolonization process is always forefront in the face of the apparent rigid diagnosis of colonial society. This instability centers Fanon's rhetorical strategy. We can read the following in *The Wretched*:

> The problem of truth ought also to be considered. In every age, among the people, truth is the property of the national cause. No absolute verity, no discourse on the purity of the soul, can shake this position. The native replies to the living lie of the colonial situation by an *equal falsehood*. (Originally cited, 44; 50; my italics)[3]

Where is truth, then, if the colonized responds with a parallel lie? It remains just outside of any of the fixed terms that constitute Fanon's description but not outside of his political discourse. To use a historian's term, durations found his rhetorical strategy (and with the word "rhetoric," I am implying more than a stylistic question). The immediacy of the anticolonial struggle contains truths, including absolute ones, even if they are of "an equal falsehood," mainly because an occupation of space is at stake and not the creation of a new one. Everything in Fanon's narrative at this moment becomes loaded with a static atmosphere.

> The oppressor, in his own sphere, starts the process, a process of domination, of exploitation, and of pillage, and in the other sphere, the coiled, plundered, creature which is the native provides fodder for the process as best he can, a process which moves uninterruptedly from the banks of the colonial territory to the palaces and the docks of the mother country. *In this becalmed zone the sea has a smooth surface, the palm tree stirs gently in the breeze, the waves lap against the pebbles, and raw materials are ceaselessly transported*, justifying the presence of the settler: and all the while the native, bent double, more dead than alive, exists interminably in an unchanging dream. (Originally cited, 44–5; 51; my italics)[4]

This is the movement of repetition. Fanon illustrates a scene of the colonial power in the movement of the cycle in which power is, among other possible forms, the power to represent. Attuned with the time of Braudelian historiography, we hear the echoes of the geographical and economic events and the weight of temporality. In a sense, we could think of existence from an impossible situation and of crossed itineraries. If Braudel can, in a way almost contemporary to Fanon, imagine life but also the enormous heaviness of the Mediterranean, it is because of a suspicion of the discursive rituals linked to the idea of historical change in Western discourses, fundamentally evident in the ideologies of a modernity that secured pristine routes for the subject. The relative disappearance of the historical subject in relation to his moral and political urgencies in Braudel and its replacement with a subject of demiurge time able to evade the activities that a history of a lifetime indicates, despite the festive tone that Braudelian historiography acquires, a problem with historicity.

The Mediterranean and the Mediterranean World in the Age of Philip II appeared in French for the first time in 1949.[5] It could not have gone unnoticed by Fanon. The colonized of *The Wretched* is a type of universal category as we saw before but so are the colonized in Algeria. He tries to discover the limits of his own representation of the world in a world that understands him within long-lasting structures. These can illuminate regions of his experience but do not say much about the possibility of historical innovation, of historical inventiveness that the metadiscoursal demands in producing him as colonized. It is a metadiscoursal to the extent that both the colonial discourse and Fanonian critical discourse take over that complex and difficult category to delimit the named "colonized," assuming his existence as such.

The specter of the historicity of the colonized as a split and partial subject must emerge from the plot of a dehistoricizing root and a radical position of the subject. If we insist on the problem of moral and political urgency, it is not coincidental with the intentionality of the Fanonian narrative that is constantly debated in the limits of an aporia, but rather by the difference that the moral and political urgency produces concerning contemporary discourses and intellectual practices in Fanon's two most important texts. This difference, clearly, is not based on the absence of such political and moral urgencies, for example, as in the discourses of history as a discipline. It suffices to recall here Marc Bloch's *Apology of History*, written in the terrible conditions of the Nazi persecution, so as not to privilege some urgencies over others.

The historiographic problem underlying the discussion of historicity in Fanon is not resolved in the direction of a method or, more loosely, of a methodology in the style of professional historiography. Fanon's approach (in some moments) differs from a Jaspersian historicity based on a discourse of philosophical rootedness that does not lead him to a way of writing about history and a historicity linked with the developments of the discipline of history. However, the double act of trust and suspicion of the subject, in considering the interior of structures that exceed the subject, affirm the historicity shown in his texts which thus appears like contemporary historical thought. A conception of historicity that contains both elements of philosophical thought and historiographic thought establishes the historical subject in Fanon's writing. Both in its nuances that bind it with daily life and with the emergent process of a consciousness able to differentiate and displace, contingency implies an empirical dimension of the subject or of subjects that cannot easily be circumvented. My reading of Lazarus discussed briefly responds to this situation.

Fanon's two most important texts are situated in this problematic. Fanon's writing may be subject to observation from its empirical component or from its poetics. In the first case, his texts authorize a critique, bearing in mind his "errors" in the reading of certain processes or of certain empirical material. Lazarus's considerations illustrate this very well regarding precolonial cultures and Algerian peasant culture with respect to *The Wretched of the Earth*. In this sense, Fanon's work is close to that of historiographic thought, as it may be the subject of and, at the same time, in dialogue with, considerations of a methodological order. However, the difference with a disciplinary thought or, rather, the differential that his writing produces with respect to it, is a poetics that appears as a condition to create the historical figures that are present in it. The colonized and the colonizer, for example, are not necessarily categories founded in an empirical historical work in which characteristics of the subjects are proven in detail but, rather, appear as totalities in Fanon's writing that invoke, paradoxically, specific and contextual modes of historicity. The contingent, then, is a metaphor for broader relationships in his texts between the historical space in which subjects are explained and the emergence of a subject in daily action, between a mode of theoretical political consciousness in line with great categories and an imagined history as production, between the apparent stability of imagining postcolonial society from the figure of national culture and the instability of a representation of a culture that is constantly recreated. Ultimately, as Parry would say, we find ourselves between an impulse and a transnational thought.

These tensions allow for a rereading of the weight of this historicity which traps the subjects in repetition because the static image of the last passage by Fanon also announces a double condition or necessity. On the one hand, it aims to recognize colonial society as a historical space (despite the immobility that Fanon assigns to it) and, on the other, to introduce in that historical space, where repetition is its visible trait, an indicator of the agency of the subjects which should not out of necessity resort to repetition.⁶ At this moment in his text, what we have are only indications of what will happen to the colonized because Fanon's description of the static environment serves as the prelude to the freedom of the subject in the historicity that produces and conditions it, whether that of colonization or of the imagination of postcolonial society. The static also reverses the image of cooperation of the colonial scenario. However, that representational power is anchored to its own history. In that sense, answers do not come from the outside but rather from the same history that colonial society produces. Therefore, it is not correct to consider alienation as a process to overcome in the beginning of colonial resistance because it articulates the actions that the colonized subject carries out. It is a paradoxical subject because it must recognize the plots of its identities and discourses and move in a progressive direction regardless of these, to be, in other words, a historical subject. However, alienation, the historical process linked to it, and the cultural project that tries to defeat it permanently displace what could be the ultimate goal: the utopian trait of Fanonian emancipatory discourse. Therefore, it becomes important to see that euchronia does not play a role in his texts. On the contrary, a historicity is permanently articulated with the new. This historicity adds a tension to Fanon's discourse between the desire to establish a new humanism, which brings forth the imagination of a "global subject," and resistance to historical or cultural determinism. But before reaching that instance, temporality must be considered trapped in the scene of repetition and, at the same time, containing in itself the event of the short term and of more profound and enduring structures.

Fanon imagines the emergence of the action of the colonized at the crossroads of different historical rhythms. He thinks of colonial society as duration in this configuration of temporality, which Braudel conceived masterfully. Thus, Fanon is forced to conceive a subject, as I said before, pregnant with the "impurities of history." These "impurities" are not necessarily residual elements that can be discarded through a judgment of the value of colonial discourse. Hence, the problem of repetition implies more than the reference to Freud's texts and, rather, a consideration of the nature of colonial discourse that must deal with the endurance and capacity of the same to be a regime of truth that conforms to subjects and the world in differentiated social and historical contexts. Bhabha highlights that a central characteristic of colonial discourse is its dependence on the concept of "fixity," which implies a mode of paradoxical representation that simultaneously connotes rigidity and implies disorder, degeneration, and repetition. The stereotype, appearing as its most important discursive strategy, is a form of knowledge that is always there, "already known, and something that must be anxiously repeated." This process of ambivalence (different from the one I explore in Fanon) assures the colonial stereotype of its strength. It insures its "repeatability" in changing historical contexts and speaks of the strategies of individualization and marginalization ("The Other Question: The Stereotype and Colonial Discourse," 66). Bhabha underscores that you cannot judge the problem of stereotypes from a previous political regulation, for example, of the good versus the bad, because that mode avoids the problem. To displace them, Bhabha states effectively, it becomes necessary to commit domination and resistance that make up the subject of colonial identification with the multiple positions of power and resistance (67).

My interest in Bhabha's argument is that when one encounters the images and the effectiveness of colonial discourse (or colonial discourses, if one wants to think contextually) in *The Wretched of the Earth* (and also in *Black Skin, White Masks* on alienation), the weight that they have on historicity and in the process of building colonial subjects, whether colonizers or colonists, cannot be ignored. Extending the theoretical licenses that I have taken in this study, Fanon's writing expresses a problem in the difficult association with repetition and the regime of truth in colonial discourse and the need to introduce in that pact what could be called a differential of emancipation, which is the imagination of possible forms of urgency of agency of subjects. Unlike Braudel, who never turned too far from a "structural" history, Fanon introduces the question of choice and, we could add, of desire. He must do so because his ability to ask, as in the final claim of *Black Skin*, "Oh, my body, makes me a man always a man who questions!" (232), enables the imagination of the cultural project and the claim to make decisions on historical grounds, as seen in the brief discussion of the question of freedom with Sartre. Both desire, which manifests itself in the colonized as the desire to displace the settler, and choice, which confronts the problem of historical affirmation, make up an ambivalent terrain, but move within the effectiveness of stereotyped images of colonial discourse as Bhabha describes them. Consider Fanon:

> The look that the native turns on the settler's town is a look of lust, a look of envy; it expresses his dreams of possession—all manner of possession; to sit at the settler's table, to sleep in the settler's bed, with his wife if possible. The colonized man is an envious man. And this the settler knows very well; when their glances meet he ascertains bitterly, always on defensive, "They want to take our place." It is true, for there is no native who does not dream at least once a day of setting himself up in the settler's place. (*The Wretched*, originally cited, 34; 39)

Further on in the text:

> What they demand is not the settler's position of status, but the settler's place. The immense majority of the natives want the settler's farm. For them, there is no question of entering into competition with the settler. They want to take his place. (Originally cited, 53–4; 60–61)

Fanon's writing introduces the problem of choice in the space of desire, that is, in the double act of seeking recognition and separation from the colonial world. The colonial world is challenged beyond any dialogic position. The gaze of the colonized, adrift but moved by desire, allows *The Wretched* to begin to articulate the space for the challenge first and the decision after.

> The native's challenge to the colonial world is not a rational confrontation of points of view. It is not a treatise on the universal, but the untidy affirmation of an original idea propounded as an absolute. The colonial world is a Manichean world. (Originally cited, 35; 41).

Desire and decision must recognize the effectiveness of the colonial world, which we call colonial discourse, in the effort to displace it and to address the ways in which it works to discover the possible ways to express its discontinuity in its own ambivalence.[7]

Parry, in an important older article, places Fanon in the center of the critique of Bhabha's theoretical position by remembering the passage of *The Wretched of the Earth* where Fanon states that the fight against colonialism is a decisive and mortal battle between two protagonists. Parry argues that Bhabha's reading does not attempt to construct a counternarrative since his project does not acknowledge claims outside of discourse and "place[s] incendiary devices within the dominant structures of representation and to not confront these with another knowledge" (43). My point is that Bhabha proposes a reading of colonial discourse, as I explained earlier regarding Edward Said's critique, where the dominant being exists within the colonizers and the colonized. Thus signifying that the colonial text is no longer a unidirectional path from the colonizer to the colonized. Though the colonial discourse tries to build the colonized as a degenerate subject (remembering the settler's discourse that animalizes the colonized, as Fanon reveals), at the same time the ambivalence of the relationship between power and knowledge divides the discursive system into its enunciations. Consequently, the natives' positions become several and scattered. When this happens, the native can resist the dominant ideology by "wrongly" appropriating its modes of construction. Thus, the natives are no longer the monolithic representation of European discourse, or the Other, but become introduced into a space of difference that reveals an important degree of autonomy. The notion of hybridization is constituted at this point. When the natives take in their hands the desire to reform the metropolitan mind, thus inverting Mudimbe's formula (*The Invention of Africa,* Ch 1), the colonial text always results in parody. They write a text that is not a copy but a different thing in itself and where the "errors" of reading expose the inconsistencies of the colonial text (as in Bhabha's description of "the English book") that disqualify its quality of Presence (Parry, 41–2), in a type of representational transparency where mediation has not operated. The operation that emerges is not the taking of power or the construction of an absolute authority against colonial discourse, as an opposite sign, but rather a "distortion" of the supposed original text supported by the colonizer as a badge of colonial authority (42).[8] Bhabha constructs the idea of mimicry to represent this act of imitation or, better said, of parody of the discourse of the colonizer. Robinson Crusoe by Daniel Defoe provides an interesting example through which to discuss Bhabha's claims on mimicry.[9] The idea is that Robinson creates a world in the text (a kind of implanting) where he locates himself in the center. Robinson's act of invention is a double act of divine invention and self-invention. It is divine invention because he is the creator of the world that surrounds him and self-invention because, in the first act of invention, he defines the representational space where he will define himself. Bhabha claims that an act of this nature disturbs the centrality of the one who produces it since "the Other" already inhabits the "I" of the creator. Thus, in the encounter with Friday (or we could say the invention of Friday), Robinson's centrality begins to lose itself. The authority of his speech (the colonial discourse) thereby weakens. Robinson, faced with the need to maintain the act of divine invention, creates Friday as a replica of himself. The latter utters the same words as his master to the extent that the voice that Robinson listens to is his own. From that perspective, Friday does not exist. Rather than a presence with its own ontology, as Fanon would say, Friday is a representation of the master's imagination. Friday will always be incomplete, partial, and insubstantial (or lacking ontology, to think with Fanon), ultimately an image. The founding act of the colonizer's discourse has created a space for him to fill. This proposal seems to prescribe perfectly the place and nature of Friday, that is, the image that this reflects is not of a presence nor the narrative of the colonial discourse itself. However, it is a distorted image that is ambivalent, doubled. For Bhabha, for example, the simple presence of the colonized within the textual structure provides evidence of the ambivalence of the colonial text that destabilizes its claim to absolute and unquestionable authority. The writing of Richard Francis Burton demonstrates a similar process.[10] According to Bhabha, gaps open in the colonial text (what he calls "the English text") that allow imagining the ways in which these are decentered and questioned.

Despite presenting the enormous strength of "mimicry" in the construction of strategies of dominium by the colonizer, Bhabha situates it in the realm of uncertainty. Using V.S. Naipaul's idea of "mimetic men," Bhabha affirms that the authorized versions of otherness are "the part-objects of a metonymy of colonial desire which alienates the modality and normality of those dominant discourses in which they emerge as 'inappropriate' colonial subjects . . . now producing a partial vision of the colonizer's presence" ("Of Mimicry and Man," 88) that destabilizes colonial subjectivity, removes its authoritative centrality, and corrupts the purity of its discourse. In this sense, the colonizer's mask of Janus leads to the production of the "mimicry" which is presented more in the form of a threat than a resemblance and more as rupture than consolidation.[11]

Returning to Fanon and his texts, the historicity which can be deduced from both the notion of contingency and that of alienation inscribes the ideas of displacement and divergence of the colonial text with sufficient weight. Moreover, to understand it as such, it becomes necessary to consider that the account of the colonized is a narrative that presents a dramatic historicity. The subjects must continually confront forces that exceed them yet take the reasons for their criticism from these. A form of representation linked to the dramatic, the subjects discover themselves in the scenario of a seemingly prescribed history in the mode of the colonial text. The script, that converts them into subordinates, also frames them as objects willing, in the narrative of that text, to reinterpret it, or better, let it circulate as pure signifier. Irony, which I have already observed is an important feature in Fanon's texts, allows this displacement as an additional process to the scattered position of colonial subjects that Bhabha finds as a result of mimesis.

Fanon sees in the extensive diagnosis of colonial and postcolonial situations with reference to national culture the risk of reassuming not only formal but also constitutive narratives of identity and homogeneous and unambiguous historicity that can contain, at least in the scenario of cultural representations and in the field of emancipation policies, the value of the contingent, of irony, and the possibility to reflect on scattered and multi-positioned subjects that the ambivalence of colonial discourse and the very discourse of alienation propitiate. Even what Fanon insistently calls national culture, beyond the arguments of Lazarus, represents in his texts an open space that is hardly contiguous to the historical dimensions that the two terms usually include.

The Wretched of the Earth reads:

> The national claims, it is here and there stated, are a phase that humanity has left behind. It is the day of great concerted actions, and retarded nationalists ought in consequence to set their mistakes aright. We however consider that the mistake, which may have very serious consequences, lies in wishing to skip the national period. If culture is the expression of national consciousness, I will not hesitate to affirm that in the case with which we are dealing it is the national consciousness which is the most elaborate form of culture . . . . National consciousness, which is not nationalism, is the only thing that will give us an international dimension. (*The Wretched*, originally cited, 226; 247)

If the paradoxes in Fanon's texts elicit surprise, regarding the idea of the infinite reproduction of metahistorical essences that assimilate the discourse of the nation, the "uses" of the discourses linked to the nation, such as the idea of national consciousness to avoid the stigma of thinking of culture from racial perspectives, for example the discourse of Africanity found in Négritude, should also surprise.

National culture in this paragraph is not a synthesis of the values consecrated in some region, mythical or not, of the past. It becomes a metaphor that provides the idea of culture with an unsuspected movement. Unexpectedly, national culture is not the space devoted to redeeming values, but to creating them in the same direction proposed by the practices of the historicity of the contingent. For this reason, Fanon's own statements contain displacement: "National consciousness, which is not nationalism." Thus, the economy of his discourse is at times by subtraction. He calls for the disincorporation of the traits that would make discourse into a repetitive space. To disembody national consciousness from the figures of nationalism does not appear as an easy equation. However, the problem consists, in that Fanon's texts must produce balance with respect to essentialist perspectives, whether these are those that come from the experiences of blackness, the philosophical discussions related to ontological problems, to the historicity of the colonized, or to national consciousness. In its midst, we find a constant, namely, a kind of political rhetorical pact that moves between distant points, from the acceptance of a powerful, but in many ways, exclusionary voice like the one found in extreme arguments of blackness or the phrase in *Black Skin, White Masks* that augurs a single destiny for the black man and, by extension, for the colonized, in the images of universality in his discourse on man, who to be sustained, requires that all the other conditions be virtually absent. This balance of Fanon is, as we will see later with respect to the subject, one of the moments that summarizes the tragic character of his texts.

V

Contingency, Identity, and Alienation
The Challenge of the Specters

> *Among me from myself to myself outside any constellation clenched in my hands only the rare hiccup of an ultimate raving spasm ... vibrating word. ...*
>
> —Aimé Césaire, *Word*

The tension between statements that appear to be mutually exclusive, or at minimum opposite, represents much of the theoretical problem in studying the work of Fanon. The narrative of the colonial society of *The Wretched*, particularly the chapter titled "Concerning Violence," and the description of why the black person is an alienated being in *Black Skin*, construct a static scenario of monumental weight.

No possibility for escape exists before the fight for recognition begins, as in the description of the city of the settler and the colonized where difference sublimates the solidity of the material structures that make up one and demerit the other (*The Wretched*, 33 and 37); or, like the tragedy of blacks existing outside of all ontology because they have not been able to inhabit and to be inhabited by a concept of "man" that includes them (*Black Skin*, 101). Despite these images in Fanon's narrative of what must be defeated, ambivalence remains because it is from the very scene of alienation, in one case, and colonial society, in the other, from where Fanon sets in motion his splintered subject. This implies that the instability that presupposes any argument of opposition for colonial discourse adds instability to the oppositional discourse itself, because the devices that domesticate "the impulse" particularly by reason of the project simultaneously destabilize the project by claiming a place for contingency in the framework of freedom in existentialist terms conceived as freedom to choose in relation to options. In this permanent process of destabilization of cultural, historical, and social assumptions, the historical subject that, at the beginning of Fanon's narrative, is a divided and limited subject, toward the end—a subject permanently open to the contextual plot of their own life and time (as is the colonized against the problem of recognition). Thus, the remaining subject cannot find a home in any determination.

Once again, Fanon's "complaint" against Sartre exhibits a new nature. It is a critique against the ascending dialectic, but it is also a greater critique of Sartre's text and the possibility of his subjects remaining enclosed in homogeneous definitions of political, cultural, and historical identity and action. Fanon knows and recognizes this as a limit and as the impossibility of an aporia.

Hence, the problem of whether Fanon presents a racialist perspective of history, as I suggested before, should be raised in other terms. The point is not simply discovering that colonialism sets up this kind of social relation but determining what Fanon does with it. In that sense, the role of "race" only has significance in the rhythms of colonial temporality. Race is immersed in the problem of recognition and alienation. First, because colonial society has developed an explanation of their relations in the terms of race and animalization. Second, because alienation renders the possibility of it being transcended. However, as I pointed out, the most important thing is not locating the place and the time of this transcendence but of finding the permanent possibility that it can happen. A dialectic links to the structures of the event, to the conditions in which both the desire and the emergent project must be negotiated. Blackness, for example, is one of the conditions that the oppositional discourse assumes when the immediacy of the colonial stage is at stake. I don't mean this in the way Sartre proposes it, which must be overcome. Therefore, the freedom of choice, particularly vibrant at the end of *Black Skin*, is no more nor less than a certain celebration of the possibility of being strategic in our conceptions of culture. Thus, the movement of *Présence Africaine* affirmed the unique condition of Africa and the Négritude movement as part of the process of renewal of cultural pride (Jules-Rosette, 32), which can be read in Fanon's case, as stated in the first pages, as part of an essentialist position that recognizes the critical limits of itself (an aporia) as a form of strategic action. Jules-Rosette discusses this point in greater detail.

Following Algirdas Julien Greimas and Joseph Courtés's concept of homologation, Jules-Rosette points out that Sartre's perspective is to place Africa (and blackness) in "contradictory relation" with Europe. However, her claim finds additional logical possibilities of opposition, namely a non-Africa versus a non-Europe. According to her, Alioune Diop, who is one of the most important members of *Présence Africaine,* believes that non-Europe is all the oppressed people of the world. From this point of departure, Sartre takes this typology and relates the African situation with the situation of the proletariat in Europe. Thus, a new homologation emerges: "Africa: Europe: Non-Africa: non-Europe." In this formula, natural Africa is considered an idyllic place, a source of strength and unity (22), and the object of European colonization. Jules-Rosette wonders whether we should consider the term non-Europe to include societies suffering from its colonial presence who would be in contradiction to the idea of non-Africa or the European masses. Sartre's answer is to homologate the two concepts, such as race and class so that, although different, the black and European proletarian are homologated in the fact that they both seek a more egalitarian and just society.

The problem that Jules-Rosette points out, and which remains with an incredible validity for our discussion of Fanon's position on blackness, is that by making such a homologation, Sartre "removes the oneness of Africa and the 'Black Man'" (32). The tone of chapter five on the vivid experience of blacks is ironic, making Fanon's challenge twofold. As I said before, Sartre's position implies a displacement of temporality in which Fanon conceives cultural and political action. If the ascending Sartrean dialectic destabilizes as a historical cultural project the spaces of representation in which a particular and ambivalent response (blackness) conforms to subordination, this does not imply that Fanon's texts remove what Parry calls "the impulse." On the contrary, they reveal the strategic uses, aporetic it could be said, that result in an expanded concept of their political and moral urgencies in which to enunciate the absolute does not necessarily mean to sanction as consecrated value.

The timing of the event or the *short-duration,* to use one of the temporal durations of the French historian Fernand Braudel, best-known for the contrary duration, the long-duration (or *longue durée*), reveals the intensity of the drama confronting a discourse that removes agency from the subordinated by introducing their subjectivity (and the constitution of the same based on their lived experience) in time in a kind of global play. Long-duration situates these agencies conceived as historically limited in stages to be overcome. This register of political and moral urgencies transforms the short-duration into something more than a response because it recognizes the difficulties in which oppositional discourse is generated: "The native replies to the living lie of the colonial situation by an equal falsehood" (originally cited, 44; 50). A lie becomes truth, partial truth, constrained to the dimensions of the process in which it is enunciated, but it nevertheless represents an extensive exercise of historical comprehension and intentionality. It is historical comprehension because it does not assign a teleological duty but only a form of action to the subjects involved. It is intentionality when it becomes possible in the constrained environment to imagine a project and submit it, in turn, to the instability of the contingent. From my point of view, the dimension of the contingent and strategic uses of the discourse of identity like blackness can be read in the following passage of Mudimbe:

> In his *Peau noire, masques blancs* [Black Skin, White Masks] Fanon accuses Sartre of treason, for Fanon does not believe that "negritude is dedicated to his own destruction." Some years later, in *Les damnés de la terre*, the West Indian theorist firmly applies Sartre's dialectical principle and bluntly states: "There will not be a black culture," "the black problem is a political." (*The Invention of Africa*, 85)

This change, also identified by Peter Rigby (270–71), could be understood as Fanon's acceptance in the face of an initial error of the process of disaggregating cultural identities when the political response to colonialism must advance beyond a moment of self-affirmation. Therefore, the most obvious difference between *Black Skin, White Masks* and *The Wretched of the Earth* is not so much what is constructed as an object in each text but the kind of demands and historical time that each one of them confronts. In other words, the dimension of the contingent varies in each text because the historical contextual conditions of its production, namely, the kind of political and moral urgency it faces differ. This does not mean establishing a sort of hierarchy between the two to trace the stages of Fanonian thought. Rather, it is a matter of considering that the interstices of expanded projects on culture and history reveal Fanon's texts. These interstices are the result of the ambivalence in which each of his statements must be negotiated. If the complaint against the erasure of the uniqueness of Négritude represents a tension with the possibilities of aperture that I am assigning to Fanon's discourse, then this is nothing more than a consequence of that opening. The aperture should not be understood as synonymous with theoretical incoherence or overcoming of thought in the chronological order of his texts, but as a permanent negotiation against the challenges proposed by the (not Jaspersian) historicity represented by the day-to-day.

In this context, what Diana Fuss calls a "second theory of white-black relations" plays a very important role. Fuss states that Fanon warns that, despite his initial assertions, black does not play the role of "other," neither imaginarily nor symbolically, for white. Fanon shows that the colonized has a different role than being the "other" for whites, because colonialism determines the limits in which this representation can be produced, and for black people, or for the colonized, there is no possibility of access to that otherness because it would imply the status of subject. On the contrary, then, excluded from the field of symbolization, the consequences are devastating; the black man cannot escape pure objectification against the cry of a child: "Mama, see the Negro! I'm frightened!" For Fuss, the white signifier "is never a 'non-black'" because in the colonial context the signifier rises beyond the concept of race and becomes a self-transparent term that does not need an external "black" sign to be denied for whites to affirm their own identity (21–2). For that reason, Fanon uses the Hegelian analogy of the master and slave as he also separates from it because while the master recognizes the slave as subject, there is no such relationship for the colonized.

> In fact, the terms the settler uses when he mentions the native are zoological terms. He speaks of the yellow man's reptilian motions, of the stink of the native quarters, of breeding swarms, of foulness.... When the settler seeks to describe the native fully in exact terms, he constantly refers to the bestiary. (*The Wretched,* original, 37, 42)

In a similar line of thought as Fuss, Natalie Melas's "Versions of Incommensurability" addresses the question of white as "other" but as it stands in comparison to blacks. Melas proposes that a space emerges in the act of comparison which loses its capacity to measure and enters a permanent flow of difference that makes it impossible to fix any standard. Melas takes Fanon's reference in *Black Skin* to the Adlerian comparison (*Moi plus large that l'Autre*—Ego Greater than the Other) (*Black Skin*, originally cited, 189; 215) that he transforms into a new relationship in which he adds the word *White* located above another new relation defined as "Ego different from the Other." Thus, Melas states that since *White* is situated outside the comparison between "I," which claims to be different from "Other," in the process *White* becomes the scale of values to establish an interior comparison. Starting from the reflection of Davis Lloyd on assimilation,[1] Melas proposes that *White* is elevated to the category of "universally representative man" that produces among blacks a permanent comparison to each other (277). The latter are only compared to *White* to establish the differences among themselves. Therefore, Melas claims that this comparison produces immeasurable subjects because they are permanently thrown into a "differential flow." When this happens, a standard can never be set, nullifying a comparison that could be measured. Difference in this context is not the separation between defined entities but "the differential effect of an impossible identification" (278–9).

Beyond the consequences that this author sees in comparative analysis with Fanon's reading, what I aim to highlight is that she indicates that the subject that Fanon imagines is partly a subject released endlessly to a differential terrain. Clearly, this process links to alienation that is produced and reproduced in the moment that *White* remains on the outside and above relations in the Antilles. However, it is no less true that what Melas calls the "differential flow" pushes these subjects permanently out of any scale of measurement. In this context of alienation constituting a divided subject and of establishing a way permanently to defer identifications, Fanon tries to think about how the colonized hold agency. Therefore, it is no coincidence that he sees in the contestation that the colonized of the colonial world make, an "untidy affirmation of an original idea propounded as an absolute" (*The Wretched*, originally cited 35; 41). There is no contradiction here because the impugnation tries to situate the subject outside the comparison that only generates differences among the subordinated. The formulation cannot be but absolute because there is an "outside" in the relationship that overdetermines it. As Melas also suggests (278), the equivalences between the colonized are minor in relation to the fact that the pattern of comparison is external and irreversible. The possibility of finding "community" in this context is reduced because a certain homogeneity of both the oppositional discourse and the field of identifications among the colonized is always deferred. However, the necessity that imposes a rigid context in this absolute formulation signifies a greater critical moment than the development of a theory of the nature of the anticolonial struggle in Fanon. From my perspective, this is because the ambivalence and tensions that his discourse generate are not random elements.

Alienation in the structure of *Black Skin* is almost a cultural starting point to establish the expanded critique of colonial society, but in two ways. First, as a signal of the inequality and distortion that it imposes on the colonized in their psychic, cultural, and social organization. Second, it is from a point of view that we could call methodological, as it provides from the "differential flow" the possibility of thinking of cultural processes as carriers of indetermination. It is obvious that this indetermination also has a limit to the extent that the central relationship that Fanon establishes is for the Antilles. The reformulation of the Adlerian schema offers no alternative to the colonized that differentiates their construction to one another by the external term of the relationship, that is, white. The "differential flow" reveals, then, the static dimension of the colonial world and its brutal manner of contrast. Fanon names this in *The Wretched* as "a positive negation of common sense is evident." He explains, "While the settler or the policeman has the right the livelong day to strike the native, to insult him and to make him crawl to them, you will see the native reaching for his knife at the slightest hostile or aggressive glance cast on him by another native" (originally cited, 47; 54). It is also evident, I believe, that permanent differentiation is a kind of mark in Fanon's theoretical text that warns of certain impossibilities in the construction of a discourse and an oppositional practice. Namely, the impossibility to sustain them without a process of "deferment" or displacement.

As I said before, Fanon's splintered subject emerges from a historical condition and the subject, in that emancipatory process stands on that historical territory. Thus, Fanon tries to build a critique of the subject while believing in it. That is why we always see him at a crossroads. There is always a suspicion from the splintered subject of colonial society, represented by the colonized, to even the postcolonial global subject. It is a counterpoint that ensures the inability to imagine him outside a varied and multi-positional environment. This very complex aspect is sometimes lost in the general realm when we read Fanon's text as an agenda. However, doubts about what happens to that subject's agency are not properly Fanonian. They belong rather to our current context of discussions, but they will nonetheless serve as a benchmark for thinking more carefully about this problem in his texts.

IMPULSES, AGENCY, AND SUBJECTS: AN UNFINISHED PLOT

In this framework of a crossroads, one can better understand the resonance of Fanon's sentence which closes *Black Skin*: "O my body, make me always a man who questions! (originally cited, 204; 232). The question of that body implies the possibility of exercising a form of existentialist freedom as it references any temptation to reduce cultural practices and discourses to a fixed sphere of representations. Let us return to Sartre and *Black Orpheus*. Alongside our prior discussion, we could say that this text displaces the accounts of Négritude from the essentialisms linked with an ontology of the Self and does so, imagining the essences as moments of a historical construction that must account for a certain instrumentality and phenomenon that one cannot grasp by an inaccessible transparency of the concepts or the meanings in a language appropriate for translation. "Black poetry has nothing in common with the effusions of the heart; It is functional, it answers a need which exactly defines it" (18).

Sartre's idea is a language without witnesses. Since Négritude is inscribed in the language of the colonizer, it must seek a zone, utopian perhaps, where its movements cannot be captured by those who do not recognize themselves in it. This gesture accompanies Sartre in almost all his reflections on colonialism and its critics. The preface of *The Wretched* shows this same gesture when he claims that it is the book of the enemy (originally cited, 13; 14). But before assigning a literal meaning to the figures that Sartre and Fanon construct in relation to blackness, it is necessary to see first that the tensions resulting from the political urgency and ambivalences of what we could call "a cultural project" articulate them. The latter, perhaps, is the least visible territory, most opaque because it implies, as I said before, endless figures of identity and difference in which the function of language is central. Not yet as a dialogic function where community speaking emerges and moves in a relational sphere but a language that, while still intimately claiming a connection with the Self, has already desisted from any enterprise outside historicity. Being age-old does not make the problem obsolete but persistent: will this cultural project allow for divergent forces or will it focus on a rigid nucleus of affirmations of identity, difference, and correspondence between the signified and signifier? As Graham Pechey points out, although he is interested in another issue (he argues about Bakhtin's treatment of language and power), "any sociopolitical project of centralization or hegemony always and everywhere posits itself against the ubiquitously decentralizing forces (centrifuges) within ideology" (62). Pechey's reading of Bakhtin in this respect is meaningful to my argument because he states that, together with the opposition that emerges from the perspective of Bakhtin between the "carnival" and the "official," there are a series of parallel oppositions within culture between self-sufficient national cultures and those that are exposed to a polyglot context (63). Pechey states that Bakhtin sees the Renaissance as the moment of passage from one state to another (ibid). Although these aspects of the Bakhtinian theories are not linked by theoretical tradition to Fanon or to Sartre, they help to reflect on the dynamics between local and transnational tensions, as well as between the recourse to so-called nativism and the heterogeneity of historical and cultural experiences. The tensions facing all oppositional discourse are fundamentally those that occur between centrifugal and centripetal forces. However, the critical problem in Fanon's reading that I am proposing is whether the tensions are resolved by renouncing the centrality of the oppositional discourse.[2] To the extent that there is a dispute over hegemony, it is tentatively fitting to think of two possibilities.[3] The first, in some ways, appears in Fanon's "complaint" against Sartre for having dismantled the illusions of the eternity of Négritude, implying with it the fact that there is no possibility of enunciating a new centrality, a substitution and, therefore, renouncing the critical spaces and the dispute over what hegemony could offer. In the second, the same Négritude cautions that the process of decentration is an irreversible act of any oppositional discourse if it is to continue being one. At this point, the novelty (and, we could say, complexity) is greater even when an element appears that converts the tension into an almost constant state of the critical task. For Fanon to resolve this tension, as he seems to suggest in multiple places in his texts (specifically toward the end of *Black Skin* and in the discussion of national culture in the *The Wretched*), implies closure to his critical project. In the face of this, I hypothesize that Fanon's writing resists any temptation of cultural and theoretical definition because his writing itself generates, as I said before, its own space of instability.

Several aspects should be considered for this to be so. First, the fact that the cognitive and political activity of the colonized makes its way into a terrain that has already defined strong "centrisms": colonial society, the history of colonial society, the blocked construction of blacks (or the "lived experience of blacks"). Second, by the fact that these historical, social, and psychological conditions enunciate a subject that does not have (and, perhaps, should not have) in its cultural repertoire, a stable and solid nucleus from which to claim and argue a position in the world that, by its main characteristic, understands as a precondition any critical experience which I tentatively called "the end of the catachresis." Thus, an enunciation that finds the perfect correspondence between the Self and the enunciation of that Being. Third, colonial alienation, which goes beyond Fanon's critique, involves an inevitable process of displacement and reconfiguration of subjects. In *Black Skin,* Fanon claims that:

> Man is a yes that vibrates to cosmic harmonies. Uprooted, pursued, baffled, doomed to watch the dissolution of the truths that he has worked out for himself one after another, he has to give up projecting onto the world an antinomy that coexists with him. (Originally cited, 14; 8)

And later he adds:

> The future should be an edifice supported by living men. This structure is connected to the present to the extent that I consider the present in terms of something to be exceeded. (Originally cited, 18; 13)

These affirmative characteristics fill the unstable terrain, which I mentioned earlier. Fanon's person, the ideal human being established as the point of arrival of his analysis, is always elusive to the extent that "truths he has worked out for himself" are permanently dissolved. However, despite the explicit reference to the error that constitutes the human being's projection of incorrect images, in this case in the Manichean structures of colonial society, the field of existential historical experience remains promising. In this sense, the future depends on a sustained construction and not of an already established "presence." Fanon's diagnosis is oriented in this direction, although some of the results are presented in the beginning of his text, as the first paragraph quoted above. His compelling statements do not close in a set of definitions and instead generate the very space of instability in his writing. For example, the human being can be a vibrant yes to cosmic energies, an almost undifferentiated, universal person, depicted from an equivalent human condition in all geography but also historical and spatially situated; they must construct their present if they want to build the future. It is by means of this process that Fanon manages to imagine history like a place of intersections and not of purifications. It is not the Hegelian spirit that passes through an ordeal ultimately to reencounter itself. For the subject to aspire to any ontology, they must first recognize their historical plot. But, to do so, they cannot ignore the history that projected them into an "antinomy that coexists in [them]." Nor can they ignore, once "discovered," the modes of that construction. They must, besides dismantling the ways in which they were constructed, recognize for themself the power of these constructions to articulate their visions of the world, their memories, and their forms of oblivion.

For that reason, alienation in Fanon's scheme is central both for his political concern and urgency and for his theoretical perspective because it not only constructs a type of "split" subject but also inscribes a history which conditions the ways the future can be imagined. However, this conditioning contains two factors. On the one hand, the fact of alienation, that is, the separation with respect to a set of practices and discourses that, for Fanon, implies "the real"; and, on the other, the inextricable link of each representation of opposition with the inscribed history in subjects by the same alienation. Therefore, Fanon attempts "nothing short of the liberation of the man of color from himself" (*Black Skin*, originally cited, 14; 8). His investigation rests on the attitudes facing "two camps: the white and the black." He explains that "The 'jungle savage' is not what I have in mind. That is because for him certain factors have not yet acquired importance" (originally cited, 17; 12). Liberating the black person from themself is not to return them to a previous state before all contact with "white civilization" but, fundamentally, to displace them from the discourses that place them in a state that does not coincide with their practices. As a result, alienation for Fanon implies a double cultural process of inscription and contact. The same element that Fanon wants to remove reveals redemption to the subject and, in doing so, a subject remains that can no longer be recognized in a fixed series of attributes.

This double process in his texts brings him closer to, and distances him from, the thought of some of the intellectuals linked to the movement of Négritude. As Richard Bjorson explains, the idea of alienation implies displacement from a supposedly normal or natural state of being. In this frame of thought, Senghor's perspective on alienation implies that alienation was the main reason for the sufferings of European (and African) society. Therefore, from the perspective of blackness, Africa would contribute a notion of humanism that would help alleviate Europe's own alienation. Thus, says Bjorson, the revaluation of the role that African culture plays would imply the awakening of black consciousness around the world (147). However, despite the negative role that Senghor and others close to *Présence Africaine* assigned to alienation, it is itself constitutive of the process by which the new black consciousness would appear. French education allowed them a separation, an externality we could say, with respect to the practices and representations of their original communities. Thus, Bjorson points out that alienation is almost a prerequisite of the movement toward knowledge and, in this way, it contributes (in a peculiar way) as a process to increasingly higher levels of consciousness.

The intellectuals engaged in the launching of *Présence Africaine* were part of this agenda (148). This point of view on alienation, whose main facets are shared by Abiola Irele, remain a central element for discussion of Fanon because his texts do not elude alienation when imagining the splintered subject of colonial society and inevitably mixed character in the oppositional contents, meanings, and practices of colonialism. This moment is at stake when I claim that Fanon's texts agree with the emergent contingent situations in reference to the strategic uses of the discourses on the identity and black consciousness of the colonized. This brings him closer to the Négritude movement while distancing him from it. It brings him closer in being in the same irreversible process of considering the problem of liberation from colonialism's historical and cultural fabric and it distances him, in that the use of these plots asserts a movement that is, one could say, aware of its own limits but which explores its significance even in regions where it risks being caught in the repetition of a set of attributes on emancipation. From that intersection, Fanon would say of the task: "Let us reconsider the question of cerebral reality and of the cerebral mass of all humanity, whose connections must be increased, whose channels must be diversified and whose messages must be re-humanized" (originally cited, 290; 314). The conscious problem of displacement linked to alienation makes this movement possible not only in its negative characteristics but as a tool of cultural critique. The discovery of a historicity that inevitably pushes subjects out of their more stable representations results from this.

Although interesting, this perspective on alienation is not novel. However, it moves from the uses that we often hear and read about it in the discourse of certain revolutionary politics, for example, which, despite pretending to be founded on historicity, present the overcoming of alienation as an ahistorical moment, as cultural nationalism also does as it separates the very concept of culture from the historical process that shapes it. Examples abound, but we cite Irele's lucid analysis of contemporary African cultural nationalism, which corresponds precisely to an extra-African process. Irele relates to Shahid Amin's study of the events in a peasant village of India in the first quarter of the century and its significance in the discourse of the Gandhian nation and in the speech of the nation of the party of Congress to the present. Amin's analysis reveals that the uses of historicity in the Gandhian discourse of the nation are based on the subjects' sectioning of instability and uncertainty produced by their practices. Furthermore, this makes it particularly interesting in the case of the Fanonian colonial subject— whose relation I am establishing—because the peasants of Chauri Chaua carry out the riots from the discourse of Gandhian nonviolence though they are unknown at first by Gandhi and the official Indian history of the twentieth century. They become reabsorbed by the discourse of the nation at the cost of removing their names from any monument or memorial act. Thus, they reread and resignify the national discourse available at that specific moment in Indian history.[4]

The consequences of facing any notion of alienation are evident. If an estrangement of certain real conditions of existence or values ultimately define what Chow calls "policies of admission," then, alienation will always be represented as a factor external to culture, as an obstruction to an occult but simultaneous transparent sense of a culture. Thus, this makes rereading impossible, and a new state of consciousness, however defined, impossible because there is no displacement, or rather, decentering. Therefore, the representation of a culture becomes a mummified representation, in the same nature that Fanon assigns to colonial society in the image of the city of the settler and that of the colonized, differing from the mode of thought that holds on to the dichotomy:

> The settler's town is a strongly built town, all made of stone and steel. It is a brightly lit town; the streets are covered with asphalt, and the garbage

cans swallow all the leavings, unseen, unknown and hardly thought about
.... The town belonging to the colonized people, or at least the native
town, the Negro village, the medina, the reservation, is a place of ill fame,
peopled by men of evil repute. (*The Wretched*, originally cited, 33–4; 39)

Seeing Fanon's image move from a critique to an ahistorical procedure of the cultural imagination as acritical truths indicates again the role that alienation plays in his discourse's plot on the subject.

As we know, Hegel's presence in Fanon's texts is not marginal. It does not matter at this point whether Fanon distances himself from the dialectic of the master and slave or if his reflections on the ontology of blacks owe to Hegel. In the case of alienation, the bond or, rather, the dialogue with Hegel is explicit. Irele, in a challenging text entitled "In Praise of Alienation," points out that, from a philosophical standpoint, the concept of alienation designates the state of consciousness in dialectical relationship between the mind (or spirit) and matter (215). Let's read a somewhat extensive quotation from Irele:

The adventure of the mind in the realm of the universe of nature is for Hegel the definition of history. What we commonly call "culture" is the result of man's transformations of nature, which remains apart from his consciousness but from which these transformations originally arise. In other words, it is through the confrontation of the mind (spirit) with matter that culture and thought are produced and that history itself is made possible; it sets in motion the historical process within which the Spirit is refined and progresses towards the final perfection of the Absolute Idea
.... The state of alienation is thus a condition for the realization of the Spirit. (215)

And further on, he adds:

In the historical context of present African development, we may now ask, Alienation for what, and in what direction? I will answer that question unequivocally: as a matter of practical necessity, *we have no choice but in the direction of Western culture and civilization.* (215; my italics)

A reminder: "For the Black there is only one destiny. And it is white" (*Black Skin*, originally cited, 16; 10). Hence, Irele resumes exploration of the problem of alienation from the very basis of the tragic Fanonian affirmation. Alienation is, at that moment, a place of possibilities to imagine the way in which history and historicity conjugate dual, partial, or splintered subjects. Alienation becomes a way of imagining culture in a historicity that is constitutive of the representations that inhabit it and conform it in temporality. Although many of the imaginings are seen as essences, these can be the goal of strategic uses. However, the expected outcome is the most important difference with Hegel's canonical texts that approach this problem. Fanon desires, as Albert Memmi and many others also do, the elucidation of the consciousness which fights against colonial alienation. However, as the cultural project becomes historicized, it comes to illustrate how, in any of its forms, alienation will always construct splintered subjects and deferred, delayed cultural meanings because alienation itself reveals the impossibility of the suspension of history in a final project, in the manner of the Hegelian Absolute Idea, or of the prescriptive utopian community.

Alienation represents a condition in the way of perceiving the agency of the colonized and of the historical subject facing the task of emancipation. Such a condition has a double characteristic as it projects the desire of Fanon's texts to completely overcome alienation yet such desire, which must be understood as the reason that makes reflection possible in the Sartrean sense of the word, is articulated in and with alienation as an organizing force in his writing. Thus, to refer to the problem of alienation as an absolute overcoming in Fanon is to cut off the dimensions his texts possess in the production of a discourse and knowledge on the colonial subject.

Conversely, Fanon's attack on alienation as a representational failure also caters to the way in which it appears in a historicity constituted by exclusion, a characteristic even in Jaspersian historicity. Presenting alienation in this way becomes the guarantor of absolutist discourses of culture and, therefore, history, rather than an open space of invention, blocked instead with the idea of the inevitable. Whatever direction alienation assumes, it occurs outside the subject. In this sense, alienation appears in Fanon as a discourse that cannot be avoided, which in turn implies the two directions that his texts approach. First, as we saw above, as a form of reflection and displacement. Second, as a phenomenon that, when presented as inevitable, abolishes any dissent and initiative by the subjects. These two instances are articulated both in the defense and critique of blackness as an absolutist discourse. However, this "initiative" does not imply that the subjects do not constitute a grid of power in their society. What we represent as agency implies a different provision of power that, at some point, can (or cannot) change the regime of truth. Agency itself constitutes one of these processes by means of which power is subjectivized.

According to Foucault in *Genealogy of Racism*, individuals are not an inert matter on which power is applied, but are the effect and, at the same time, composition of power (32). However, the tension between policies of confinement and of emancipation for the subject in Fanon's texts is not due to a lack of definition of his political vision, which is explicit on more than one occasion, but depends rather on the historicity that inevitably crosses and constitutes the subject. Thus, the agency of the colonized is a terrain of extreme tensions which necessarily summarize the reasons why a cultural project is defended. At the same time, the contents of the historical processes make it impossible to not consider these tensions given the conditions that they delineate. In other words, the theoretical teaching of Fanon's texts proposes not to see alienation only as a form of confinement, although the goal is to overcome it, but as the foundation of policies of openness or emancipation.

> The problem considered here is one of time. Those Negroes and white men will be disalienated who refuse to let themselves be sealed away in the materialized Tower of the Past. For many other Negroes, in other ways, disalienation will come into being through their refusal to accept the present as definitive. (*Black Skin,* originally cited, 190; 226)

Overcoming alienation, therefore, depends on two factors that are included in it: one, as an essentialized past in which one cannot think in strategic terms; two, a sacralized present from which there is no projection. The effective counterparts of these two factors are the past as a place of revaluation and inscription of new social historical meanings and the consideration of the present as a temporal place that recalls the actuality and deferment of each event, in other words, its historicity.

Temporality provides the means by which discourse confronts the fixation of identity (or of identities). The conjugation in future time to discuss disalienation raises several issues such as the recognition that disalienating is not a finished process. Indeed, it is only in its beginnings. More importantly, this conjugation reveals that alienation can be understood as a form of historical movement as a double object. On the one side, in a dialectic that needs it in order to establish the accomplishment of its possibilities and, on the other, of the historicity that Fanon recognizes in the actions of the present. Hence, the "lived experience of the black man" is not a claim for forms of cultural authenticity but by the contingency of the present and consequently the demystification of the past as an impregnable fortress of identity. The past is no longer a timeless inscription of an essence that, by being out of history, claims it as property, but also, and fundamentally, of a past consecrated in the terms of a tradition of rationality. Tradition can represent the dialectic in a paradoxical way: at the same time rejecting the consolidation of a narrative, it affirms a sense for history, thus conjugating a historical account of the most intense origins. That moment becomes a statement that represents an unstable space for any figure of identity.

> And so it is not I who make a meaning for myself, but it is the meaning that was already there, pre-existing, waiting for me . . . . The dialectic that brings necessity into the foundation of my freedom drives me out of myself. It shatters my unreflected position. Still in terms of consciousness, black consciousness is immanent in its own eyes. I am not a potentiality of something. I am wholly what I am . . . . But I will be told, your statements show a misreading of the processes of history. (*Black Skin*, originally cited, 124; 134–5)

> Exactly we will reply, the black experience is not a whole, for there is not merely one Negro—there are Negroes. (Originally cited, 125; 136)

Ross Posnock has aptly pointed out a similar path for *The Souls of Black Folk* by W.E.B. Du Bois. Posnock posits that Du Bois's work could be considered a founding text of inauthenticity. Du Bois privileged action over identity but, at the same time, kept open the question of not dissolving "double consciousness" in a new unity to unlock the main problem of paralysis in black agency.

Du Bois proposed from the initial pages of *The Souls of Black Folk* to establish the double condition of black Americans. This condition could, at one point, give access to historicity and the rejection of the discourses of authenticity emerging from the colonizing space of American modernity and as the response of black leaders of the late nineteenth and early twentieth centuries. Du Bois provocatively claimed the duality, best expressed in the English word "doubleness," to represent the historical tension in which the action of Blacks could be interpreted and thought. But the two souls, American and Black, were constituted in one body as a testimony of its historical conflict (5, 6, 7).

Similarly, half a century later, Fanon defied the ideologies of authenticity by rejecting the ways in which these ideologies construct the colonized (327). The defiance is manifested in Fanon's writing in counterpoint procedures which organize his texts and the theory produced by them in the form of ambivalence. In this direction, Fanon's dispute with Sartre presents an additional dimension: Sartre's inscription of blackness in the itinerary of a teleological dialectic which prefigures a society without racism is, for Fanon, the inevitable memory of the absolute fact of the figurative contact with alienation.

The reductionism of an autonomy of blackness as a cultural project of historically relevant scope that operates in *Black Orpheus* nonetheless reminds Fanon of the inevitable facet of the colonial process. Any attempt at decolonization, namely, to the extent that the belief in a subject is sustained, cannot be thought out without the historicity that constitutes it to dispute it from the representations of identity to an emancipatory project. This problem also corresponds to *Black Orpheus*. Sartre raises a Négritude that is, in various ways, a kind of autonomous language with its own articulations and zones of occlusions. However, the same movement conjoins blackness with a language that cannot be thought of outside a dialogic dimension and outside a negotiating space where conflicts and tensions are present. The authenticity of that language arrives from the possibility of its insertion in history, in a field where it can be questioned or tested as a structure of feeling or as a cultural discourse. Sartre's ascending dialectic partly provides this function, but only in part because its own structure must necessarily deny the terms that constitute it. In other words, a society without racism must leave out (or, we could say, forget) any form of representation based on particularisms linked to a notion of race. Fanon's ironic stance in the face of such a dialectic and the rigidity in which the discourse of blackness may fall, also comes from the conscious fact that its "language" is inhabited more by specters, by enunciations and concrete practices of colonization and alienation as a psychological, historical, and cultural process. Fuss has observed that Fanon's discontent with Sartre for his critical support of Négritude is not precisely because he uses dialectics, but because Sartre does not know the profound asymmetry of the colonial regime. The negative role that fits blackness in this dialectic as a denial of white racism, which will produce by synthesis a new humanism or the post-racial society, implies assimilation for Fanon (23). Such a situation means, in Fanon's texts, the evidence that there is no "self-sufficient home" when the starting point for the theoretical and political imagination is and has been that of a subject historically defined, traversed, by the "impurities of history." It would seem difficult to present the tensions and ambivalences of Fanon's discourses as a dispute between closed terms or categories of nativism-cosmopolitism and thus abandon them by reason of their Manichean logic. The central fact remains that the so-called nativism, like the Sartrean dialectic (beyond constituting a certain process of reading essentialist, reductionist forms of thinking about history and culture), serve to imagine possible forms of opposition and responses to specific modes of domination.

Thus, ambivalence and tension assume a character that transcends Fanon's particular sphere. Nativism and a certain universalist sense present a problem between concepts of culture that have a strong orientation toward dehistoricization, or that are formulated ahistorically, and conceptions of culture that position even essentialisms as historical products with concrete consequences in the organization of knowledge and cultural and discursive practices. My point is to recover the historical articulation of what we call "the essentialist dimension" of a discourse and not reject it by that specific dimension. In this context, the question of centrifugal forces of any cultural practice enters again proposing, as Fanon does, the possibility of thinking that nativism, even those closed in a logic of exclusion, can be in a certain moment the foundation of these centrifugal forces: as in the Bakhtinian carnival.

Fanon states in the chapter "On National Culture" that "the native literature of the last twenty years is not a national literature but a Negro literature. The concept of negritude, for example, was the emotional if not the logical antithesis of that insult which the white man flung at humanity" (*The Wretched*, originally cited, 194; 212). Blackness then, with all the globalizing and essentialist dimensions that it at times reveals, implied for Fanon that in opposing "the white man's contempt showed itself in certain spheres to be the one idea capable of lifting interdictions and anathemas" (originally cited, 194; 212). But the permanent counterpoint formula that does not abandon his texts also allows him to criticize the moment when that same blackness appears like a new centrism, like the Bakhtinian "the official."

> On the whole, the poets of negritude oppose the idea of an old Europe to a young Africa, tiresome reasoning to lyricism, oppressive logic to high-stepping nature, and on one side stiffness, ceremony, etiquette, and

skepticism, while on the other frankness, liveliness, liberty, and—why not?—luxuriance: but also irresponsibility. (Originally cited, 194; 213; my italics)

Furthermore, he states, "this historical necessity in which the men of African culture find themselves to racialize their claims, to speak more of African culture than of national culture will tend to lead them up a blind alley" (*The Wretched*, originally cited, 195–6; 214). The reading of *Black Skin,* specifically chapter five, divulges further suggestions in relation to this passage of *The Wretched.* But the question of national culture and the misfortunes of national consciousness remain for future discussions. For now, I am interested in highlighting the fact that the "license" that Fanon gives to blackness and nativism depends almost exclusively on the way he conceives of historicity, with the ambivalence and tensions that I discuss here.

In this register, a new tension is inscribed which Sartre emphasizes in *Black Orpheus*: the tension that inhabits the body of the colonized involves the impossibility of a language capable of transparency and precision in every enunciative act. Therefore, the recourse to Négritude will be fundamentally poetic and will be shown in Sartre's presentation as a scenario abandons prose.

> As everyone knows, every poetic experience has its origin in this feeling of frustration that one has when confronted with a language that is supposed to be a means of direct communication (24).

> As soon as we experience a first frustration, this chattering falls beyond us; we see the whole system, it is no more than an upset, out-of-order mechanism whose arms are still flailing to indicate existence in emptiness; in one fell swoop we pass judgment on the foolish business of naming things; we understand that language is in essence prose, and that prose is in essence failure; Being stands erect in front of us like a tower of silence, and if we still want to catch it, we can do so only through silence: "to evoke, in an intentional shadow, the object by allusive words, never direct, reducing themselves to the same silence" (25).

> It is through having had some contact with white culture that his blackness has passed from the immediacy of existence to the *meditative* state. But at the same time, he has more or less ceased to live his negritude. In choosing to see what he is, he has become split, he no longer coincides

with himself. And on the other hand, it is because he was already exiled from himself that he discovered this need to reveal himself. (Originally cited, 18; 20; my italics)

The black man who asserts his negritude by means of a revolutionary movement immediately places himself in the position of having to meditate. (Originally cited, 17; 19)

In this movement, neither the home nor its broadened metaphor, the community, can remain immune. Fanon's ironic complaint against Sartre is felt in a moment of discovery. Sartre claims the articulation of blackness with a historical project and reclaims these essences constructed in the temporal but questioned, since the very beginning, the project that conceived them. There is a negativism, a dialectic which Fanon realizes when he proposes an abandoned Being after his illusions of constructing a self-representation fail or, rather, after all representation of himself becomes impossible. Just as Sartre considers that the language of blackness contains a kind of hidden code, untranslatable for the gaze of the European, similarly, Fanon sees this experience linked in a figure of resistance and of opposition who, in the absence of available languages, must create a new one.

For this reason, the mode to control the "impulse" contains an irony since, from the beginning, it seems to be inhabited by the same discourses that he rejects, namely, those that make the colonized a subject without agency. In this context, ambivalence refers to a problem more important than that of indecisiveness, that is, to the very reasons for indefiniteness. Fanon warns of the foundations of the problem he faces. If he reinforces the essentialist dimensions of "nativism," these become moved from the periphery to the center in the production of meaning and, in a certain way, develop the capacity to hegemonize any representation outside of them.

If his critique devastates these discourses, it risks not situating them historically and not perceiving the specific forms in which they are articulated with oppositional modes reinforcing the thesis which assures that these movements slip down the sides of rationality. In Fanon, there is no solution to this conflict, only a way of action in the face of this dilemma. This way of action, which for me is a central element in Fanon's theoretical development, is of the permanent balance between the two positions expressed earlier. What is the central problem in this ambivalence? The main problem is that Fanon, as I said above, simultaneously conducts a critique of colonial society and its assumptions that hold the existence of a subject, which must survive and own agency even in a fragmented world that does not offer sanctuary for any illusion of emancipation. Thus, the dilemma is to sustain a perpetual decentering that avoids the establishment of new centers but maintains a notion of the subject that risks claiming the unification of historical and cultural narratives. A paragraph, which I quoted before in a partial way, illustrates exactly what I am explicating here:

> Today we are present at the stasis of Europe. Comrades let us flee from this motionless movement where gradually dialectic is changing into the logic of equilibrium. Let us reconsider the question of mankind. Let us reconsider the question of cerebral reality and of the cerebral mass of all humanity, whose connections must be increased, whose channels must be diversified and whose messages must be re-humanized. (*The Wretched*, originally cited, 290; 314)

All the duties that are present in this paragraph and that exceed, without doubt, the dimensions of the day-to-day of the contingent, also express a double content in the Fanonian critique. While preserving the claims to reestablish the world from a kind of collective "I" (remember here the mention of Cioran and intellectuals of the periphery), Fanon must sustain a permanent critique of any form of construction of the subject that involves an almost exclusive concentration of attributes. Fanon claims a movement that has multiple directions. It is directed against the univocal discourse of political and cultural identities, but, at the same moment, it cautions that the ways in which a univocal discourse articulates the world can be present even in those who defy its restrictions and constraints.

Fanon's doubts and the prescriptive tone, which the final passages of *The Wretched* sometimes assume, are part of this tension inhabited between the drives of different orders at stake in his texts. If there is a tragic scene of Fanonian representation of the history of decolonization, it is in the fact of not being able to renounce the reasons that construct the subjects as "subjects," as we saw in the definition of Foucault, already subjected by control and dependence or subjected by a consciousness and self-knowledge of their own identity. It is a tragic situation in Fanon's narrative because his texts traverse long itineraries to find a subject in the folds of colonial discourse, expressly pointing out this problem, for example, in the search for recognition. However, his search results, as the whole of his narrative, are not clearly defined nor separated from the reasons for the critique of colonial discourse and regime.

More than the projected desire in retrospect of many of its readers to find a kind of abandonment of the subject on the part of Fanon, he attempts to put it in movement, knowing that its construction depends always on the fact of being inhabited, as Berman states in everyday life by the "demons that hover." In response, Césaire requires the word to vibrate.

VI

Memory, Oblivion, and the Subject

> *We're not on the maps. They erased us from the map, but we no longer recriminalize those who erased us. It's about building our own geography, plotting our own cities, telling our histories. To think of the world from here, from the so-called nothing, from the named no one, from nominal none toward the whole world.*
>
> —Marcelo Eckhard, *Barbarie* [Barbarism]

Let us now return to the tension that dwells in the body of the colonized. The objectification of which the colonized is object makes it present, in the black person of *Black Skin* to be precise. Located above and behind noticeable traits of color, a set of characteristics distributes fixed attributes on the surface of the category "colonized." In the same movement, as surface effect, phenomenological in more than one sense, it assigns direction and meaning to the life of the colonized: "For the Black there is only one destiny. And it is white" (originally cited, 16; 10).

While that phrase serves as a metaphor for colonial desire that develops in the colonized, it is also the critique (and consciousness) of a new impossibility. Not defining the colonized (which I would consider as a category of experience) from the place of attribution to supposed histories and solid origins signals that this fate, which becomes white, is consumed in the disappearance of remembrance and the memory of the colonized.

The question that has been repeated over a thousand times in the scenario of postcolonial critique is: "What are the cultural materials and symbolic values that make up remembrance and memory?" Let's consider that it is not the reissue of supposedly timeless values, but, instead, of conceiving the response in political terms and as a strategy of power to colonial discourse/s, and how the metaphorical disappearance of remembrance and memory does not inevitably refer to the repetition ad nausea in the binary logic that Fanon explicitly finds in colonial society.

However, a reflection on memory and remembrance implies a consideration in Fanon of the function of oblivion. To talk about the memory of the colonized as an activated memory in the direction of a politics is, in some sense, oxymoronic. The word "certain" places the solidity of the previous statement in doubt. However, the oxymoronic appears, as I pointed out earlier, in the moment in which the question of those lost memories and remembrances is being argued. If we consider that an inherent agency exists, then there would be no reason to broach the discussion. The answer would be that it does not matter what (subordinated, oppressed) conditions the subjects are under, because they will always find an answer, sometimes totalizing, sometimes fragmented, toward what constitutes itself as the reason for the situation in which they find themselves. Thus, we could see the development of imperialism, colonization, and postcolonial nationalisms as a history of the responses of societies and subordinate groups to each of these processes.

One of the challenges that can be undertaken (and many have) is to show how those answers were effectively given. Implicit, however, is that these memories are articulated with the process that subordinates. Therefore, we cannot leave aside what has been said at different times in this study—namely, that Fanon agreed with a subject that is not separated from colonial history and that colonial history has a lot to do with the way that the subject imagines the answers to the colonial discourse and regime. This aspect is crucial in the conception of historicity of *The Wretched* and in the existentialist revelation in *Black Skin*.

In the project of *The Wretched* an attribution on the part of Fanon is at stake in the process that is slowly articulated from recognition to national consciousness. We could say here, relying on Yosef Yerushalmi, that *halakhah*, in this case of the colonial society, cannot be held as a project of the organization of memory and remembrance.[1] Fanon attempts to demonstrate that a distinct possibility of organizing the past and giving it guidance exists, but in an orientation that, paradoxically, does not appear to be restrictive because the sense of history (*halakhah*) contains a direction even when its project is broad. Fanon's position links to both the fact of ambivalence and the tensions that we have already discussed as a perspective of historical process as displacement.

Fanon, then, elaborates a *halakhah*, but stripped of one of its attributes: selectivity. I think what Fanon "sees," as Gordon says, is the absence of an inherent agency in subjects. Additionally, he also "sees" the historicity of any project, even the constructing of an agency. For this reason, the historicity that emerges from *The Wretched* has a heroic and founding dimension since it must articulate the available forms of remembrance and memory by constructing forms of oblivion. Additionally, Fanon's texts oscillate between ways of conceiving agency. However, it is necessary to clarify that oscillation here does not mean an oscillation between an ontology of Being and an experiential historical dimension. Fanon's work has a strong contextual and historical concern, including in *Black Skin* where there is a defined presence of psychoanalytic and psychological analysis.

Therefore, no possible metaphor exists between figures of identity conceived ontologically and their agency. The problem is particularly complex on this point. With the process of emancipation of the colonial subject, Fanon manifests his belief in an unfragmented subject or, better yet, in the concrete existence of a subject. Critique of colonial modernity does not necessarily derive from the abolition of the subject as a historical category. However, the agency that Fanon finds in the colonized is not a territory without answers that is solid and enduring. There is, on the one hand, an agency that is available in the fact of the subject's freedom to imagine a project, as we saw in relation to the freedom of Sartrean existentialism. On the other hand, this agency is manifested in the process of traversing and building a historical process constitutive of alienation and of overcoming it in the displacement of Manichean representations of culture both in colonial and in the postcolonial (here I refer to the historical period) society. Again, Fanon appears to move in the territories of ambivalence. The question of whether or not there is an inherent agency in subjects is at times supported in his texts, especially when his enunciations deal with the man who interrogates at the close of *Black Skin*.

However, an agency conceived only in the historical process predominates in Fanon's texts. Inherent agency, however, should not be understood in the terms of an ontology of Being, of a metahistorical immanence, even when, at the precise moment of the historical crossroads, it may have that connotation. Regardless, it is in this tension between the possible forms of agency in the process of decolonization when, once again, the same counterpoints that cross the work of Fanon are produced. Alienation, for example, in this process of understanding how agency is constituted in the colonized subject, is a central topic, because it characterizes the form in which forgetting is treated. Alienation, a term that Fanon uses with meanings close to those of the Marxist tradition, produces in the colonized a kind of forgetfulness.[2] (Fanon delimits the subject by referring almost exclusively to Antillean examples.) Thus, a forgetting that remembers: the forgetting of the Créole in relation to the French, the forgetting of the colony in relation to the metropolis, the forgetting of the origin of the Senegalese in the face of a Martinique one, the forgetting of the black man in front of the white man. In these instances, alienation is a process in which the reason of oblivion is always present as an inextricable function (not only linked to memory) of what it replaces. Becoming white to move away in the representation of the condition of colonized implies recognizing that one remembers, in some way, the condition that one wants to leave but, in turn, that difficulty of becoming, by the Adlerian relation that Fanon criticizes and modifies for the colonial world, is the memory of an impossibility. In this sense, any project of overcoming alienation travels in the direction of the Fanonian project to solve some type of remembrance.

Lewis Gordon, in *Fanon and the Crisis of European Man*, assigns the concept of Sartrean bad faith a central role in Fanon's theoretical and philosophical structure (16–24). If we contrast bad faith, basically the ability to not say or tell the truth even if you know what it is, with Fanon's decolonization project, then we could see that the latter would be a way of overcoming the bad faith that immobilizes the subject, both in the static landscape of colonial society and in its ability to be considered an agent of history. Of course, this reading is possible when one considers that memory and memories have some historical and cultural efficacy. That is the role of a "consciousness":

> If culture is the expression of national consciousness, I will not hesitate to affirm that in the case with which we are dealing it is the national consciousness which is the most elaborate form of culture. The consciousness

of self is not the closing of a door to communication. Philosophical thought teaches us, on the contrary, that it is its guarantee. National consciousness, which is not nationalism, is the only thing that will give us an international dimension. (*The Wretched*, originally, 226; 247)

Although the utopian register of this position is evident, it does not promise the subject a world of existential or ontological tranquility. On the contrary, Sartre presents reflection on blackness as a constant task. Otherwise, the claim that dwells in the phrase "white fate" would become the only possibility of the historical imagination. Hence, the emergence of an emancipated humanity would enter an opaque zone; however, it is not explicitly present in Fanon's texts.

A retrospective problem that undoubtedly affects the present appears: silence as a possible figure of resistance becomes a characteristic of bad faith and disarticulation of an agency in whatever way the agency is conceived. Silence forms complex figures of identity and difference referring to the identifications and founding moments of an extensive critique of colonial society. Silence therefore demonstrates an impossibility: to recover an alleged lost voice in the colonial process, yet it also signals the need to establish new spaces for collective enunciation. The latter may highlight a manipulation of the "agency" of the colonized, complicated by the development of the colonial project first and by the discourse of the nation after. For example, Gayatri Spivak has pointed out the problems of female agency at the heart of this problematic by extending the question to whether the subaltern can speak (283). Spivak wondered whether the closure that the imperial project exerts on female agency leaves any possibility of imagining a space for enunciation or action for women's agency. This closure is a consequence of an international division of labor. Though her answer is negative, it implies a growing complexity, mainly because what it refers to is a critique of the idea of the appropriation of the "Other" by assimilation. Spivak, following Derrida, will say that *catachresis* is read in the origin of this problematic (308).

Spivak's controversial affirmation is made in a different context from Fanon's. She develops her work within the framework of poststructuralism and in the field of feminist and postcolonial studies in the present. However, despite seeming extemporaneous, its inclusion in the reading of Fanon that I propose here is a good reference in considering what is involved in the problem of agency in a colonial situation. Spivak's claim, that the "'the subaltern cannot speak,' means that even when the subaltern makes an effort to the death to speak, she is not able to be heard, and speaking and hearing complete the speech act" (85). Clearly, this "effort to death" is a conscious act where the intent to speak and be heard is not a residual effect. The subaltern cannot speak because women's agency (her subject of study) has already been closed by the imperial project and the international division of labor. Spivak subscribes in large part to the position of the Subaltern Studies Group. The subaltern, according to Epifanio San Juan, is subordinated and oppressed in different ways by the colonial and postcolonial regimes for which the "'supplement' of resistance acts like a contrapuntal chord" (85). The category "subaltern" refers then to "the demographic difference between the total Indian population and all those whom we have described as the 'elite'" (San Juan quoting Spivak, 85). The agency of change in the decolonizing formations is sought in the insurgent subalterns, conceived as the product of "a network of differential, potentially conflicting strands" (San Juan). However, the subaltern woman from a disadvantaged nation of the Third World carries, on top of her, centuries of history of Western imperialism. Because, for Spivak, "speaking" and self-representation by definition mean access to symbolic and political power, her conclusion is pessimistic: the subaltern cannot speak. If the subaltern can speak, explains Spivak in subsequent interviews, then she is no longer a subaltern (2–3).[3] Beyond this latter clarification, the problem of voice and speech is directly imbricated with Fanon's problematic in his two main texts. In *Black Skin*, speech becomes another way in which the history of alienation and the difficulties faced by the colonized subject is manifested:

> To speak means . . . to support the weight of a civilization . . . . A man who has a language consequently possesses the world expressed and implied by that language . . . . Every colonized people—in other words, every people in whose soul an inferiority complex has been created . . . finds itself face to face with the language of the civilizing nation; that is, with the culture of the mother country. (*Black Skin*, originally cited, 34; 17–18)

Thus, Spivak's claim regarding the impossibility of the subaltern speaking possibly resonates with Fanon. Spivak's argument, as she recognizes, leads one to consider that the quality of the subaltern or colonized ceases at the time when the subaltern is heard, that is, at the time that a relationship is established in which the speech of the subaltern or the colonized acquires symbolic and political relevance.

From this point of view, it is possible to connect the polemic raised by Spivak's famous phrase to my discussion of agency in Fanon. Without broadly subscribing to this claim about the subaltern's condition, and whether their voices can be heard, certainly this problematic directly links to the displacement and ambivalence in Fanon's discourse. First, because Fanon must conceive, as I have said on several occasions, a subject that is already crossed and constituted by the "impurities of history" and by the traversal of various forms of organization of knowledge, passing through representations of identity in the sphere of culture to subordination in the economic order. That is, he must carry the "baggage" of a history of subordination and alienation from which he must emerge as a subject capable of responding, even though he is still subject to the colonial regime. Therefore, despite the tone and emancipatory intent in Fanonian discourse, there is always the suspicion of a possible loss against the weight of colonial history. There is always, we could say, the possibility that the colonized, to use the term closest to Fanon, cannot speak.

But I think that Spivak's discussion raises another very interesting dimension: there is naiveté in considering that the subaltern has a voice in all times and places. This naivety is based on a belief that an almost ontological agency exists in subjects. The possibility of considering Spivak's posture can contribute to understanding Fanon's approach, which posits both a belief in the subject and in their agency as the result of an intention. Consequently, conscious action must be carried out with a certain directionality and sense, especially at the moment of thinking of a possible postcolonial community, because one of the characteristics of the imagination of the postcolonial community is that it proposes a double act of displacement and restitution. It is a displacement of the direction of colonial discourse and the silences that inhabit it, since the restitution of a place of enunciation differs from colonial silence and univocality. As a response, it can show that some originality and dominance in the invention of a community remains at stake. It is the restitution of the place of enunciation, but it is not from a lost voice (or narrative) that could be restored in the present intact. Let's read Fanon in this moment in *Black Skin*:

It was not the black world that laid down my course of conduct. My black skin is not the wrapping of specific values. It is a long time since the starry sky that took away Kant's breath revealed the last of its secrets to us. And the moral law is not certain of itself.

As a man, I undertake to face the possibility of annihilation in order that two or three truths may cast their eternal brilliance over the world.

Sartre has shown that, in the line of an unauthentic position, the past "takes" in quantity, and when solidly constructed, *informs* the individual. He is the past in a changed value. *But I, too, can recapture my past, validate it, or condemn it through my successive choices.* (Originally cited, 201; 227–8; second italics are mine)

Beyond the paradox in this, the quote announces a difficulty: that of narrating the community when this narrative must be built in intimate relation with what it opposes. As Simon Gikandi observes in Chinua Achebe's texts, inventing an African narrative involved writing against the colonial discourse and decentralizing it to evoke alternative spaces of representation (6). The two acts involved, opposition and decentration, carry an inevitable link. However, that supposedly paradoxical link from a critical project, such as Fanon's, can produce a space where the difference imprisoned by a monolithic and unmistakable representation emerges. However, this difference can never be thought of from the reassuring shores of a conjugated, singular identity.

The metaphor of colonial silence also refers to this reduction in alternative areas of evocation. Homi Bhabha characterizes this silence thus: "It is a silence that turns imperial triumphalism into the testimony of colonial confusion and those who hear its echo lose their historic memories" ("Articulating the Archaic," 124). Additionally, the memories are lost in a space of indecision, in a certain impossibility of cultural translation, if the word in the colonial context is linked exclusively to a project of signification and not of the signifier.

A key point of Fanon's theoretical strategy considers the impossibility of restituting a presence. If we contemplate this aspect in his texts, but especially in *Black Skin* and in *The Wretched*, we quickly find that the texts become marks of the displacement and the construction of history. Displacement, or as I have said before, the decentering of oppositional discourses, has an objective to maintain its critical character and to suspect attempts to restore or institute a Being "available" for the postcolonial society that serves as a reminder, on more than one occasion, of the universe of representations of colonial society.

Fanon's texts point to the construction of history to the extent that what links to the word "construction," in addition to the project, is the possibility of provisionally naming what is in fact provisional, contextual, spatially and historically located (the best example is perhaps that of Négritude) and the displacement or decentering of which is a new possibility or almost a condition in the constitution of a postcolonial subject.

The final passages of Fanon's two texts quoted here signal this movement. It is also announced in the dynamics that Gordon analyzes in terms of an existentialist phenomenology in Fanon, highlighted as what he "sees" in *Black Skin*. Fanon "sees" a process of estrangement of the "colonized" with respect to the place in which they live or an estrangement from or toward themselves. The estrangement is perceived through a series of phenomena linked to the factuality of the concrete existence of the colonized. *The Wretched* does not restitute any history because the descent (through which the only destiny that Fanon sees for the black person is to become white), highlighted by the existentialist phenomenology, has already happened. There is also no restitution or possibility of establishing—once and for all—the terms of a postcolonial society. There is never a primacy of presence, nor of a being conceived in ontological terms.

If we propose another untimely jump with the attendant risks of anachronism, it is possible to consider Fanon's position, through several links to the Derridean critique of logos. Without wanting to make Fanon appear as a poststructuralist *avant la lettre*, if we consider the dimension that historicity acquires in his texts, we can certainly observe that there is never a presentation of the absent in the terms of a correspondence between the attempt to enunciate the absent and absence itself, as for example, a precolonial past, which, in Derrida, could be related to the presentation, the perpetual situating in the present time of the logos, by means of the phone, which is, inevitably, a process of representation. As such, rather than make meaning emerge from a supposedly representative transparency, it becomes constituted in the series of signs. It is the Derridean "différance" which contains the following two terms: to defer and differentiate.

Fanon seems to propose an idea of historicity that may result in a first reading as a claim of "present perpetual time." However, he assigns this to colonial society as his specific way of representing himself. This model of historicity is always outside and above the existentialist phenomenology that Gordon attributes to his texts. Thus, it produces in the field of colonial society, the idea of a direct correspondence between what that society "claims to be" and its form of representation that, in that context, would be "presentation." On the contrary, the historicity in Fanon is a process that provokes the inevitable displacement of any utterance that is assumed as restoration of the absent in an extensive sense. The historicity displaces any illusion of restoration of the absent as presence, either as a narrative of the past or a kind of condensation of the Self. That is why historicity is founded and set in motion at the time when the struggle for liberation occurs. Without forgetting the obvious link of this passage with the idea of Marxist class struggle, the important point here is that this historicity does not resist being fixed or defined, as it does not resist any notion of community forged in the imaginary of the idea of national liberation. Thus, Fanon sees with interest "the pitfalls of national consciousness" although the most programmatic part of his writing seems to define the so-called national culture and its modes of consciousness. Fanon cautions that any illusion of perpetuating the dominion of representation betrays the critical space that its analysis has opened. In this sense, its exploration produces meaning in the fact of displacement and in the difference between signs, where the seduction of a sign is not allowed, invoking the restoration of an "absence" arrogated by the simple fact of enunciating all meaning.

This case is paradigmatic in how Fanon conceives national culture because it does not grant any meaning to a supposed intrinsic characteristic of the two words. The words, national culture, can only hold meaning in the chain of signs (deferring/differing) in which they inscribe, after all, a historicity.

This way of reading Fanon's texts, although provisional, could be key in considering the struggles against the confinements that his writing deploys and in helping us to understand how, in the heart of specific contexts and moral and political urgencies, there is always room to avoid making the margins into a new center.

By Way of Conclusion

This is an open-ended history. If the preceding pages have any meaning, it is to explore the Fanonian tributaries of thought in relation to our political, theoretical, and moral concerns. One of them is, without a doubt, the possibility of discussing categories of the subject. Clearly, I have not dealt with the problem of the subject in relation to the vast literature that social theory, within which I include historiography, has produced. This was neither the space nor the time to do so. That absence is also due perhaps—and I say only perhaps—to our contemporary discussions of identities, cultural representations, historicity, and subjects conformed in the historical and cultural processes of the second half of the twentieth century, topics which deserve to be thought from the dialogues, conflicts, and tensions proposed by works such as Fanon's. For this reason, our title enunciates a kind of play between politics and poetics in the imagination of the subject. A poetics, because we treat Fanon's writing as a space in which we generate not only strong definitive statements in more than one sense but also a politics linked to forms and as the outcome of a writing that offers a critical perspective on confinement. The reference to the disciplines is explicit. It is not about considering whether Fanon's writing can be "used" in relation to disciplinary developments (as we saw, there is more than one possible example of this) but, to regard that each of those particular "uses," questions the forms and procedures of the disciplines. Their uses are questioned in both the mixture and renovation that Fanon produces with theory, for example, in developing thought, together with Said, that is impossible to degrade when theory travels and transforms. It also stimulates thought regarding the possible ways to generate and sustain, what Said calls, moral communities. In this sense, the originating marks circulating in the theories and texts on Fanon's writing matter from the standpoint of their transformation. Readers can conclude from my reading that there are no explanatory ends or homogeneous lines of analysis based on the path of a specific theory. If so, one can say, Fanon's specters have worked correctly.

It is interesting to think about the space of the supposed incompatibilities among Fanon's readers, that is, among all of us. As I said, in this work, forgetfulness reveals what is forgotten. If the readings of Bhabha, for example, disappear the Sartrean existentialism that inevitably inhabits Fanon's texts, the disappearances reappear when one reads Fanon. In the imagination of postcolonial situations and in contexts of dissemination but, above all, of fragmentation of the idea of the subject, Fanonian historicity is in tension or conflict with Sartrean historicity. The problem is not that theorists orient their theories to support their theoretical projects, as Parry's and Lazarus's critique of Bhabha, thus resulting in a poststructuralist Fanon *avant la lettre*. The problem is that Fanon's writing links to the regime of ambivalence which allows unforeseen drifts against readings that demand precision in the definition of contexts. The regime of ambivalence, which must be discussed because of Chow's reflections, is not an easy territory to contextualize. However, perhaps the most interesting aspect of ambivalence in Fanon's writing, and its derivations in the theoretical project in question, is that it becomes a strategy in the same way that we discussed the issue of essentialisms.[1] Fanon's writing is doubly ambivalent from the point of view of a poetics and from the point of view of a politics. A poetics privileges his writing as an evocation of possible worlds, in the sense that Barthes assigns to the literary utopia. Fanon's writing reveals an ambivalent mark not from a defined authorial intentionality but in his interweaving in the regime of representations what his discursive objects propose. We could say that colonialism and the associated figures in the two central texts of this discussion compel Fanon not to house his writing in the homogeneous and univocal. It is precisely the presence, whether deferred or not, of the images of colonial society that range from white masks to the wretched of the earth, which distributes ambivalence in his writing.

We have seen how, despite the obvious intentionality of certain Fanonian passages at domesticating the pressurized uncertainty, his same writing makes it difficult to sustain such intentionality. This study attempted to center itself in this terrain, putting into question the zones that seem clearly to follow a route of reaffirmation and certainty by showing that they are also spaces of uncertainty where ambivalence takes its place in the region of politics. It is not ambivalence, in the sense that there is no clarity toward where Fanon's cultural and political project was aimed. It would be presumptuous to deny that. But ambivalence is evident in the constitution of the plot of that process. Again, Fanon's writing places matters in the realm of doubt and negotiation of meaning, where the univocal and the register of a possible prescriptive utopia are developed. It becomes, intentionally or not, a strategy. It is from this perspective that he establishes the reading of blackness and the dispute over historicity with Sartre. That is also a starting point for thinking about how the contingent becomes a key element of history in Fanon, as in Bhabha's day-to-day Bhabha's day-today. If this argument is carefully followed, perhaps it becomes possible to better understand that a historicity founded on the contingent, to name it polemically, is a process in which meaning is deferred and where it is impossible to consolidate a consecrated narrative of identities or a homogeneous narration of national culture.

I have not completely explored this last point regarding mimesis in the *Wretched of the Earth*. Although among other arguments in Fanon's text we find a discussion of national consciousness, and of the weaknesses of the same, there is no projection of the political and cultural fiction that offers closure to the problem of national culture. Imagining Fanon's national culture from its warnings is perhaps one of the best critical exercises regarding the historical processes that developed especially in the post-independence African continent. However, the ambivalent nature of Fanon's texts, represented with value of cultural critique, makes a closed ending almost impossible. Think of the two endings of *Black Skin, White Masks* and *The Wretched of the Earth*. In the first text, Fanon proposes:

> At the conclusion of this study, I want the world to recognize, with me, the open door of every consciousness. My final prayer: O my body, make of me always a man who questions! (Originally cited 204; 232)

In the second:

> For Europe, for ourselves, and for humanity, comrades, we must turn over a new leaf, we must work out new concepts, and try to set afoot a new man. (Originally cited, 292; 316)

Two endings that could share the same text, two endings that flee like maroons from the determinations that a singular way of seeing the world can impose. The two endings are not concessions with existentialism, as suggested by Sekyi-Otu in the case of *Black Skin*. Rather, they reveal the itineraries of ambivalence in Fanon's writing and the type of subjects that emerge from that situation. As suggested in the introduction of this study, this is a situation that does not respond easily to the theoretical determination of a specific cast.

If we recover Fanon for our contemporary discussions, it is not, after all, in a spirit of restoration; or not, at least, in a spirit of restoring discourses or discursive practices, be they academic or of any other nature, that do not seem to correlate with our current practices. Fanon is recovered, as suggested by the idea of the specter, because his writing offers more than one possibility for discussing and evaluating the spoken and unspoken presumptions about culture, politics, and academic disciplines. As such, focusing on the methodological, theoretical, and factual errors of his texts is to become immersed in a task without a future. Fanon's "use" as a resource, that is, as a document that has something to say about the period of national independences, may be a useful path for certain readings, such as that of Lazarus, but, in the intermediate term, it narrows the cultural and political rhetorical possibilities of his texts. To consider his texts as similes of academic monographs over an historical period could never confront the numerous investigations, fieldwork, and extensive archival explorations carried out by historians, anthropologists, sociologists, and others in universities. First, his texts were not conceived with that logic. Second, they do not respect the formalities that pertain to academic work. Third, his texts do not intend to concentrate on a case study, even if many of its readers affirm that they do. The Antilles, Algeria, and the rest of Africa are undeniable references, but they are not undertaken through a contemporaneous strict methodology of social scientific research. These three places are tropes for a reading that, paradoxically, is not territorialized in such a simple way.

A frequent attitude links the indetermination of the contexts with a certain absence of embodied, lived discourses. This is similar, as we saw in the introduction and in this conclusion, to what Edward Said recognizes as a prejudice in his own text. The idea affirms that a theory displaced from the conditions that gave it birth, displaced from its original subjects and objects, is a theory of a second order and, thus, degraded. Fanon's writing resists that charge which reveals the general aim of this study, of presenting questions that exceed certain intellectual geographies and originating conditions. It resists the claim because his writing spreads itself in unsuspected directions. It allows its "use" as a source, as a reference for a field of study, as a text that debates contemporary culture as well as other contemporary texts, and allows, as I said at the beginning of this study, theoretical leave and methodological flexibility. From Marx to Freud, through Lacan, Sartre, Hegel, and others, Fanon produces huge political fictions that remain open despite his frequent tone of affirmation. Finally, it could be said that Fanon's writing affirms precisely what is unstable.

Frantz Fanon
A Biography[1]

If, as Arnold Krupat says, we must inquire from the policies of fixation and travel (115), then, there is nothing better than to think of Fanon from his environment. Fanon was born in Forte de France, Martinique, on July 20, 1925. His family could be considered fervent French patriots who belonged to the middle class of the island (Onwanibe, vii). His family and their territorial belonging, in some way, configured part of Fanon's future, especially his political future. His thought, as my study proposed, was decentered. This decentration of his native Fort de France, clearly evident in his writings after *Black Skin, White Masks*, despite everything, involved his native land because of the universal nature of his appeals. The founding of a new humanism could only be directed toward different historical cultural spaces, which included Martinique. Fanon grew up in a family of five siblings and attended a segregated secondary and high school. In 1944, he enlisted in the French Army and fought against the Germans in the remainder of World War II. For his bravery in combat, he received a medal of courage. His participation in this war has to be read in at least two ways. First, his participation can be understood as a continuation of a patriotic response to German aggression against France, and second, as a response to all forms of oppression. Both dimensions are actively involved in the development of posterior Fanonian thinking. It is from the disenchantment occasioned by his experience as a French soldier and as an intellectual shaped in France that his writings, particularly in *Black Skin, White Masks*, related to alienation appear. Regarding the struggles against oppression in any of its forms, the quoted texts but also the later ones, especially from *The Wretched of the Earth*, display links with those early positions.

After the war, Fanon studied medicine and psychiatry at the University of Lyon where he was an active student responsible for the publication of the mimeographed newspaper called *Tam-tam*.

He took up residence in Saint Alban in 1952 where he was immersed in the study of psychiatry. That same year, he returned to Martinique where he worked at the hospital in Vauclin. During his stay in France, he was a regular participant in many contemporary intellectual encounters. Through those early incursions and in his university life, he was influenced by Maurice Merleau-Ponty and Jean-Paul Sartre, Karl Jaspers, Søren Kierkegaard, Friedrich Nietzsche, and the G.W.F. Hegel in the French reading of Sartre and by the prominent figures of the Négritude movement, generally associated with the journal *Présence Africaine* and figures such as Aimé Césaire, Cheikh Anta Diop, and Léopold Sédar Senghor, among others. From contact with that intellectual universe and his practice as a resident physician, Fanon published his book, *Black Skin, White Masks*, in 1952.

In 1953, he married Marie-Josphe (Josie) Duble, a woman from Lyon with whom he remained for the rest of his life. In trying to broaden his perceptions of the problem of patients in colonial territories, that is, when trying to link disease with colonialism, Fanon accepted in the same year a contract with the Blida-Joinville hospital in Algeria. During his residency there, the results of his research convinced him of the dimensions of the colonial regime and how it disarticulated people's psychic structure. At the same time, he reaffirmed his commitment to the cause of the Algerian resistance against French colonialism. See the last part of *The Wretched of the Earth* for more regarding his reflections related to his medical practice.

In 1954, he attended the birth of the Algerian revolution and the violent repression by the French colonial forces. For that reason, in protest he resigned from his position in the hospital and became the editor of the National Liberation Front (Front de Libération Nationale) newspaper known as the *Moudjahid*, which was published in Tunisia.

The impulse he gave to the newspaper was decisive in the constitution of a public discourse for those who daily faced the colonial regime. Drawing on accounts from that time, some of his biographers describe the cooperative work Fanon developed within the working group of the newspaper.

In 1956, he was an active participant in the Black Writers' Congress in Paris where all the important names of the Négritude movement gathered. In 1958, he attended the Conference of All African Peoples in Accra, Ghana. This was only one of many conferences and meetings that Fanon attended on behalf of the Algerian National Liberation Front. He faced serious risks to his life on several occasions, for example, on the border of Morocco and Algeria where, in 1959, he escaped death from an exploding mine. In that same year, he published *L'an V of the Révolution Algérienne*, known in Spanish as *Sociología de una revolución* (Sociology of a Revolution) and in English *A Dying Colonialism*.

In 1960, he became a representative of the interim Government of Algeria in Ghana. In 1961, he traveled to Rome where he held a meeting with Sartre and Simone de Beauvoir. She offers an extensive and interesting description of Fanon's personality and of this encounter in her book *The Force of Circumstance*, which I have quoted in this study. It is fair to state that, for Fanon, Sartre was one of the most important, if not the most important, interlocutor in the intellectual world of the time. That same year Fanon's illness, leukemia, manifested itself. He was referred to the National Institute of Health hospital in Bethesda, Maryland, in the United States to receive adequate medical care. However, his illness was terminal. He died on December 6, 1961. His body was sent to Algeria and buried with honors.

This brief account does not describe or do justice to Fanon's intellectual or personal vitality. Perhaps the best of homages extend beyond those that our academic practices suggest: to speak of Fanon, to think about Fanon, to argue with Fanon, to write about Fanon. To pay tribute to a specter that can still guide some of our most complex questions about culture, history, and politics, while destabilizing our strongest certainties. This is a specter that besieges us kindly but without tranquility in an end/beginning of a century that, as Fanon's writings accomplish, evokes the privileges of ambivalence and the possibilities of the subject.

Works of Frantz Fanon[1]

IN SPANISH

Los condenados de la tierra, Julieta Campos (trad.), Méxicom, Fondo de Cultura Económica, 1994.
Piel negra, máscaras blancas, G. Charquero y Anita Larrea (trads.), Buenos Aires, Schapire Editor, 1974.
Por la revolución africana: escritos políticos, México, Fondo de Cultura Económica, 1965.
Sociología de una revolución, Víctor Flores Olea (trad.), México, Era, 1968.

IN FRENCH (ORIGINAL)

Frantz Fanon: Écrits sur l'aliénation et la liberté, eds. Jean Khalfa and Robert Young. Paris: Éditions la découverte, 2017.[2]
L'An V de la révolution algérienne, Paris, Francois Maspero, 1959.
Les damnés de la Terre, Paris, Francois Maspero, 1961.
Peau Noire, masques Blancs, preface and afterword by Francis Jeanson, Paris, Editions du Seuil, 1965.
Pour la Révolution africaine: Ecrits politiques, Paris, Francois Maspero, 1969.

IN ENGLISH (FOR THIS TRANSLATION)

Black Skin, White Masks. New York: Grove Press, 1967.
The Wretched of the Earth. New York: Grove Press, 1963.

Notes

FOREWORD

1. Italo Calvino, *Por qué leer los clásicos*, tr. Aurora Bernárdez (Ciudad de México: Tusquets, 1994). Available in English as *Why Read the Classics*, trans. Martin McLaughlin (Boston: Mariner Books, 2014), 5.
2. Italo Calvino, *Por qué leer los clásicos*, 15; 5.
3. Michel de Certeau, *La invención de lo cotidiano, I. Artes de hacer*, trans. Alejandro Pescador (Ciudad de México: Universidad Iberoamericana, 1996), 145–65. Available as *The Practice of Everyday Life*, 3rd edition, trans. Steve Rendall (Berkeley: University of California Press, 2011).

INTRODUCTION

1. This observation is shared by those responsible for the compilation of works on Frantz Fanon titled *Fanon: A Critical Reader*, edited by Lewis Gordon, T. Denean Sharpley-Whiting, and Renée T. White. The editors suggest in their introduction that the presence of Fanon's name in the works of what they call the fifth stage of Fanon studies indicates that his texts can serve to further reflect on African literature, the philosophy of human sciences, and the phenomenology of experience. The chapters in the volume, as the editors point out, share Fanon's preference for free thinking (7). Although I will later briefly discuss these stages, the idea of a use of Fanon that always serves to go "beyond" is present in texts of other traditions, including in a book that the contributors of this compilation almost abhor: *The Fact of Blackness*, edited by Alan Read,

specifically the essay of Homi Bhabha, "Day by day . . . with Frantz Fanon" and that of Stuart Hall, "The After-Life of Frantz Fanon: Why Fanon? Why Now? Why *Black Skin, White Masks?*" Hall reiterates the idea that a reading is always a new text, a point that highlights the attempt to "colonize Fanon's work became in-process from the moment of his death, and the identification of Fanon's writing in terms of his 'Marxist themes' in the decades of the '60s and '70s was, in and of itself, already the product of a re-reading" (15–16). The existentialist turn adopted in the works by Gordon, for example, and which organize the theoretical and philosophical preferences in *Fanon: A Critical Reader*, can be seen through a similar lens. In my work, I try not to generate that hiatus from which theoretical and political duties are distributed according to theoretical political backgrounds, whether Marxist, poststructuralist, postcolonial critique, existential phenomenological, etc. Nevertheless, I extend myself with the organization of Fanonian themes in the two decades after his death and, at that point, my reading could also be said to posit and distinguish preferences. But I do not support the widespread belief that certain dialogues are impossible nor support some almost banal accusations. Namely, there are many that do not respect and distort his texts in making themselves readers of Fanon. I am thinking here of the reproach of Bhabha for trying to create a Fanon for his theoretical project, the reproach of Robinson by those who would divert Fanon from the route of revolutionary readings, the reproach directed to the intellectuals close to postcolonial critiques, although theirs are marked by similar differences. Regardless, I maintain that there is an unacknowledged, great debt to Sartre, present in the analysis of some of Fanon's readers.

2. A translation of Homi K. Bhabha's book, *The Location of Culture*, which contains this essay, was published by Ediciones Manantial in Buenos Aires in 2002 with the title *El lugar de la cultura*. The translator of this edition is César Aira. In this study, I used the English edition because a Spanish translation was not yet available. I kept the references to the Routledge edition for that reason. Aira's translation is good and I recommend it. My only reservations concern the translation of Guillermo Gómez Peña's poem, on page 23. Aira writes the whole poem in Spanish pointing out which parts were in Spanish in the original. This undermines the bilingualism of the poem, or its border language, which gives the poem its cultural aesthetic value. The best option might have been to keep the poem as it is in the original.

3. I am paraphrasing the title of the book compiled by Nigel G. Gibson, *Rethinking Fanon: The Continuing Dialogue.*

4. I am taking advantage of the interesting discussion raised with the Spanish translation of *Specters of Marx* by José Miguel Alarcón and Cristina de Peretti. They translate the *hanter, hantise, hanté (e)* as "besiege," "siege," "besieged" in trying to represent the condition of specters and the way in which they inhabit a place in Derrida's text (Derrida, 17–18).

5. Throughout this study I use the Spanish version of both texts. I have crosschecked the translation of *Le damnés de la Terre* (*The Wretched of the Earth*) by Juliet Campos with the original in French published in 1961 by François Maspero. The translation by Campos is, to the extent that any translation can be, faithful to the detail and tone of different particularly complex passages in the original. For *Peau noire, masques blanches* (*Black skin, White masks*), I use the translation by G. Charquero and Anita Larrea. In this case, I have compared it with the 1965 French version with the preface and afterword by Francis Jeanson. In a few instances, I offer additional clarifications about a particular expression, though it does not weigh heavily against the general context of the translation. However, I have preferred to maintain the conjugation of the second person singular of the pronoun *you* while the translators use the pronoun *vos*. I make this clarification because it applies to the phrase "mama, see the negro!" which I quote on several occasions.

6. Gordon, Sharpley-Whiting, and White present this biographical moment in the study of Fanon as a separate stage to which those of theoretical political reflection of liberation movements are linked (5).

7. Gordon, Sharpley-Whiting, and White state verbatim: "Postcolonial studies have fortunately not marked the final stage of Fanon's studies . . . . The past ten years [mid-1980s through mid-1990s] have sometimes been described as seeing a 'resurgence' in Fanon's thought . . . . however, what each stage represents is an ongoing dialectical process" (6–7). A dialectical process, fair to say, that buries the old theses, especially if they emerge from postcolonial studies.

8. Except for Rey Chow, the works of these other authors are included in the volume edited by Alan Read, *The Fact of Blackness: Frantz Fanon and Visual Representation.*

9. *Translator's note*: In *What Fanon Said* (2015), Gordon argues there is actually a sixth stage that identifies the prior five; see 4–5.

10. I am referring to the work of Floyd W. Hayes, "Fanon, Oppression, and Resentment: The Black Experience in the United States"; Stanley O. Gaines Jr., "Perspectives of Du Bois and Fanon on the Psychology of Oppression," and Richard Schmitt, "Racism and Objectification: Reflections on Themes from Fanon." Most of the works consulted on the Fanon-Du Bois connection concentrate on the subjects described by these titles. In this study, I have not included more than marginal references to the work of Du Bois, only when it has had to do with Fanon or as it has been read as part of a possible intellectual genealogy from Fanon, as in the reading by Ross Posnock that we will engage later.

11. Thinking contextually may be a duty, but it does not necessarily mean assigning the full meaning (possibly an erroneous metaphor) of a theory to an era with certain configurations referred to as "the real thing." Benita Parry, who

I will discuss extensively in chapter two, in her "Resistance Theory: Theorizing Resistance or Two Cheers for Nativism," defends, following Stuart Hall, a contextual dimension of knowledge while bearing in mind its dispersion and dissemination, particularly as produced by Fanon. The interesting point of this theoretical wager by Parry, which has many antecedents, but that she finds correctly and with clarity in Édouard Glissant and Stuart Hall, is the fact of thinking of histories as discontinuities and not necessarily as histories that reaffirm an essential content. This argument runs throughout my study. It is nuanced by the problem of being strategic and of thinking about our readings as possibly "absolutist," even those that propose total dispersion, and also as contextualized knowledge. Historians, perhaps more accustomed by disciplinary duty to think of temporality, quickly warn of the tension between the context in which events unfold (I include knowledge, and specifically theories) and the readings that we make of these. The history of ideas, conceived in these terms, is not so much a revision of genealogies that show the specific contexts in which they are structured and developed as a permanent interaction of our theoretical thoughts. New contextualization may possibly emerge from the knowledge in question in its most absolute dispersion and dissemination. Edward Said raises an interesting and polemical discussion in "Travelling Theory," a chapter of his book *The World, the Text, and the Critic*. Said states that a bias traversed his analysis in the fact that every recorded human experience produces a theory specific to it and that its strength depends on it being simultaneously connected and compelled by its real historical circumstances (197). Something like the value of a theory lies precisely in its genesis. Therefore, later versions of a theory, traveling in different contexts to that which gave it reason to exist, cannot have the same force because the situations have changed and consequently the theory experiences a sort of deterioration, filtered by a substitute academician from the real thing. Said reflects on this dimension to discuss again the subject/object relation in Lukács's most important texts but, fundamentally, in terms of *History and Class Consciousness* and his lectures that make him the Adorno of *Philosophy of Modern Music* and the Frantz Fanon of *The Wretched of the Earth*. To not extend his quotation, Said's review of the first article on traveling theories finds that such deterioration does not occur. Both the use of Lukács by Adorno to understand the place of Schoenberg in the history of music, and the use that Fanon makes of figures of thought from Europe on the dialectic of the subject/object transposed to the context of the relationship between colonizer/colonized, reveal what theory is capable of when it is not trapped in a universalizing turn (214). Moreover, Said proposes in his final argument that the task is not simply to distinguish the uses and borrowing but to distinguish the moment in which theories undergo a kind of reignition that would indicate, among other things, the existence of a possible moral community (*ibid*). That is another reason why, in this study, I speak of fragile theoretical positions. Not because of a congenital weakness of second order theories, or as degraded, as reviewed by Said, but because in the space of some theoretical permissiveness these signs of community may appear. In other words, there is the reignition of theories.

12. The chapters by Robert Bernasconi, Paget Henry, Sonia Kruks, Eddy Souffrant, and Maurice Stevens indicate and reflect this with certain intensity.

13. Less organized by stages, as is arguably the case with Gordon, Sharpley-Whiting, and White, Alessandrini's volume tries to recover the most important nuclei of analysis on Fanon by referring to cultural studies. The writings on Fanon's legacy, especially Rey Chow's "The Politics of Admittance: Female Sexual Agency, Miscegenation, and the Formation of Community in Frantz Fanon" (which, in the rest of this study, I quote directly from the author's book *Ethics After idealism*) and that of Terrie Goldie, "Saint Fanon and 'Homosexual Territory'" are examples. There is a section dedicated exclusively to discussing the limits of cultural studies uses of Fanon that highlights the article by Gibson mentioned in the main text and that of E. San Juan, Jr., entitled "Fanon: An Intervention into Cultural Studies." San Juan focuses on what he calls Fanon's materialistic hermeneutics, which functions as an antidote to the formalist conservatism of disciplines (127). See also, the text by Kobena Mercer, which refers to the problem of cultural politics and its future, "Busy in the Ruins of a Wretched Phantasia," and of Samira Kawash, "Terrorists and Vampires: Fanon's Spectral Violence of Decolonization."

CHAPTER I

1. It is interesting, as I said before, to see that Jean-Paul Sartre has a minor place in the development of current postcolonial studies. Directly stated, he is not a member of the postcolonial "pantheon." This is a conspicuous absence considering the proximity of his politics to the construction of difference and in relation to the existence, or inexistence, of a historical subject.

2. Most of the English translations for this chapter, except that of Sekyi-Otu (1996), note "The fact of blackness." The problem with this translation is that, in a way, it essentializes the situation that Fanon intends to represent. In the original it is called "L'expérience vécue du Noir." From my perspective, we see that there is an attempt to represent a historical and existential experience that remains outside the English version. In other words, "blackness" is not "*le noir.*" "Le noir" [black or the black] appeals to a subject, and "blackness" to a condition.

3. See chapters II and III of *Black Skin, White Masks*.

4. In the 1974 Schapire Editor Spanish edition, translated by G. Charquero and Anita Larrea, which I use for all the quotations of *Black Skin, White Masks*, they translate the expression to: "Very rich Banania." Banania was a brand of French powdered chocolate the label of which had the representation of a Senegalese soldier in which his "black" features (especially wide lips) were exaggerated, in what is called pejoratively "Petit Nègre" in which he declared "*Y a bon Banania!*" The expression can be translated as "is good the Banania" or "There is good Banania." I thank Bertrand Douet and Dominique Lieutet for a conversation in the Patagonian winter of 1996, where they explained to me (before I got my hands on the Spanish translation) what the Banania was all about. Fanon uses this image with great force amid an existentialist argument revealing that the construction of the Other in a stereotyped way in the colonial imaginary is produced even in the smallest details. [*Translator's note*: the English version used throughout in this translation is by Charles Lam Markman, New York: Grove Press, 1967.]

5. To consider this argument in more detail, I recommend the full reading of Sartre's text. However, the most significant passages that apply to Fanon are those that refer to the anti-Semitic construction of Jews (83–4) and Jews' response to that construction. More than a response, it considers the conditions in which anti-Semitism is produced against the accusation of Jews as a kind of metaphysical inauthenticity (164). Fanon's idea of an absence of an ontology in the colonized, which I'll discuss later, is directly related to the idea of metaphysical inauthenticity.

6. See the interesting book by Charles F. Wallraff, *Karl Jaspers: An Introduction to His Philosophy*.

7. Jaspers's position on existentialism and its impact on modern culture can be clearly seen in the text "What Is Existentialism?" Jaspers has sympathy for the way Sartre treats the concept but warns that "man" must always be in search of his absolute Other with whom he can compare himself. Jaspers states: "becoming existential means to accept and be the deep seriousness that man is. And to be a man is to be in relation to that Being by which and in which we are. There is no existence without transcendence" (*Lectures and Essays*, 437). As seen here, the possibility of transcendence that Jaspers's claims, becomes impracticable in Fanon's logic to the extent that what characterizes the colonial world is not a cognitive activity in relation to the supposed Being but a close relationship with the problem of alienation. This separation characterizes the particularity of Fanon's project to a large extent. If alienation is separation, it is also a source of tensions and indeterminate impulses. The subject that is produced at this crossroads organizes, from my fin de siècle reading, Fanon's writing and his postcolonial inheritance. It could be said that alienation imposes limits on transcendence.

CHAPTER II

1. Geismar refers to Césaire's characterization of Fanon in the following manner: "Césaire drew sharply on Fanon's spirit and dedication, but not so much his political attitude" (30).
2. The article is on the role Marx's writings played in contemporary historiography. Hobsbawm differentiates between uses of Marxism associated with the development of forms of analysis within the historical discipline from uses related to the political struggle. Generally, the famous economic reduction from Marx's perspective is much more pronounced in the latter. However, the main distinction is in using the categories of Marxist analysis in relation to empirical material, in the first case, versus a certain construction of political doctrine, in the second. This distinction relates, in Eric Hobsbawm's case, with the double question of his condition as historian and with his rupture with Stalinist currents in the 1950s. The title of the article is "Karl Marx's Contribution to Historiography."
3. On this point, Hayden White observes that a characteristic of Carlyle, for example, with respect to Novalis (another of the great romantics) was the belief that historical experience and the meaning of the human life could only be found inside of humanity (White, 147).
4. Burton's writing exemplifies how the more rigid statements regarding difference, or rather, more rigid in terms of the construction of difference, can contain their own instability, or disintegration in the context of seemingly mimetic situations or of a displacement of restricted notions of "home." Richard F. Burton wrote in the multiformed space of the nineteenth-century British Empire, apparently preserving the traits of a classic colonial gaze as the gaze which orders the spaces and the subjects that inhabit them for the eye of the observer. However, in several passages, the certainties which seem to indicate a control of the originality and hierarchy of its discourse with regard to what it describes are destabilized both by the answers in mimetic form which it receives as by the same mimesis that he carries forward, such as the displacement of the point of enunciation of the idea of Great Britain to that of the Empire. Another possibility, when thinking about the reflections of Homi Bhabha on mimesis, as I discuss in this study, is that Burton is camouflaged rather than disguised with the so-called "natives," which implies that the discourse of the imperial traveler can suffer the same process as the colonial discourse suffers when the "natives" blend in with it. In other words, originality and centrality are lost. For a more extensive discussion about Richard F. Burton and his writings, see my book, *El viaje de la escritura. Richard Francis Burton y el este de África*.
5. It seems that Marx, however, had some problems getting into the library because he did not have the proper attire, a sort of raincoat of the time. I owe

this reference to Adrian Cangi in a friendly talk traveling between Rosario and Buenos Aires, after a colloquium on the essay in the first city.

6. Marshal Berman draws in detail the clashes (and in many moments the struggles for recognition) with the social authority contained in Dostoevsky's book, *Memories of the Subsoil*. The street articulates the moment and the space in each of the relationships that are established among the members of different social classes in nineteenth-century St. Petersburg (Berman, 226–36). The fact of thinking about the spaces of modernity from the political and cultural metaphors that the street offers makes Berman's book extremely interesting, if impossible to completely comment on here.

7. See Marshall Berman's "The Signs in the Street: a Response to Perry Anderson," in the edited volume by Nicolás Casullo, *El debate modernidad posmodernidad* (The Modernity-Postmodernity Debate).

8. Memmi's case is perhaps one of the most interesting for the analysis of the role that identities play in the colonial regime. Memmi often reflects on being Jewish while, at the same, criticizing colonial relations in the context of Tunisia, which assures him a paradoxical situation. He perceives he holds a privileged status with respect to the Muslim population. Yet, this status does not ensure the complete separation of his subordination nor does it allow him to be completely part of the colonial settlers. The idea of being "fully a part" is a metaphor with which I try to represent the main characteristic of the alienation by the colonial regime that Fanon observes. The emerging subjects of it, but, perhaps, of any other historical and cultural situation, are always split or partial subjects. This incompleteness, not seen in a negative way, implies that interstices constitute the strategies and the identity processes where, in addition to the attempts to exorcise alienation, emerge the complex procedures of identities to resist and shape the contemporary world: irony, tragedy, mimesis, fragmentation.

9. Epiphany, *Epipháneia*, means "manifestation." In the Christian tradition this idea is used to commemorate the emergence and manifestation of Jesus in the world. As such, the term expresses the emergence of the new and different.

10. References to the etymology of epiphany were drawn from Guido Gómez de Silva, *Breve diccionario etimológico de la lengua española* (A Brief Etymological Dictionary of the Spanish Language) and Lisandro Sandoval, *Diccionario de raíces griegas y latinas y de otros orígenes del idioma español* (A Dictionary of Greek and Latin Roots and Other Origins of the Spanish Language).

11. But ultimately utopia is a form of unresolved continuity.

12. For a historical political study in Spanish of the work of the Asadato Hasan Manto, see Susan Devalle's *Saadat Hasan Manto. Antología de cuentos* (Anthology of Stories).

13. The image of the tree may be one that most strongly refers to the idea of rooting. It is no coincidence that Deleuze and Guattari, in *A Thousand Plateaus*, used the metaphor of a tree to represent the idea of modern knowledge and the cultural pretensions that are linked to it. The tree represents order and hierarchy, identity, direction, and sense of history, in an organically functioning matrix. The rhizome represents the open and uncertain space of any development, the de-hierarchization of the world, territoriality that can only be apprehended in instances, at specific crossroads. These visions are pertinent to consider, and not as an annotation, the figures of identity in the texts of Manto and Fanon. Obviously, it is difficult to think about ephemeral territories when what appears with insistence on the surface of discourses is a sense of direction, however, the general attempt of this study is to see what happens when we decide to see texts that simulate adopting the figure not of the tree but that offer instead, with great seduction, the possibility of being rhizomatic.

14. See Wilda Western's book, *Alquimia de la nación* (Alchemy of the Nation), especially the first part.

15. Although there were many before him, Fanon's life could be understood as an example of modern and colonial transhumance and as a sort of anticipation of the movements of people from the imperial regions to the metropolises. A discordant pattern characterizes his displacement. Fanon does not end up in the cultural and geographical metropolis but in one of the most tumultuous places in the colonial world, Algeria. However, living at the margins, as Cioran would say about Borges, helps him to see better what metropolitan culture is about. Cioran's argument with respect to Borges is interesting to contrast with those who reclaim territorialities. Cioran writes to Fernando Vater, telling him that his interest in Borges lies in the fact that the latter is "destined, forced to universality, forced to exercise his spirit in all directions, even if to escape the asphyxiation of Argentina" (156). Without imagining similar trajectories between Borges and Fanon, Cioran's capacity to see how decentering allows thought on greater situations applies. There is a kind of universality for peripheral intellectuals. Some of the readings that attempt to capture Fanon in a kind of forgetfulness of the universal, of the categories of man, humanity, for example, lose sight of this process. As well as the fact that Fanon almost always represents multi-positioned intellectuals whose ways of thinking and strategies of writing converge and diverge with images of the world that do not necessarily respond with extreme fidelity to the trajectories that each one of them would have separately, whether in political, cultural, or disciplinary terms. It is precisely this condition, by which the most oriented texts can be read as disseminated texts, flowing in the least envisaged directions, even at the expense of the alleged intentions of their writers. Yet, it is also necessary to say that Cioran's perspective should not be taken as a rule. Ultimately, as he states,

it all depends on whether this curiosity for the universal bears the mark of "I." Curiously, the periphery from which these intellectuals write is represented to give value to that universal drive as an empty space where a powerful and farcical "me" gives it content. However, he is not referring to a colonial image in the sense of a discourse that devastates a geography, but of a situation, which, I think, is Fanon in Fort de France. This is a situation that spurs displacement because what is at stake is more than the problem of understanding the periphery. It is about being critical of it. In that sense, Fanon's texts move as a double critique.

16. It is interesting to review this idea in relation to Stephen Tyler's claims about the origins of the postmodern world. Tyler narrates, from the texts by Habermas (1975, 1984) and Lyotard (1979), with style and irony on the progressive separation of science's primeval attempts to give an account of the real and the adoption by the real of a model of language in an auto-perfectionist form that closes the passage to communication by reason of representational efficacy of the concepts, which converts language itself into an object of description (298–9). This characteristic of the discourse of science has a presence in all the readings that I discuss here. However, Tyler adds a new element for their analysis, namely, that they try to exorcise Fanon's conceptual and rhetorical anomaly not in the direction of a self-perfecting language (which exists in his clear, explicit statements) but in his capacity to account for the real, although what is at stake are precisely the greater or lesser approximations of Fanon's writing to the canon of several traditions. In that sense, Perinbam's reading is the best example. To show that Fanon's critics were wrong in ascribing his stances on violence to a kind of political hallucination, Perinbam reconstructs Fanon's background of thought in the plots of modernity and attempts to return his legitimacy to him from there. Nevertheless, the paradox is that legitimacy is found not in relation to the "real" but in relation with traditions drawn from these plots.

17. This concept is treated in several of the discussions in the anthology edited by Carlos Reynoso titled *El surgimiento de la antropología posmoderna* (The Emergence of Postmodern Anthropology), which recovers most of the articles of the text, *Writing Culture: The Poetics and Politics of Ethnography*, edited by James Clifford and George E. Marcus from the talks presented in the New Discussions of American Anthropology held in the second half of the 1980s. Stephen Tyler makes an extensive defense of the collective authorship of ethnographic texts from the argument that ethnography privileges discourse rather than text, favoring dialogue and not monologue, emphasizing "the cooperative and collaborative nature of the ethnographic situation in contrast to the ideology of the transcendental observer" (301). Despite the many problems that this idea generates (because ultimately the ethnographies that Tyler refers to end up as texts), many of them are covered by Dennis Tedlock in the same

book (295–6). I am interested in understanding the limits of Tyler's argument, especially the reference to the transcendental observer. This aspect is very interesting when considering texts with eccentric discourses like those of Fanon which must, according to criteria such as Lucas's, be part of a tradition. This incorporation produces a kind of estrangement in Fanonian discourse. If it exists, that is, if it has legitimacy, it is in relation to a context of authority granted by a tradition's past and not by the dialogues, conflicts, and tensions that his writing produces. In view of the dimension of this problem, it seems to me that there is no qualitative difference between the ethnographic situation of the transcendental observer to which Tyler refers and the situation of a text written in the interstices of anticolonial discourses but subjected to the inflexible rule that dictates that its meaning always occurs through being linked with reason as a certain theoretical political tradition.

18. This note could be an article but, to avoid such a thing, I would like to say that, for example, the works of Fernand Braudel, Georges Duby, Marc Bloch, and Lucien Febvre cannot be thought without the decisive role historical time plays in them and their analytical forms. Consider, for example, the levels of Braudelian temporality and architecture in the pinnacle of his work, *The Mediterranean*, and the rhythms of Georges Duby's thought on the social history of the order of the Cistercian in the low Middle Ages. See specifically the chapter "Monarchism and the Economy" (272–87) in the book, *Hombres y estructuras de la Edad Media* (Men and Structures of the Middle Ages). Also consider the dialogue between present and past of Marc Bloch in *The Historian's Craft*, and the Modernist passion of Febvre in *Combates por la Historia* (*A New Kind of History*), which argues for a new time as a central task of the historian. Each of these historiographic experiences relies on the methodological efficacy of handling temporality. However, as an additional warning, the notion of Braudelian time acquires at times, a metahistorical presence.

19. In fact, she is the English translator of Derrida's book, *Of Grammatology*. The English version is 1985. Additionally, it was published in Spanish, translated by Oscar del Barco, in 1971. This last edition is the one I use in this study.

20. Their work has been published in the magazine *Subaltern Studies: Writings on South Asian History and Society*. It has in recent years been a place of reference for those who discuss topics such as the categories of domination and subordination in a wide range of sources, situations and histories. The objective of the group was to propose a new critique of the perspectives of colonial and national historiography. The Subaltern Studies Group (their name) was founded in 1982. Some recognizable names are Ranajit Guha, Partha Chaterjee, Gyanendra Pandey and Gayatri Spivak, among others.

21. Madan Sarup is a bit surprised by Spivak's idea (41) because it is expected that a discourse related to deconstruction would emphasize the

specific and not the type of issues linked to the ideas of a universal intellectual like Sartre or, why not, Fanon. This surprise, however, is not necessarily negative.

22. I use the English version published by *Présence Africaine*. It was, regrettably, impossible to know during the writing of this work if there was a version published in Spanish. When I finished, I discovered the existence of such a translation published by Editorial La República del Silencio in Buenos Aires in 1960, but I could not find a copy. Although I did not use this edition, for the reader's convenience I refer henceforth to the translated title: *Black Orpheus*.

23. Gunther Grass reconsiders the question of Adorno in an essay titled "Writing After Auschwitz," first published in German in 1990, proposing that the absolute suspension of writing after Auschwitz operates as an impossibility, both for him and for Adorno. To suspend writing as an absolute act is neither more nor less than the metaphor of the horror of doing so in reality. Therefore, as in Adorno's title, Grass thinks that to stop writing absolutely after Auschwitz is universal suicide. This presents the possibility of horror against its suspension, but what is essential is that it refers to the double impossibility that I mentioned in the main text, in which the absolute phrase is the condition of an ethic that disbelieves absolutisms. I do not refer to a specific page in Grass's text because his argument is present everywhere.

24. Husserl, in many ways, tried to think of the radical foundations of the enterprise of philosophical reason. The question was to find absolute evidence that, just as a phenomenon would justify itself, an apodictic search would give science and reason its meanings. Thus, it was represented as the appropriate method for a consciousness that attempted to describe the analysis of essences. The phenomenological reduction gave him access in philosophical terms to a position that would be neither objectivist nor metaphysical, neither psychologistic nor subjective. The process followed by Husserl ranges from the non-psychological analysis of consciousness, through the non-psychological consciousness to a transcendental consciousness. The reduction, then, is a process that goes against the natural tendencies of the mind, leaving aside all psychological forms. Reducing did not mean leaving aside. On the contrary, it implied, in some way, to capture the phenomenon by way of consciousness, not the thing as it was but the immanent reality of the world. What is trapped in the reduction is the whole of everything empirical, rational, and even judgments about the world. The ultimate goal of this process was to shed light on this essential and intentional contact between the world and consciousness, a dimension which, in the perspective of Husserl, was not present in objectivism or naturalism. Thus, the world in the act of reduction remains where it is and each act of knowledge refers to a subject and a term that originates and supports the foundation of meaning (Thévenaz, 45, 46, 47). In the sense of overcoming subjectivism and a consciousness linked to the psychology, Husserl postulated

the necessity of a universal (transcendental) subjectivism. The same displacement was affirmed for objectivism and relativism (Husserl, 71).

CHAPTER III

1. Thinking of cultural critique, I want to point out that Fanon's project is not reducible to a specific field of political action or, more generally, of experience.

2. Marx's echoes or his specter appears, as Derrida would say. Marx's famous phrase in the general introduction to the critique of political economy resonates here by indicating the way in which the Marxist tradition intersects in Fanon's writing: "No social order is ever destroyed before all the productive forces for which it is sufficient have been developed, and new superior relations of production never replace older ones before the material conditions *for their existence have matured within the framework of the old society. Mankind thus inevitably sets itself only such tasks as it is able to solve*" (67, italics of mine). These echoes of Marx' specter might mean that Fanon read *The German Ideology*, particularly the sections on consciousness and its empirical dimensions. See *The German ideology*, chapter I, the section "on the production of consciousness" ["The Essence of the Materialist Conception of History: Social Being and Social Consciousness"] (39–54). But most important is the attempt to not prescribe the future that appears in the phrase "In no fashion should I undertake to prepare the world that will come later." This implies an element of tension for the remainder of Fanon's project. I would say this is a qualification for not being reduced to certain clear traits of emancipatory discourse. As we will see later, the doubts about the dimension that nativism acquires in their discourse, the reductionism, in a certain way, of "national consciousness" lurks in the texts. However, the condition of historical and cultural experience will always be present as a mode of control. It is a mode of paradoxical control in the instability it produces in the explicit statements that seem to orient his texts toward programmatic contents, especially in *The Wretched of the Earth*.

3. The tragedy that accompanies the irony appears earlier in *Black Skin*. It will not be in Chapter V where it manifests itself but in the first, when Fanon says: "The educated Negro, slave of the spontaneous and cosmic Negro myth, feels at a given stage that his race no longer understands him...and it is with rage in his mouth and abandon in his heart and he buries himself in the vast black abyss. We shall see that this attitude, so heroically absolute, renounces the present and the future in the name of a mystical past" (originally cited, 19; 14). The idea of the evolved (*evolué*) also fits the cultists of Négritude.

4. It would be useless to offer a definition of "irony" in this context for the simple reason that this trope often depends on the position of the reader or, we

could say, of the conditions of the reading. On the other hand, the term is the result of a long historical, philosophical, and literary tradition and it would be impossible to summarize it here. However, with the only purpose of clarifying the main mode of use of the term in my text, I will say that when I refer to irony, I mean the expression of an idea whose literal sense is different or often opposite to what ultimately is meant or expressed. The way of interpreting it frequently depends on the keys that tacitly contribute to the context (Azaustre Galiana and Casas Rigall, 25). However, as I said before, at least two contexts are at play, writing and reading.

5. Raymond Williams in *Marxism and Literature* coined "structures of feeling." To explain it briefly, the concept speaks of meanings and values in the way they are actively lived and felt and the relationships that are established between them. The structures of feeling address this space of representations and practices where consciousness is, fundamentally, a practical awareness linked to the way people perceive the world in the flow of "a living continuity and interrelated" (155). Parry's idea, if my reading is correct, is that blackness as such is not a fixed form, but what Williams would say is precipitous, in process, at least until the time when Fanon writes *Black Skin, White Masks*. This implies that Parry is announcing the emergence of new forms and social and cultural practices. Of interest, Parry's conceptual option does not set blackness in the established definition and unpacks the use and its reading of reductionisms. However, when she analyzes the tension that the structure of feeling produces in Fanon, her argument pushes her toward a fixed analysis.

6. See the introduction of V. Y Mudimbe to *The Surreptitious Speech* (xvii–xxvi). In the same text, see the articles of Bernard Mouralis, Denis-Constant Martin, and Christopher Miller.

7. I include blackness in this list because it also has a history. I think that leaving it alone in the field of "nativisms" loses sight of it assuming a central role in the configuration of postcolonial texts. The task is not to establish hierarchies and qualities of these discourses, but rather to understand their articulations.

8. This privileged character of ambivalence, in my case, counters any construction of the sexual or ethnic community that requires fixed attributes for those who possess the relevant identity. In that sense, privilege means having more elements to be able to decenter the pretensions of homogeneity that inevitably reduce the attributes of belonging to a few. Chow's use of this idea is that ambivalence is something that can be denied for black or colonized women or the colonized in postcolonial society in Fanon. However, privilege must be put in quotation marks. We can celebrate the decentering in our representations of identities but that does not necessarily mean assigning a positive value to instability per se. One can have this, as Chow says, when we think of communities as open-ended which ensure, at least partially, the absence of

comprehensive policies of exclusion, but for those who live in unstable social, political, and cultural processes, certain marks of stability and less ambivalence are necessary. I think here, for example, of the global immigrants of the present. Yet again, it could be argued that it is a lack of ambivalence that causes community-based exclusionary policies. However, when ambivalence is located, in representational terms, only on the side of subordinate subjects, its political effectiveness is different. That is also my reading of Shohat's idea with regard to the inscription of a community's past.

9. Much of this debate has been settled since the original Spanish publication of this book. More accurate readings were established about the translation from French into English of expressions such as "Les nègres." Lewis Gordon, for instance, engaged Ronald T. Judy's discussion of a Fanonian nomenclature. The point most relevant to this discussion is the fact that it was often assumed that Fanon used gendered words that were not actually gendered (Gordon, 2015: 22). This poses complex challenges for translations into Spanish, which in this sense is very close to French, since, at the linguistic level, the idea that the masculine gender represents the universal persists. In recent years, there has been strong critical activity by feminists and LGTBQ + collectives to respond through creating and promoting inclusive forms of language.

10. The book in question is titled *Je suis martiniquaise* ("I am Martinican [woman]").

11. Kobena Mercer, with notable sharpness and irony, reminds readers that postcolonial theory has overlooked chapter six note 44 on homosexuality as a source of anxiety in Fanon's theorizing (125). Fanon's note: "Let me observe at once that I had no opportunity to establish the overt presence of homosexuality in Martinique. This must be viewed as the result of the absence of the Oedipus complex in the Antilles. The schema of homosexuality is well enough known. We should not overlook, however, the existence of what are called there 'men dressed like women' or 'godmothers.' Generally, they wear shirts and skirts. But I am convinced that they lead normal sex lives . . . . In Europe, on the other hand, I have known several Martinicans who became homosexuals, always passive. But this was by no means a neurotic homosexuality: For them it was a means to a livelihood, as pimping is for others" (*Black Skin*, 180).

12. See, later in this study, the discussion that these two authors offer about the problem of alienation.

13. Patrick McGee proposes to think of hegemony (a concept that must be treated carefully when thinking about colonial situations) as a path that is not one-way. The idea, associated with the problem of writing, is that a hegemonic construction not only captures those who appear to be subordinates of it but also those who have hegemonic control (125).

14. I would like to point out that the use of the singular in this case is intentional, since it responds more precisely to the idea contained in discourses on identity in so-called "nativisms."

15. My reading here has a strong and indispensable debt to Andrew Dobson's *Jean Paul Sartre and The Politics of Reason: A Theory of History*.

16. Lack in the sense of absence and not in the sense of error.

17. This is the place and the time to clarify that my reading of Sartre does not seriously regard the changes that the same philosopher later made to his concepts. I am simply using those passages that, from my point of view, appear more committed to Fanon's reading. An important note is the fact that the postwar work of Sartre will broaden the horizon of what he calls the situation and historical contexts. However, it could be ensured that Fanon had read all of Sartre's major works. An interesting fact about this can be seen in the meeting that they held in Italy referenced by Simone de Beauvoir in *The Force of Circumstance*, in which Fanon, already very ill, was impressed by the philosophy of Sartre. In that meeting he asked about *Critique of Dialectical Reason*, especially the analysis of "fraternity-terror." His interest was related to Lumumba's assassination. According to Beauvoir, Fanon saw that, before reaching any brotherhood, "the Negroes were going to kill each other" (677).

18. I abstain from saying "notion" or "concept" of freedom since it was never Sartre's task to find a definition of freedom in those terms.

19. It seems that the ending of both of Fanon's two most important texts refer to the same problem. In *The Wretched*, speaking of the solutions that should bring presence to the third world from a new global historical subject, Fanon points out: "What matters is to stop talking about output, and intensification, and the rhythm of work. No, there is no question of a return to Nature. It is simply a very concrete question of not dragging men toward mutilation, of not imposing upon the brain rhythms which very quickly obliterate it and wreck it" (originally cited, 209; 314). It is important to note here that Fanon's options for "nativisms" (an extremely fraught term of prejudices) should be contextually thought in relation to the concrete process that Fanon describes. When I refer to the context, in this case, I want to signify the specific contexts that Fanon's texts build and to the fact that Fanon treats certain subjects always in relation to a historical process. Later we will briefly see the problem of temporality but, for example, the discourses of opposition from the colonized are formulated as absolute at the time when they oppose the colonial regime. There is no such formulation when Fanon tries to think of postcolonial society.

CHAPTER IV

1. I refer here to Shahid Amin's book, *Event, Metaphor, Memory: Chauri Chaua, 1922–1992*; for commentary, see my article review "Historias de subalternos o cómo imaginar la nación desde la discontinuidad: una lectura" (Stories of Subordinates or How to Imagine the Nation from Discontinuity: A Reading).

2. Manthia Diawara, in an interview by V. Y. Mudimbe, points to similar theoretical perspectives of blackness and the European discourse of the Other. In relation to the annotation of Lazarus on Fanon's construction of a national consciousness which becomes or is unambiguous, Diawara states that blackness was caught in essentialist notions (also *Présence Africaine* as a place that reflects the discourse of blackness). He points out that, in response to the Manichean perspectives presented by Eurocentric visions of Africa and the perspectives of the Enlightenment, *Présence Africaine* was committed to relativism, but the paradox was that the categories used, for example blackness, found a solid foundation in the existing literature from the illustration and the re-thematization by Gobineau. Hence the use that blackness gave to the concepts of identity and race were "totalizing and Ethnocentric" (386–7).

3. Sekyi-Otu aptly points out that the "truth" of the nation in Fanon is not simply the consideration of an unambiguous reality. It represents a set of particular interrelated histories and shared projects (p. 37). It is also interesting to highlight Sekyi-Otu's critique with the reading of Christopher Miller in *Theories of Africans*, on the paragraph quoted in the main text. Miller cites the quote "the native replies . . . by an equal falsehood" to argue that Fanon defends a notion of truth that is exclusivist and dismisses peculiarities (34–5).

4. The scene Fanon describes is reminiscent of several passages in Albert Camus's *The Stranger*, a book that Fanon must have read. Although the main character (Meursault) is not exactly the colonized, he is somehow outside the expectations of colonial society. He looks at the world as if it happens without him being involved with it. The separation between Fanon's and Camus's texts can be seen better in the role that they assign to the subject. Camus's disbelief of any promise of redemption represents the environment of colonial society. The world is alien for Meursault and its discourses are also. Life and death are confused in a homogeneous scenario. The main continuity is, in some way, the repetition ad nausea of the context. It is a repetition that, despite its futility, produces positive acts: it threatens the lives of those who inhabit it. Therefore, the image of the static represents more than a pastoral, as can be seen in representations of the "natives" in the nineteenth century: it poses a threat.

5. The title of the Spanish version is *El Mediterráneo y el mundo mediterráneo en la época de Felipe II*. It was published by the Economic Culture Fund in Mexico in 1953. Those responsible for this excellent translation were Mario Monteforte Toledo and Wenceslao Roces. The title and publication information of the original French edition are included in the references section.

6. The reference to Freud here is inevitable. Reiteration or repetition refers to the way in which Freud conceives the distance between repetition and remembrance ("to remember, to repeat and to play"). For Freud, thinking from a psychoanalytic dimension, repetition blocks memory and, therefore, makes the past occur as the present, forgetting it justifiably as the past (Hornstein,

171). This is a central argument for the emancipation discourse that Fanon builds, if and when it is noted that the appeal in this case is to a collective subject. Reiterating the logic of colonial discourse is a kind of "pathology" in postcolonial societies. For this reason, I venture to say that displacement is a form of historicizing, as it relocates what corresponds in the past and frees the present from a mimetic act. Luis Hornstein, quoted here, uses an expression that reflects this point well: "Remember to Forget" (171). The static scene threatens to dissolve memory and convert time to a circle that no one leaves, as in the Moebius strip where there are no "outsides," "insides," "beginnings," or "endings." The static image is, on the other hand, a metaphor for mobility without change. Toward the end of *The Wretched of the Earth*, Fanon claims to "flee from this motionless movement where gradually dialectic is changing into the logic of equilibrium" (314).

7. An important annotation on the problem of colonial discourse, it is not a question of replacing the word colonialism, in terms of its historical implications, for the seemingly more complex concept of colonial discourse. In reality, the idea of colonial discourse evokes a long dialogue between postmodern and poststructuralist thinking and the analysis of colonial discourse. Ania Loomba makes this point, indicating that although the linkages are not always clear, for example, Foucault's theories derived from the Eurocentric models of prison reform (i.e., conceived from those cases), colonial situations permanently overlap. The idea is that colonial discourse implies a form of thought where intellectual, economic, and political processes are thought of as ensembles working in the direction of forming, perpetuating, or dismantling colonialism. There is an attempt, following colonial discourse, to think of the spaces where ideas, knowledge, and power intersect. Loomba points out that this intention was also present in nationalist ideologies, but that what studies of colonial discourse are trying to do is to deepen the analysis of colonial epistemologies and connect them to the history of colonial institutions (54).

8. I deal with this discussion in other parts of this study. For the most complete set of Bhabha's arguments, see "Of Mimicry and Man: The Ambivalence of Colonial Discourse" in *The Location of Culture*. For a perspective that partially recovers the "wrong" modes of appropriation of so-called natives (a term that has an extremely heavy burden, at least in Spanish), see the already classic book by Walter García Canclini, *Hybrid Cultures: Strategies for Entering and Leaving Modernity*. As you can see, Canclini's title suggests, I believe, that the "wrong" appropriations of the dominant discourse can be strategically thought. It can also be read as a parody of the supposed ability to subvert the "original" text.

9. I take this example from the website, "Postcolonial Studies," at Emory University. I could have followed the examples that Bhabha used, of Macauly, for example, but the idea of using the metaphor of the colonial text in the figure of Robinson Crusoe seems closer to our readings.

10. See my book, *El viaje de la escritura. Richard Francis Burton y el este de África* (The Journey of Writing: Richard Francis Burton and East Africa).

11. Deleuze and Guattari precisely point out that mimicry, or mimesis, is a "bad concept, since it relies on a binary logic to describe phenomena of an entirely different nature" (16). In the case of their critique of the model of representation, it does not appear as an image that reproduces the world, i.e., as its mirror, but connects with it through the rhizome. It is, according to them, to think of aparallel developments. They affirm the idea to reinforce the lines of escape of each body and to not concentrate it in the order of a hierarchy and in the figure of resemblance, of mimesis. They give a good example: "The Pink Panther imitates nothing, it reproduces nothing, it paints the world its color, pink on pink; this is its becoming-world, carried out in such a way that it becomes imperceptible itself, asignifying, makes its rupture, its own line of flight, follows its 'aparallel evolution' through to the end" (16). If we stop for one more moment to consider the problem of mimesis, we can see that in the imitation of colonial discourse, the repetition of its gesture without a meaning that centers it, authorizes and gives originality to what occurs in precisely a type of aparallel evolution that Deleuze and Guattari point out. The idea of aparallel evolution does not mean that there are no contacts or connection, rather there is difference, pure difference, but without the attribute nor the duty of having to prescribe a starting point of one with respect to the other.

CHAPTER V

1. See "Race Under Representation" for this author.
2. The centrality of all discourse is a key issue in postcolonial critique. See Pechey's article "On the Borders of Bakhtin: Dialogization, Decolonization."
3. The use here of the concept of hegemony is somewhat complex because while I am talking about a dispute to impose (by consensus and coercion) the visions of the world that held colonial societies, the material and political reality of these societies is not close to the key concepts and processes associated with Gramsci's perspective on hegemony: Political society and civil society. Gramsci in *Il Risorgimento* observes a correspondence between the development of civil society and "the role of hegemony that the dominant group exerts throughout society" (70). In the colonial context, hegemony as a concept encounters, as part of the analysis of developed capitalist societies, problems in specifying the concrete spaces that both civil society and the state occupy when there is no option for either factor. However, the way in which colonial discourses are embodied can link to one of the facets that the term has from the Gramscian perspective. Namely, "as a particular mode of leadership that is not based on the use of coercion or violence, but on the systematic spread of the world view of the ruling class" (100). For a discussion of the notion of

the "subaltern" related to the concept of hegemony in Gramsci see *Beyond Postcolonial Theory* by Epifanio San Juan. My use of the concept here is more sui generis, in that I am not carrying out the analysis of a specific historical process looking for the ways in which hegemony is articulated and the forms that assume the counterhegemonic practices of certain social groups. Rather, I discuss the forms that assume the tensions of Fanon's oppositional discourse regarding the need to define or not define the enunciations of oppositional practice, to define in terms of regulating the syntax and semantics of that discourse.

4. Amin's proposal implicitly contains Bhabha's idea of imitation (mimicry) by means of which the colonial discourse unfolds. The presence of the colonized in the text of the colonizer undermines the authority or the authenticity of it. For Bhabha, the resistance of the colonized introduces an element of destabilization in the affirmations of the colonial text. In a sense they are the signs of a discontinuous history. For my argument here, the imitation responds to the logic that Bhabha assigns to it, that more than to represent, the mere act of repetition causes its originality to be lost, and its centrality to be decentered (88). The repetition of the Gandhian discourse of the nation by the peasants of Chauri Chaura registers in this direction. Amin shows how the discourse of the nation tries to avoid, even in its monuments, a certain hybrid condition of its narration. However, repetition always opens a critical space not controlled by the hegemonic textual authority. Thus, the same ones that before the revolt were active members of the movement of noncooperation (and were those that had erected Gandhi as the Mahatma), when producing a repetition of the discourse of the nation, write a differentiated text generating its unfolding. Obviously, the history that Amin constructs also attempts to show how the "text" of the nation is disturbed in perceiving the unfolding and loss of authority.

CHAPTER VI

1. I use this metaphor of the *halakhah* from a text by Yosef Yerushalmi, "Reflections on Forgetting," where alongside other historians, he discusses the "Uses of Forgetting." Drawing from the tradition of the Torah, in which the term refers to Jewish law, Yerushalmi rescues the concept of *halakhah*, which also has the meaning of "sense" or of an organizing principle of history, to express its desire to find some guiding criterion on the reflections of the past, beyond a "possible excess of historiography," in a Nietzschean manner. Yerushalmi makes an extremely metaphorical use of the concept to illustrate a theoretical but also ethical position against arguments that, in some way, call for silence. My use has the same meaning.

2. It is, from my perspective, the notion of estrangement. Although Marx develops the concept in terms of the estrangement of the proletariat from the

productive forces and the process of production, the metaphor of estrangement is functional in Fanon's text. What he highlights is the estrangement of the colonized, in terms of representation, from the material and symbolic conditions of colonial society.

3. Dennis Walder points out that Spivak's strategy is premised on the fact that most of the subalterns' accounts have been constructed by colonizers or by the indigenous elite. Once the Other has been "Orientalized," one must ask the question: "can the subaltern speak?" (111).

BY WAY OF CONCLUSION

1. I am referring back to the problem of Spivak's strategic essentialisms discussed earlier in this work. As a brief reminder, when I speak of strategy, I refer to the conscious act of exploring and using the essentialist character of certain ideological positions or of certain discourses on identity in order to show, precisely, the historical character that they possess. A "use" that is linked to the problem of locating discourses in the area where both the dominant discourse and those in a resistant situation are articulated and produced.

FRANTZ FANON

1. This short biographical synopsis is fundamentally based on Richard C. Onwuanbe's *A Critique of Revolutionary Humanism*. For more extensive references and more detail as to the events of Fanon's life, see the quoted texts of Caute, Geismar, Gendzier, Hansen, and Zahar.

WORKS OF FRANTZ FANON

1. I refer here to his best-known works. I do not include, for example, those of which he was coauthor. Also, wherever possible, I mention the publication in Spanish. I do not cite his articles in the *Moudjahid* and other magazines. For the purposes of references, you can see a complete list of his articles in the edited book already quoted by Anthony C. Alessandrini.

2. Published after the original, Spanish publication of this study.

Bibliography

Amin, Shahid. 1995. *Event, Metaphor, Memory: Chauri Chaura, 1922–1992.* Berkeley: University of California Press.
Anderson, Benedict. 1993. *Comunidades Imaginadas.* México: Fondo de Cultura Económica.
[———. 1993. *Imagined Communities.* New York: Verso Books.]
Alessandrini, Anthony C. 1999. *Frantz Fanon: Critical Perspectives.* New York: Routledge.
Barthes, Roland. 1998. *El placer del texto y lección inaugural.* México: Siglo XXI.
[———. 1973. *The Pleasure of the Text.* New York: Hill and Wang.]
———. 1979. "Lecture in Inauguration of the Chair of Literary Semiology, Collège de France, January 7, 1977". Trans. by Richard Howard. In *October* vol. 8 (Spring): 3–16.
Benjamin, Walter. 1998. *Poesía y capitalismo. Iluminaciones II.* Madrid: Taurus.
[———. 1969. *Illuminations: Essays and Reflections.* Trans. by Harry Zohn. New York: Schocken Books.]
———. 1971. *París, capital del siglo XIX.* México: Madero.
[———. 1969. "Paris, Capital of the Nineteenth Century". In *Perspecta* vol. 12: 163–172.]
Berman, Marshall. 1991. "Las señales en la calle" en Nicolás Casullo (comp.) *El debate modernidad posmodernidad.* Buenos Aires: Puntosur.
———. 1989. *Todo lo sólido se desvanece en el aire. La experiencia de la modernidad.* México: Siglo XXI.
[———. 1988. *All that Is Solid Melts into Air: The Experience of Modernity.* New York: Penguin Books.]

Bhabha, Homi k. 1996. *The Fact of Blackness. Frantz Fanon and Visual Representation.* Ed. by Alan Read. Seattle: Bay Press. 186–205.

———. 1994. *The Location of Culture.* New York: Routledge. 123–138.

———. 1994. "Interrogating Identity. Frantz Fanon and the Postcolonial Prerogative". In *The Location of Culture.* New York: Routledge. 40–65.

———. 1994. "On Mimicry and Man: The Ambivalence of Colonial Discourse". In *The Location of Culture.* New York: Routledge. 85–92.

———. 1994. "The Other Question. Stereotype, Discrimination and the Discourse of Colonialism". In *The Location of Culture.* New York: Routledge. 66–84.

———. 1991. "A Question of Survival: Nations and Psychic States". In *Psychoanalysis and Cultural Theory: Thresholds.* Ed. by J. Donald. London: Macmillan/ICA. 89–103.

Bjorson, Richard. 1992. "Alienation and Disalienation: Themes of Yesterday, Promises of Tomorrow". In *The Surreptitious Speech: Présence Africaine and the Politics of Otherness 1947–1987.* Ed. by V. Y. Mudimbe. Chicago: Chicago University Press. 147–156.

Bloch, Marc. 1965. *Introducción a la historia.* México: Fondo de Cultura Económica.

[———. 1964. *The Historian's Craft: Reflections on the Nature and Uses of History and the Techniques and Methods of Those Who Write It.* Trans. by Peter Putnam. Toronto: Alfred A. Knopf.]

Braudel, Fernand. 1990. *La Méditerranée et le monde méditerranéen à l'époque de Philippe II.* París: A. Colin.

[———. 1995. *The Mediterranean and the Mediterranean World in the Age of Philip II.* Trans. Siân Reynolds. Berkeley: University of California Press.]

Camus, Albert. 1982. *El extranjero.* Madrid: Alianza Editorial.

[———. 1989. *The Stranger.* Trans. by Matthew Ward. New York: Vintage Books.]

Carlyle, Thomas. 1976. *Los héroes. El culto de los héroes y lo heroico en la historia.* México: Editorial Porrúa.

Caute, David. 1970. *Fanon.* London: Wm. Collins & Co. Ltd.

Chow, Rey. 1998. *Ethics after Idealism: Theory, Culture, Ethnicity, Reading.* Bloomington: Indiana University Press.

Cioran, E. M. 1992. *Ejercicios de admiración y otros textos. Ensayos y retratos.* Barcelona: Tusquests Editores.

Clifford, James. 1995. *Dilemas de la cultura. Antropología, literatura y arte en la perspectiva posmoderna.* Barcelona, Gedisa.

[———. 1988. *The Predicament of Culture: Twentieth-Century Ethnography, Literature, and Art.* Cambridge: Harvard University Press.]

Clifford, James and George E. Marcus. Editors. 1986. *Writing Culture: The Poetics and Politics of Ethnography*. Los Angeles: University of California Press.

Coetzee, J. M. 1982. *Waiting for the Barbarians*. New York: Penguin Books.

Coletti Pischel, Enrica. 1970. "'Fanonismo' y 'Cuestión colonial'" Traducción de Miguel Camperchioli, en Peter Geismar, Peter Worsley y Collotti Pischel, *Frantz Fanon y la Revolución Anticolonial*. Buenos Aires: Ediciones del Siglo. 19–30.

Conrad, Joseph. 2007. *The Heart of Darkness*. London: Penguin Classics.

Córdoba, Ricardo. 1970. "Prólogo" en Peter Geismar, Peter Worsley y Collotti Pischel, *Frantz Fanon y la revolución anticolonial*. Buenos Aires: Ediciones del Siglo. 7–30.

De Beauvoir, Simone. 1986. *Las fuerza de las cosas*, Ezequiel de Olaso (trad). México: Editorial Hermes.

[———. 1965. *The Force of Circumstance*. Trans. by R. Howard. New York: Harper Collins.]

De Certeau, Michel. 1993. *La escritura de la historia*. México: Departamento de Historia Universidad Iberoamericana.

[———. 1988. *The Writing of History*. Trans. by Tom Conley. New York: Columbia University Press.]

Defoe, Daniel. 2012, *Robinson Crusoe*. London: Penguin English Library.

De Lauretis, Teresa. 1990. "La esencia del triángulo, o tomarse en serio el riesgo del esencialismo: teoría feminista en Italia, los EUA y gran Bretaña" en *Debate Feminista*, núm. 2, septiembre: 77–115.

[———. 1994. "The Essence of the Triangle or, Taking the Risk of Essentialism Seriously: Feminist Theory in Italy, the U.S., and Britain". In *The Essential Difference*. Ed. by Naomi Schor and Elizabeth Weed. Bloomington: Indiana University Press.]

Deleuze, Gilles and Félix Guattari. 1988. *Mil mesetas. Capitalismo y esquizofrenia*. Valencia: Pre Textos.

[———. 1987. *A Thousand Plateaus: Capitalism and Schizophrenia*. Minneapolis: University of Minnesota Press.]

De Oto, Alejandro. 1999. "Historias de subalternos o cómo pensar a la nación desde la discontinuidad. Una lectura" en *Estudios de Asia y África*, núm. 3, septiembre–diciembre: 611–622.

———. 1996. *El viaje de la escritura. Richard Francis Burton y el Este de África*. México: El Colegio de México.

Derrida, Jacques. 1998. *Espectros de Marx. El Estado de la deuda, el trabajo del duelo y la nueva Internacional,* José Miguel Alarcón y Cristina de Peretti (trads.). Madrid: Trotta.

[———. 1994. *Specters of Marx: The State of the Debt, the Work of Mourning, and The New International*. Trans. by Peggy Kamuf. New York: Routledge.]

———. 1971. *De la gramatología*, Oscar del Barco, Conrado Ceretti (trad.). Buenos Aires: Siglo XXI.
[———. 1976. *Of Grammatology*. Trans. by Gayatri Chakravorty Spivak. Baltimore: Johns Hopkins University Press.]
Devalle, Susana. 1996. *Saadat Hasan Manto. Antología de cuentos*, Daniel de Palma (trad. Del urdu). México: El Colegio de México.
Diawara, Manthia. 1992. "Analysts". In *The Surreptitious Speech. Présence Africaine and the Politics of Otherness 1947–1987*. Ed. by V. Y. Mudimbe. Chicago: Chicago University Press. 382–403.
Dobson, Andrew. 1993. *Jean Paul Sartre and the Politics of Reason*. Cambridge: Cambridge University Press.
Dostoevsky, Fyodor. 1994. *Notes from Underground*. London: Vintage Classics.
Du Bois, W.E.B. 1989. *The Souls of Black Folk*. New York: Penguin.
Duby, Georges. 1989. *Hombres y estructuras de la Edad Media*, Reyna Pastor (pról.). México: Siglo XXI.
Febvre, Lucien. 1993. *Combates por la historia*. Barcelona: Planeta Agostini.
[———. 1973. *A New Kind of History: From the Writings of Lucien Febvre*. Ed. by Peter Burke. New York: Harper and Row.]
Feuchtwang, Stephan. 1987. "Fanonian Spaces". In *New Formations* vol. 1 (Spring): 124–130.
Foucault, Michel. 1996. *Genealogía del racismo*. La Plata: Editorial Altamira.
———. 1988. "Por qué estudiar el poder: la cuestión del sujeto," en Hubert L. Dreyfus y Paul Rabinow, *Michel Foucault: Más allá del estructuralismo y la hermenéutica*. México: Universidad Autónoma Nacional.
[———. 1982. *Beyond Structuralism and Hermeneutics*. Ed. by Hubert L. Dreyfus and Paul Rabinow. Chicago: University of Chicago Press.]
[_____. 1982, Summer. "The Subject and Power," *Critical Inquiry* vol. 8, no. 4: 777–795.
Freud, Sigmund. 1914. "Recordar, repetir, reelaborar. (Nuevos consejos sobre la técnica del psicoanálisis; II)" en *Sigmund Freud, Obras completas*. Buenos Aires: Amorrortu, vol. XII, 1990: 146–157.
[———. 1914. "Remembering, Repeating and Working-Through (Further Recommendations on the Technique of Psycho-Analysis II)". In *The Standard Edition of the Complete Psychological Works of Sigmund Freud, Volume XII (1911–1913)*. Downloaded Nov. 15, 2018: https://www.marxists.org/reference/subject/philosophy/works/at/catharsis.htm]
Fuss, Diana. 1994. "Interior Colonies: Frantz Fanon and the Politics of Identification". In *Diacritics* vol. 24, no. 2–3: 20–42.
Gaines, Jr., Stanley O. 1996. "Perspectives of Du Bois and Fanon on the Psychology of Oppression". In *Fanon: A Critical Reader*. Ed. by Lewis R.

Gordon, T. Denean Sharpley-Whiting, Renée T. White. Oxford: Blackwell Publishers. 24–35.

Galiana, Antonio Azaustre and Juan Casas Rigall. 1994. *Introducción al análisis retórico: tropos, figuras y sintaxis del estilo.* Santiago de Compostela: Universidad de Santiago de Compostela.

García Canclini, Walter. 1995. *Culturas híbridas. Estrategias para entrar y salir de la modernidad.* México: Grijalbo.

[———. 1995. *Hybrid Cultures: Strategies for Entering and Leaving Modernity.* Trans. by Christopher L. Chiappari and Silvia L. Lopez. Minneapolis: University of Minnesota Press.]

Gates, Jr., Henry Louis. 1991. "Critical Fanonism". In *Critical Inquiry* vol. 17 no. 3: 457–470.

Geismar, Peter. 1970. "Frantz Fanon: evolución de un revolucionario" Juan Gelman (trad.) en Peter Geismar, Peter Worsley y Coletti Pischel, *Frantz Fanon y la revolución anticolonial.* Buenos Aires: Ediciones del Siglo. 19–30.

———. 1969. "Frantz Fanon: Evolution of a Revolutionary". In *Monthly Review* vol. 21 no. 1: 22–30.

Gendzier, Irene. 1973. *Frantz Fanon: A Critical Study.* New York: Pantheon.

Gibson, Nigel. 1999. "Fanon and the Pitfalls of Cultural Studies". In *Frantz Fanon: Critical Perspectives.* Ed. by Anthony C. Alessandrini. New York: Routledge. 99–125.

———. 1999. Editor. *Rethinking Fanon: The Continuing Dialogue.* New York: Humanities Books.

Gikandi, Simon. 1991. *Reading Chinua Achebe: Language & Ideology in Fiction.* London: J. Currey.

Ginzburg, Carlo. 1986. *El queso y los gusanos.* Barcelona: Muchnik Editores.

[———. 1980. *The Cheese and the Worms: The Cosmos of a Sixteenth-Century Miller.* Trans. by John Tedeschi and Anne C. Tedeschi. Baltimore: Johns Hopkins University Press.]

Goldie, Terrie. 1999. "Saint Fanon and 'Homosexual Territory'". In *Frantz Fanon: Critical Perspectives.* Ed. by Anthony C. Alessandrini. New York: Routledge. 75–86.

Gómez de Silva, Guido. 1988. *Breve diccionario de la lengua española.* México: Fondo de Cultura Económica.

Gordon, Lewis. 2015. *What Fanon Said: A Philosophical Introduction to His Life and Thought.* New York: Fordham University Press.

———. 1995. *Fanon and the Critic of European Man. An Essay on Philosophy and the Human Sciences.* Nueva York: Routledge.

———. 1996. "Fanon's Tragic Revolutionary Violence". In *Fanon: A Critical Reader.* Ed. by Lewis Gordon, T. Denean Sharply-Whiting, and Renée T. White. Oxford: Blackwell Publishers. 297–308.

Gordon, Lewis, T. Denean Sharply-Whiting, and Renée T. White. Editors. 1996. *Fanon: A Critical Reader*. Oxford: Blackwell Publishers.
Gramsci, Antonio. 1954. *Il Risorgimento*. Turín: Einaudi De.
Grass, Günter. 1999. *Escribir después de Auschwitz*. Barcelona: Paidós.
[―――. 1990. "Writing After Auschwitz". In *Two States-One Nation?* Trans. by Arthur S. Wensinger. Boston: Houghton Mifflin Harcourt.]
Greimas, A. J. and J. Courtés. 1979. *Sémiotique: Dictionnaire raisonné de la théorie du langage*. París: Hachette.
Grüner, Eduardo. 2002. *El fin de las pequeñas historias. De los estudios culturales al retorno (imposible) de lo trágico*. Buenos Aires: Paidós.
Guha, Ranajit and Gayatri Spivak. Editors. 1988. *Selected Subaltern Studies*. New York: Oxford University Press.
Hall, Stuart. 1997. "Cultural Identity and Diaspora". In *Contemporary Postcolonial Theory*. Ed. by Padmini Mongi. New York: Bloomsbury Academic. 110–121.
―――. 1996. "The After-life of Frantz Fanon: Why Fanon? Why Now? Why Black Skin, White Masks?". In *The Fact of Blackness: Frantz Fanon and Visual Representation*. Ed. by Alan Read. Seattle: Bay Press. 12–37.
Hansen, Emmanuel. 1999. "Frantz Fanon: Portrait of a Revolutionary". In *Rethinking Fanon: The Continuing Dialogue*. Ed. by Nigel C. Gibson. New York: Humanities Books. 49–82.
Harris, Leonard and Carolyn Johnson. 1996. "Foreword". In *Fanon: A Critical Reader*. Ed. by Lewis R. Gordon, T. Denean Sharpley-Whiting, and Renée T. White. Oxford: Blackwell Publishers. xiv–xxi.
Hayes, I., Floyd W. 1996. "Fanon, Oppression, and Resentment: The Black Experience in the United States". In *Fanon: A Critical Reader*. Ed. by Lewis R. Gordon, T. Denean Sharpley-Whiting, and Renée T. White. Oxford: Blackwell Publishers. 11–23.
Hobsbawm, Eric. 1983. *Marxismo e historia social*. México: Universidad Autónoma de Puebla.
[―――. 1968. "Karl Marx's Contribution to Historiography". In *Marx and Contemporary Scientific Thought: Papers from the Symposium on the Role of Karl Marx in the Development of Contemporary Scientific Thought*. The Hague: Mouton.]
hooks, bell. 1996. "Feminism as a Persistent Critique of History: What's Love got to Do with It?" In *The Fact of Blackness. Frantz Fanon and Visual Representation*. Ed. by Alan Read. Seattle: Bay Press. 76–85.
Hornstein, Luis. 1990. "Recordar, repetir y reelaborar: una lectura" en Silvia Bleichmar et al., *Lecturas de Freud*. Buenos Aires: Lugar Editorial. 171–210.
Husserl, Edmund. 1992. *Invitación a la fenomenología*. [Invitation to Phenomenology]. Barcelona: Paidós.

Irele, Abiola. 1992. "In Praise of Alienation". In *The Subrreptitious Speech: Présence Africaine and the Politics of Otherness 1947–1987*. Ed. by V. Y. Mudimbe. Chicago: Chicago University Press. 201–234.

Jaspers, Karl. 1972. *Conferencias y ensayos*. Madrid, Gredos.

———. 1968. *Origen y meta de la historia*. Madrid: Ed. Castilla S. A. (Revista de Occidente).

[———. 1953. *The Origin and Goal of History*. England: Routledge.]

———. 1953. *La filosofía desde el punto de vista de la existencia*. México: Fondo de Cultura Económica.

[———. 1971. *Philosophy of Existence*. Trans. by Richard F. Grabau. Philadelphia: University of Pennsylvania.]

Jules-Rosette, Bennetta. 1992. "Conjugating Cultural Realities: Présence Africaine". In *The Surreptitious Speech: Présence Africaine and the Politics of Otherness 1947–1987*. Ed. by V. Y. Mudimbe. Chicago: Chicago University Press. 14–44.

Kawash, Samira. 1999. "Terrorists and Vampires: Fanon's Spectral Violence of Decolonization". In *Frantz Fanon: Critical Perspectives*. Ed. by Anthony C. Alessandrini. New York: Routledge. 235–257.

Kiros, Teodros. 1985. *Toward the Construction of a Theory of Political Action; Antonio Gramsci*. New York: University Press of America.

Kruks, Sonia. 1996. "Fanon, Sartre, and Identity Politics". In *Fanon: A Critical Reader*. Ed. Lewis R. Gordon, T. Denean Sharpley-Whiting, and Renée T. White. Oxford: Blackwell Publishers. 122–133.

Krupat, Arnold. 1992. *Ethnocriticism: Ethnography, History, Literature*. Los Angeles: University of California Press.

Lazarus, Neil. 1999. "Disavowing Decolonization: Fanon, Nationalism, and the Question of Representation in Postcolonial Theory". In *Frantz Fanon: Critical Perspectives*. Ed. By Anthony C. Alessandrini. New York: Routledge. 161–194.

Levinas, Emmanuel. 1993. *Entre nosotros*. Valencia: Pre-textos.

[———. 1998. *Entre Nous: on thinking-of-the-other*. Trans. by Michael B. Smith and Barbara Harshav. New York: Columbia University.]

Lloyd, David. 1991. "Race Under Representation". In *Oxford Literary Review* vol. 13 no. 1–2: 62–94.

Loomba, Ania. 1998. *Colonialism/Postcolonialism*. New York: Routledge.

Lucas, Philippe. 1973. *Sociología de la descolonización*. Buenos Aires: Ediciones Nueva Visión.

Martin, Denis-Constant. 1992. "Out of Africa! Should We Be Done with Africanism?" In *The Surreptitious Speech. Présence Africaine and the Politics of Otherness 1947–1987*. Ed. by V. Y. Mudimbe. Chicago: Chicago University Press. 45–56.

Marx, Karl. 1982. *Introducción general a la crítica de la economía política*, Umberto Curi (intr.). México: Siglo XXI editores.
———. 1973. *La ideología alemana*. Buenos Aires: Ediciones Pueblos Unidos.
[———. 1998. *The German Ideology*. New York: Prometheus Books.]
Mastrogregori, Massimo. 1998. *El manuscrito interrumpido de Marc Bloch. Apología para la historia o el oficio de historiador*. México: Fondo de Cultura Económica.
McClintock, Anne. 1999. "Fanon and Gender Agency". In *Rethinking Fanon: The Continuing Dialogue*. Ed. by Nigel C. Gibson. New York: Humanities Books. 283–293.
McGee, Patrick. 1992. *Telling the Other: The Question of Value in Modern and Postcolonial Writing*. Ithaca: Cornell University Press.
Melas, Natalie. 199. "Versions of Incommensurability". In *World Literature Today* vol. 69 no. 2: 275–280.
Memmi, Albert. 1965. *The Colonizer and the Colonized*. New York: The Orion Press.
Mercer, Kobena. 1999. "Busy in the Ruins of a Wretched Phantasia". In *Frantz Fanon: Critical Perspectives*. Ed. by Anthony C. Alessandrini. New York: Routledge. 195–218.
———. 1996. "Decolonisation and Disappointment: Reading Fanon's Sexual Politics". In *The Fact of Blackness: Frantz Fanon and Visual Representation*. Ed. by in Alan Read. Seattle: Bay Press. 114–131.
Miller, Christopher. 1992. "Alioune Diop and the Unfinished Temple of Knowledge". In *The Surreptitious Speech: Présence Africaine and the Politics of Otherness 1947–1987*. Ed. by V. Y. Mudimbe. Chicago: Chicago University Press. 427–434.
———. 1990. *Theories of Africans: Francophone Literature and Anthropology in Africa*. Chicago: University of Chicago Press.
Mouralis, Bernard. 1992. "Présence Africaine: Geography of an 'Ideology'". In *The Surreptitious Speech. Présence Africaine and the Politics of Otherness 1947–1987*. Ed. V. Y. Mudimbe. Chicago: Chicago University Press. 3–13.
Mudimbe, V. Y. 1992. "Introduction". In *The Surreptitious Speech: Présence Africaine and the Politics of Otherness 1947–1987*. Ed. by V. Y. Mudimbe. Chicago: The University of Chicago Press. xvii–xxvi.
———. 1988. *The Invention of Africa: Gnosis, Philosophy and the Order of Knowledge*. Bloomington: Indiana University Press.
Nietzsche, Frederick. 1962. *Obras completas. Consideraciones Intempestivas, tomo I*, Eduardo Ovejero y Maury (trad., introd. y notas). Buenos Aires: Aguilar.
Parry, Benita. 1997. "Resistance Theory/Theorizing Resistance, Or Two Cheers for Nativism". In *Contemporary Postcolonial Theory*. Ed. by Padmini Mongia. New York: Bloomsbury Academic. 84–109.

———. 1995. "Problems in Current Theories of Colonial Discourse". In *The Post-Colonial Studies Reader*. Ed. by Bill Ashcroft, Gareth Griffiths y Helen Tiffin. New York: Routledge. 36–45.
Pechey, Graham. 1987. "On the Borders of Bakhtin: Dialogization, Decolonization". In *Oxford Literary Review* vol. 9 no. 1–2: 59–85.
Perinbam, Marie. B. 1982. *Holy Violence: The Revolutionary Thought of Frantz Fanon, an Intellectual Biography*. Washington: Three Continents Press.
Posnock, Ross. 1997. "How It Feels to Be a Problem: Du Bois, Fanon, and the 'Impossible Life' of the Black Intellectual". In *Critical Inquiry* vol. 23: 323–349.
Pratt, Mary Louise. 1992. *Imperial Eyes: Travel Writing and Transculturation*. London: Routledge.
Rigby, Peter. 1992. "Practical Ideology and Ideological Practice: On African Episteme and Marxian Problematic – Ilparakuyo Maasai Transformations". In *The Surreptitious Speech: Présence Africaine and the Politics of Otherness 1947–1987*. Ed. by V. Y. Mudimbe. Chicago: Chicago University Press. 257–300.
Said, Edward. 1999. "Travelling Theory Reconsidered". In *Rethinking Fanon: The Continuing Dialogue*. Ed. by Nigel C. Gibson. New York: Humanities Books. 197–214.
———. 1993. *Culture and Imperialism*. New York: Knopf.
———. 1983. *The World, the Text, and the Critic*. Cambridge: Harvard University Press.
Sandoval, Lisandro. 1930. *Diccionario de raíces griegas y latinas y de otros orígenes del idioma español, tomo I*. Guatemala: Tipografía Nacional.
San Juan, Jr., Epifanio. 1999. "Fanon: An Intervention into Cultural Studies". In *Frantz Fanon: Critical Perspectives*. Ed. by Anthony C. Alessandrini. New York: Routledge. 126–145.
———. 1998. *Beyond Postcolonial Theory*. New York: St. Martin's Press.
Sarmiento, Domingo Faustino. 1961. *Facundo*. Buenos Aires: CEAL.
Sartre, Jean Paul. 1998. *El ser y la nada*. Buenos Aires: Losada.
[———. 1956. *Being and Nothingness*. Trans. by Hazel E. Barnes. New York: Washington Square Press.]
———. 1976. *Black Orpheus*. París: Présence Africaine.
———. 1954. *Réflexions sur la question juive*. París: Gallimard.
[———. 2009. *Reflections on the Jewish Question*. Trans. by Jonathan Judaken. Lincoln: University of Nebraska Press.]
Sarup, Madan. 1999. "Imperialismo y cultura" en Santiago Castro-Gómez, Oscar Guardiola Rivera y Carmen Millán de Benavides (eds.). *Pensar (en) los intersticios. Teoría y práctica de la crítica poscolonial*. Bogotá: Centro Editorial Javeriano. 21–43.

Schmitt, Richard. 1996. "Racism and Objectification: Reflections on Themes from Fanon". In *Fanon: A Critical Reader*. Ed. by Lewis R. Gordon, T. Denean Sharpley-Whiting, and Renée T. White. Oxford: Blackwell Publishers. 35–52.

Sekyi-Otu, Ato. 1996. *Fanon's Dialectic of Experience*. Cambridge: Harvard University Press.

Shohat, Elle. 1992. "Notes on the 'Post-Colonial'". In *Social Text* vol. 31–32: 99–113.

Souffrant, Eddy. 1996. "To Conquer the Veil: Woman as Critique of Liberalism". In *Fanon: A Critical Reader*. Ed. by Lewis R. Gordon, T. Denean Sharpley-Whiting, and Renée T. White. Oxford: Blackwell Publishers. 170–178.

Spivak, Gayatri. 1993. *Outside in the Teaching Machine*. New York: Routledge.

———. 1990. *The Post-colonial Critic: Interviews, Strategies, Dialogues*. Ed. by Sarah Harasym. New York: Routledge.

———. 1988. "Can the Subaltern Speak?". In *Marxism and the Interpretation of Culture*. Ed. by Cary Nelson and Lawrence Grossberg. London: Macmillan. 271–313.

Stevens, Maurice. 1996. "Public (Re)Memory, Vindicating Narratives, and Troubling Beginnings: Toward a Critical Postcolonial Psychoanalitical Theory". In *Fanon: A Critical Reader*. Ed. by Lewis R. Gordon, T. Denean Sharpley-Whiting, and Renée T. White. Oxford: Blackwell Publishers. 203–219.

Tedlock, Dennis. 1992. "Sobre la representación del discurso en el discurso" en Carlos Reynoso (comp.), *El surgimiento de la antropología posmoderna*. Barcelona: Gedisa. 295–296.

Thévenaz, Pierre. 1962. *What is Phenomenology and Other Essays*. Chicago: Quadrangle Books.

Tyler, Stephen. 1992. "La etnografía posmoderna: de documento de lo oculto a documento oculto" en Carlos Reynoso (comp.), *El surgimiento de la antropología posmoderna*, Barcelona: Gedisa. 297–314.

Vergés, Francoise. 1996. "To Cure and to Free: The Fanonian Project of Decolonized Psychiatry". In *Fanon: A Critical Reader*. Ed. by Lewis R. Gordon, T. Denean Sharpley-Whiting, and Renée T. White. Oxford: Blackwell Publishers. 85–99.

Walder, Dennis. 1998. *Post-colonial Literature in English, History, Language, Theory*. Oxford: Blackwell.

Wallraff, Charles. 1997. *Karl Jaspers: An Introduction to His Philosophy*. Princeton: Princeton University Press.

Western, Wilda. 1997. *Alquimia de la nación*. México: El Colegio de México.

White, Renée T. "Revolutionary Theory: Sociological Dimensions of Fanon's Sociologie d'une revolution". In *Fanon: A Critical Reader*. Ed. by Lewis R.

Gordon, T. Denean Sharpley-Whiting, and Renée T. White. Oxford: Blackwell Publishers. 35–52.
Williams, Raymond. 1980. *Marxismo y literatura.* Barcelona: Edicions 62 s/a.
[———. 1977. *Marxism and Literature.* Oxford: Oxford University Press.]
Worsley, Peter. 1970. "La teoría revolucionaria de Frantz Fanon" Juan Gelman (trad.), en Peter Geismar, Peter Worsley y Coletti Pischel, *Frantz Fanon y la Revolución Anticolonial*. Buenos Aires: Ediciones del Siglo. 31–58.
Yerushalmi, Yosef H. 1989. "Reflexiones sobre el olvido" en *Usos del olvido. Comunicaciones al coloquio de Royaumont.* Buenos Aires: Ediciones Nueva Visión. 13–26.
Young, Lola. 1996. "Missing Persons: Fantasising Black Woman in *Black Skin, White Masks*". In *The Fact of Blackness: Frantz Fanon and Visual Representation*. Ed. by Alan Read. Seattle: Bay Press. 86–101.
Zahar, Renate. 1974. *Frantz Fanon: Colonialism and Alienation.* London: Monthly Review Press.

Index

Achebe, Chinua, 126
Adlerian, 99, 101, 122
Africa, 96, 97, 106, 113, 132; African narrative, 126; African Revolution (Algerian War), 19–20; country of the mind, 68; non-Africa, 97; post-independence, 131
Africanity, 93
Alessandrini, Anthony, 9
Algeria, 86, 132; independence, 24
alienation, 1, 13, 16, 25, 27, 31–32, 57, 61, 64–65, 79–80, 84, 88, 92–93, 95–96, 100, 105–10, 112, 121, 122, 124; colonial, 104, 109; disalienation, 82, 110
All that is Solid Melts into Air, 30
ambivalence, 10, 23, 25, 30–31, 55–61, 66, 79, 81–82, 84, 88, 90–93, 95, 98, 101–2, 112–16, 121, 125, 130–31
Amin, Shahid, 107
anachronism, 7
Anderson, Perry, 30
animalization, 96
anomaly, 23–25, 27

anti-colonial, 22, 33; revolution, 20; struggle, 85, 101
anti-imperialist, 79
Antilles, 21, 27, 100, 101, 122, 132
antimodern, 16, 20
assimilation, 80, 81, 100, 112, 123
au-delà, 33
authorial authority, 1, 6, 8, 64–65, 130; Fanon the author, 2

Bakhtin, Mikhail, 103
Bakunin, Mikhail, 28–29
"barbarie", 119
barbarity, 30
Barthes, Roland, 130
Baudelaire, Charles, 28–29
Beauvoir, Simone de, 72
becoming, 58
"In the Beginning: The Search for Roots, 1925–1952", 23
Being, 12–13; "Some" and "Certain", 56
Benjamin, Walter, 29
Berman, Marshall, 30, 117
Bhabha, Homi, 2, 8, 9, 76–79, 81, 88–93, 126, 129–31

The Birth of The Clinic, 27
Bjorson, Richard, 64, 105–6
Black, 16, 97; agency, 111; consciousness, 106; subject, 14
Black Americans, 8
blackness, 14, 23, 59, 60, 62, 67, 68, 71, 94, 96–98, 102, 109, 112–15, 123, 131; fact of, 72; representation of, 63; structure of feeling, 58; use of, 66; visceral attachment, 66; and whiteness, 65
Black Skin, White Masks, 2, 5, 8, 13–14, 16–17, 22, 25–26, 29, 56, 57, 61, 63, 65, 67, 72–73, 84, 89, 94–96, 98–105, 108, 110–11, 114, 119–21, 124–27, 131–32
Bloch, Marc, 13, 86
borders, 16, 33–34
Braudel, Fernand, 85, 86, 88, 89, 97
Burton, Richard Francis, 28–29, 92

Capital, 30
Carlyle, Thomas, 25–26
catachresis, the end of, 104
Césaire, Aimé, 21, 55, 66, 95, 117
Chauri Chaua, 107
Chow, Rey, 7, 60–62, 81, 107, 130
Clifford, James, 21
Coletti Pischel, Enrica, 20, 25
colonial discourse, 33–34, 60, 88–93, 95, 117, 120, 125–26; anti-colonial, 22, 33; desire, 119; European, 56; history, 120, 125; identification, 89; modernism, 10; occupation, 55; silence, 27, 66, 125–26; situation, 76, 85, 93, 98; society, 13, 34, 84, 87, 88, 95, 101, 104, 106, 107, 116, 120–23, 126–28; subject, 56, 107; violence, 23
colonialism, 19, 33–34, 79, 90, 96, 98, 99, 102, 106, 130
colonialist, 31

colonization, 82, 87, 97, 112, 120
colonized, 16, 25, 31–32, 86–92, 94–96, 99–101, 104, 106, 107, 109, 110, 112, 114, 115, 119, 121–26; consciousness of, 22–26, 30, 32; societies, 55; subject, 10, 14
colonizer, 31, 87, 89, 91, 92, 102
The Colonizer and the Colonized, 31–32
community, 59, 60, 62, 70, 100, 102, 125, 126, 128; moral, 129
confinement, 129; logics of, 4
Conrad, Joseph, 28
consciousness, 22–26, 30, 32, 69, 75–76, 80–82, 84, 107–9, 111, 116, 119, 122, 128; absolute, 58; Black, 106; colonized, 26, 28; political, 87
Cordoba, Ricardo, 19, 20, 24
cultural authenticity, 111; determinism, 88; identities, 98; imagination, 1, 108; politics, 9; project, 102, 103, 109, 110, 112; traversals, 4
culture, 80–82, 87, 93, 94, 96, 98, 103, 107–9, 113, 122, 123, 125; national, 2, 131; postcolonial, 8; precolonial, 87
"*Culture and Imperialism*", 77

dasein, 14, 16
de Certeau, Michel, 29
decolonization, 82–84, 112, 116, 122
decolonized, 79, 83
Defoe, Daniel, 91, 92
dehistoricization, 113
Derrida, Jacques, 3, 27, 123, 126; Derridean difference, 127; Derridean imagination, 3
deterritorialization, 32
dialectic/al, 6, 14, 16, 67, 68, 72; Sartrean, 113
Diop, Alioune, 97

displacement, 3, 5, 13–14, 17, 25–28, 30, 34, 60–65, 92–94, 101, 104, 106, 107, 109, 121, 125, 126, 128
Dobson, Andrew, 69–71
"The Dog of Tithwal", 34
dominant being, 31, 33
domination, 81, 85, 88, 113
Dostoevsky, Fyodor, 30
Du Bois, W. E. B., 8, 59; double consciousness, 111

Eckhard, Marcelo, 119
egalitarian, 97
Ego different from the Other, 100; Greater than the Other, 100
El Moudhajid, 20
emancipation, 80, 82, 89, 93, 106, 109, 110, 116, 121
emancipatory process, 101
emancipatory project, 112
"emergent everyday", 76
"emergent insurgent", 78, 81
enlightenment, 32
epiphany, 32–34
essentialist and essentialism, 59, 65, 66, 130; dimension, 113
eternal, 15–16
ethics, 63
euchronia, 88
Europe, 97, 106, 113, 116; non-Europe, 97
existence, 12, 15–16, 19, 20, 31, 57, 72; consciousness of, 58
existentialism and existential, 11–12, 14, 20, 23, 57, 58, 60, 66, 67, 72, 131; existential phenomenology, 127, 128; Sartrean, 72, 121, 130. *See also* phenomenological existentialism

Facundo: Civilization and Barbarism, 30
Fanon and the Crisis of European Man, 12
"Fanon and the Pitfalls of Cultural Studies", 10
Fanon death, 20, 24; eras and traditions, 5; historical Fanon, 2; invented Fanons, 9; studies, 5; "use" of, 1, 8, 129, 132
Fanonian colonial subject, 107; critical discourse, 86; emancipatory discourse, 88; Hegelian dialect, 82; national culture, 78; spaces, 55, 56; subaltern, 77; thought, 129; writing, 5; zones, 4
Feuchtwang, Stephen, 55
finite man, 15
flaneur, 28–29
Foucault, Michel, 17, 27, 110, 116
Frantz Fanon and the Crisis of European Man, 8
"Frantz Fanon: Evolution of a Revolutionary: A Biographical Sketch", 20
freedom, 57, 62; existentialist, 102; Fanon's critique of, 72; Sartre, 68–71
Freud, Sigmund, 23, 88, 132; psychology and French Freudians, 56
Fuss, Diana, 9, 99, 112

Gandian discourse, 107
Gates Junior, Henry Louis, 7, 9
Geismar, Peter, 20, 22, 23
Gelman, Juan, 20
gender, 60; "generic man", 62; politics of sexuality, 62;

representation of Black women, 66; women's agency, 62
Gendzier, Irene, 20, 22–24, 27
Genealogy of Racism, 110
Geschichtlichkeit, 14–15
Geschichtsbewusstein, 14
Gibson, Nigel C., 9
Gikandi, Simon, 126
Gordon, Lewis, 8, 12, 27, 33, 57, 121, 122, 127, 128; and Sharpley-Whiting and White, 7–9
Greimas, A. J. and J. Courtés, 97
Guevara, Che, 20
Guha, Ranajit, 79

Haitian literary movements, 58
halakhah, 120, 121
Hall, Stuart, 58
Hansen, Emmanuel, 9
Harris, Leonard and Carolyn Johnson, 3
haunt (haunted, haunting), 3
The Heart of Darkness, 28
Hegel, Georg W. F., 14–15, 23, 108, 109, 132
Hegelian, 56, 58, 64, 67, 71, 84; Absolute Idea, 109; analogy, 99; master and the slave, 14, 71; spirit, 24, 105
hegemony, 79, 81, 103
Heidegger, Martin, 12
heterological study, 2
hierarchy, 21–22, 26
historical affirmation, 89; comprehension, 98; condition, 101; consciousness, 15–16; determinism, 88; estrangement, 13–14'; intervention, 83
historicism, 26–27, 29

historicity, 1, 2, 10, 14–17, 19, 26, 29–30, 33–34, 57, 86–89, 92–94, 102, 106, 107, 109–12, 114, 120, 121, 127, 128, 131; colonization, 66; displaced historicity, 57, 65, 68; universalizing, 56
historiography/ic, attitude, 6; gradation, 6; thought, 7, 129
history, 63, 66–67, 127; dialectic of, 9; Fanon, 71; impurities of, 88, 113, 125; longue durée (long duration), 97, 98; natural, 55; Nietzsche, 72; open-ended, 129; psychiatry, 8; teleology, 67; thought, 7, 129
Hobsbawn, Eric, 21
homologation, 97
homophily, 62
homophobia, 7
hooks, bell, 7, 62–63
humanism, 82, 88, 105, 112; classical, 10, 16
Husserl, Edmund, 12

identity(ies), 3, 67, 78, 81, 83, 93, 95, 98, 99, 102, 103, 106, 110–12, 116, 121, 123, 125, 126, 129, 131; Black, 59; coherent, 59; discourse on, 65–66
"Imperial Eyes", 28
India, 107
Indian Revolution, 58
international division of labor, 123, 124
Irele, Abiola, 64, 106–8
irony, 57, 58, 60, 66, 67

JanMohamed, Abdul, 7
Jaspers, Karl, 14–17, 26; Jaspersian historicity, 86, 99, 109

Jules-Rosette, Benetta, 68, 96, 97; on Alioune Diop, 68

Kantian moments, 63

Lacan, Jacques, 132
Lazarus, Neil, 78–81, 87, 93, 130, 132
Les Temps Modernes, Présence Africaine, 23
Levinas, Emmanuel, 63–64
liberation, 13, 20–21, 24, 26; liberationist, 79; movements, 81; theories of, 58; theorist, 7
lived experience, 56
Lloyd, Davis, 100
local authority, 29
Location of Culture, 33
Lyotard, Jean-François, 7

"Mama, see a Negro!", 56, 64
Manichaeism, 31
Manichean, 60, 63, 90, 104, 113, 121; Manichean world, 13, 76
manifestation, 32–34
Manto, Saadat Hasan, 34
marronage, 21, 131
Marx, Karl, 3, 23, 28, 30, 132
Marxism, 11, 21, 23, 60, 66; vulgar, 21
master and the slave, 14, 71
McClintock, Anne, 9
Melas, Natalie, 99, 100
Memmi, Albert, 31–32, 34, 80, 109
memory, 16, 120–22, 126; of the colonized, 119, 120
Mercer, Kobena, 7, 62
Merleau-Ponty, Maurice, 12, 23
methodological, 7–9, 132
Miller, Christopher, 78, 82
mimesis, 131
mimetic men, 92

mimicry, 91, 92
misogyny, 7
modernity, 15–16, 28–30, 85, 121; end of, 4
Mudimbe, V. Y., 91, 98

Naipaul, V. S., 92
national independence(s), 132
nationalism, 29, 79, 81, 93, 94, 123; bourgeois, 79; postcolonial, 120
native, 83, 85, 90, 91, 98, 99, 101
native-cosmopolitism, 113
nativism and nativist, 58, 59, 66, 69, 103, 113–15
Négritude, 13, 21, 58, 66, 93, 96, 98, 99, 102, 103, 106, 112–14, 127
new humanism, 9, 12, 23, 26, 60
Notes from Underground, 30

ontological dimension, 66
ontological matrix, 12
ontology, 13–14; lack of and negation, 56; resistance, 57, 71
Orientalism, 30
the Other, 70, 71, 91, 123; problem of, 69
Otherness, 68, 99

Pan-Africanism, 58
Parry, Benita, 7, 24, 58, 59, 66, 73, 90, 97, 130; and multivalence, 59
Pechey, Graham, 103
peculiarity, 15–16
pedagogy, 4
phenomenological existentialism, 8, 127–28
poetics, 2, 129, 130
Poetry and Capitalism, 29
political and cultural imagination, 17, 26, 30
political and moral urgency(ies), 2, 3, 6, 16–17, 19–20, 22, 66–67

Posnock, Ross, 67, 111
postcolonial analysis, 59; community, 70, 125; critical thought, 80; criticism and critique, 7–9; global subject, 101; imagination, 80; national culture, 80; postcoloniality, 81; processes, 66; situation, 93; society, 87, 88, 121, 126, 127; subject, 63
post-European Humanism, 58
postmodern, 7
postmortem (theoretical and political) duties, 8
postmortem ethics, 11, 20, 22, 24, 26, 28, 33, 81
post-racial society, 112
poststructuralism, 123
poststructuralist, 11–12, 79
Pratt, Mary Louis, 28
The Predicament of Culture, 21
Présence Africaine, 59, 68, 96, 97, 106
psychoanalysis, 30, 60

race, 96, 99, 112
racial epidermal schema, 13, 16
racialist, 96
racialization, 77, 78
Reflexions sur la question juive, 14
remembrance, 120–22
representation, 9, 64–66; cultural, 129–30; self-representation, 56–57, 124
resistance, 88, 89; collective, 59; opposition, 60
reversibility, 63–64
revolution, 19; theory, 5
revolutionary, 21–22, 25, 27, 29
Rigby, Peter, 98
Rimbaud, Arthur, 28, 30
Robinson, Cedric, 7

romantic hero, 19, 24–25
romanticism, 20–22, 28; moralistic, 21; unhappy romanticism, 72

Said, Edward, 7, 9, 30, 77, 91, 129, 132
Sarmiento, Domingo Faustino, 28, 30
Sartre, Jean Paul, 4, 11–12, 19, 23, 56, 58, 62, 67–71, 89, 96–98, 102, 112, 114, 115, 123, 126, 132; *Being and Nothingness*, 68; Black Orpheus, 59, 67, 72, 102, 112, 114; Husserl, 68; non-being, 69; *Reflections on the Jewish Question*, 71
Sartrean historicity, 130; proximity, 8
sees, 12–14, 17, 27, 29, 57
Sekyi-Otu, Ato, 73, 82, 132
the Self, 102, 104, 128
self, 14–15, 30
self-invention, 91
separation, 12–13, 16
settler, 89, 90, 95, 98, 101, 107
Shohat, Ella, 59
silence, 27, 66, 123
slavery, 21
Sociologie d'un revolution, 8
specter, 3, 4, 10, 86, 112, 129, 132
spectral, 4
Spivak, Gayatri, 7, 66, 123–25
stereotype, 14, 89
subaltern, 66, 124, 125; classes, 79; consciousness, 77, 78; subjects, 34
subject, (the), 1, 10, 17, 25–26, 28, 31–33, 65, 129, 130; global, 88; splintered, 101, 106, 109
The Subject and Power, 17
subordination, 13, 25, 31

territorialism, 81
territorialization (territorialized), 27–28, 31, 65, 132
time and temporal(ity), 5, 12, 15, 25–26, 30–31, 34, 57–58, 96
"Toba Tek Singh", 34
tragedy, 57, 58, 72
transcendence, 15–17, 71, 72
translation (failed), 3; cultural, 4; problem of, 5
triple person, 14–17, 30, 56
Tunisian independence, 32

uncertainty(ies), 2–4, 132
unisonant, 79, 80
universal, the, 67
universalist, 113
univocal discourse, 116
utopia, 130, 132
utopian desire, 65
utopian principle, 55

Vergès, François, 8

"Walking in The City", 29
white, 100; civilization, 105; culture, 114; fate, 123; racism, 112; white-Black relations, 99
White, Haden, 26
White, Renée T., 8
Wolfgang von Goethe, Johann, 25, 28
The Wretched of the Earth, 2, 5, 13, 19, 22, 25, 32, 71–73, 75–77, 79, 80, 82–84, 87, 89, 90, 93, 95, 98–103, 113, 114, 116, 120–23, 126, 131; "*Les Damnes de la Terre*", 98

Y'a bon Banania, le petit déjeuner dynamique, 14
Yerushalmi, Yosef, 120
Young, Lola, 7, 61

Zahar, Renate, 27

About the Author

Alejandro J. De Oto is CONICET researcher and professor of methodology and epistemology in the department of philosophy and the department of history at the Universidad Nacional de San Juan, Argentina.

About the Translator

Karina Alma is assistant professor in the Chicana/o and Central American Studies department at the University of California, Los Angeles, and coeditor of *U.S. Central Americans: Reconstructing Memories, Struggles, and Communities of Resistance* (2017).

www.ingramcontent.com/pod-product-compliance
Lightning Source LLC
Chambersburg PA
CBHW020120010526
44115CB00008B/908